Phiz: 'Christmas Eve at Mr. Wardle's', illustration for *Pickwick Papers* (C53)

Victoria and Albert Museum

Charles Dickens

An exhibition to commemorate
the centenary of his death

June–September 1970

London 1970

Designed by HMSO: Philip Marriage

Printed in England
for Her Majesty's Stationery Office
by Lonsdale & Bartholomew Printing Limited,
Leicester (text),
and The Curwen Press Limited, London,
(illustrations)
Dd 646891 10M 6–70

Foreword

In 1876 the bequest of John Forster, the life-long friend and biographer of Dickens, brought to the then South Kensington Museum what is still the largest collection in the world of original Dickens manuscripts. The centenary of Dickens's birth in 1812 was celebrated by an exhibition in the Victoria and Albert Museum, and it seemed appropriate that the centenary of his death in 1870 should also be commemorated in this way. Accordingly in 1968 a committee was set up under the chairmanship of Graham Reynolds, Keeper of the Department of Prints and Drawings and Paintings, to plan a centenary exhibition. The quality of the resulting exhibition is a tribute to the scholarship, enthusiasm and hard work of the members who generously agreed to serve on it. Although the nucleus of the exhibition is provided by Forster's benefaction, more than a third of the exhibits have been lent by private owners or institutions. The exhibition differs from that of 1912 in that it is addressed to a wider world than that of Dickens specialists. Its purpose is to portray one of the greatest creative artists of the nineteenth century against the background of the life and social history of his time.

JOHN POPE-HENNESSY
Director

CHARLES DICKENS CENTENARY EXHIBITION COMMITTEE

GRAHAM REYNOLDS *Chairman*
Keeper, Department of Prints and Drawings, and Paintings

ANTHONY BURTON
Assistant Keeper, Library, Victoria and Albert Museum

EDWARD CROFT-MURRAY, CBE
Keeper, Department of Prints and Drawings,
The British Museum

CHRISTOPHER FIRMSTONE
Exhibition Designer

SUSAN LAMBERT
Research Assistant, Department of Prints and Drawings

OLIVER MILLAR, CVO
Deputy Surveyor of the Queen's Pictures

RICHARD ORMOND
Assistant Keeper, National Portrait Gallery

VICTOR PERCIVAL
Officer in charge of the Wellington Museum.
Exhibitions Officer

DR MICHAEL SLATER
Lecturer in English, Birkbeck College.
Editor of the *Dickensian*

COLIN SORENSEN
Co-Director, The Paul Mellon Foundation for British Art

DR ROY STRONG
Director, National Portrait Gallery

KATHLEEN TILLOTSON
Hildred Carlile Professor of English in the University
of London at Bedford College

ANGUS WILSON
Professor of English Literature, University of East Anglia

Introduction

It is the aim of this exhibition to illustrate the many and varied contacts Charles Dickens had with the life of his times. Since he was in the first place the creator of a world of the imagination, the centre of interest is provided by the manuscripts and texts of his novels, and their contemporary illustration. But his activity was so remarkably diverse that a setting showing something of the appearance and preoccupations of the period is needed to give an impression of his intense absorption in many different spheres.

Sections of exhibits which represent phases of this wide range are here interspersed with portraits, and with scenes and letters recalling important episodes in his life, such as his courtship, the visits to America, and the Staplehurst railway accident.

His methods of composition are illustrated in a section 'Dickens at work': planning, writing, correcting and revising are shown in examples of manuscripts, proofs and early editions. Such a demonstration of Dickens's creative activity could only be made from the resources of the Forster Bequest, and a special section has been devoted to reflecting Dickens's warm relationship with his first biographer, and Forster's own activity as a literary man.

Dickens's contacts with the British artists of his own time were more extensive than is sometimes realised, and are represented here through paintings by Maclise, Stanfield, Egg, Frank Stone, Frith and other contemporaries. From almost the beginning of his career the illustrations to his novels were subject to his criticism and approval; they are an extension of his printed word, shown by a selection of the plates and by some original sketches by Cruikshank, Phiz and Fildes.

Another facet of Dickens's contact with his public is seen in his long association with the stage. Part of this exhibition illustrates his interest in the theatre in all its phases; his early attempts as a playwright, his enthusiastic promotion of amateur theatricals, and the Readings which added so much to the excitement and stress of his later life. His work as an editor is illustrated by exhibits showing his relationship with his contributors. The magazines he conducted were one vehicle for the conveyance of his views on social reform, and these are given more extensive treatment in the section of the exhibition devoted to novels of his middle period, in which he treated more extensively of social themes: *Dombey and Son, Bleak House,*

Hard Times, Little Dorrit. His concern for improved sanitation, the reform of the law, and administrative reform was shared by many of his contemporaries, as the pamphlets, reports, drawings and illustrations in this section reveal. Paintings and texts which concern his collaboration with the Baroness Burdett Coutts in her philanthropic activities are also shown in this section. The representation of Dickens's most extensive circle of friends can only be a partial one, being confined in the main to portraits of the better-known amongst them. But an attempt has been made to give as wide a selection as possible of portraits of Dickens himself, showing his changing appearance from youth to middle age. At the end a small open library section has been added, furnished by the generosity of a number of publishers, where, after looking at the exhibits, visitors to the exhibition may, if they wish, look at the novels themselves and some recent critical and biographical writings.

That it has been possible to assemble such a diverse and relevant group of paintings, drawings, manuscripts and relics is due to the generosity of many lenders. They are headed by Her Majesty The Queen who has graciously lent three paintings and a drawing. Other collectors who have liberally entrusted their possessions to the Museum are:
Mr Roger W. Barrett, Mrs J. Brain, Mr W.J. Carlton, Lady Cobbold, Mr Cedric Dickens, Mr Harry Dickens, Captain Peter Dickens, Mrs J.E. Egerton, Sir Arthur Elton, Sir Paul Fildes, Lady Galway, Mrs Patrick Gibson, Professor Gordon Haight, Mr Hippisley Coxe, Mrs Terence McHugh, Major Sir Charles Pym, Mrs S.A. Radcliffe, Sir David Scott, Mrs A. Waley, Mr H.C.D. Whinney, Dr Margaret Whinney.
Museums, libraries and other bodies who have lent to the exhibition are:
The Athenaeum, Bedford College Library, Birmingham City Art Gallery, Bodleian Library, British Museum: Department of Prints and Drawings; Department of Printed Books; Department of Manuscripts, British Railways Board, The Dickens House, Fitzwilliam Museum, Graves Art Gallery, Lady Lever Art Gallery, London Museum, City of Manchester Art Galleries, Manchester Central Library, Marylebone Cricket Club, National Portrait Gallery, City of Nottingham Museum and Art Gallery, Pierpont Morgan Library, Portsmouth City Museum, Principal Probate Registry, Public Record Office, Rector and Churchwardens of St. Luke's Church, Chelsea, Royal Holloway College, Southampton Art Gallery, Sun Life Assurance Society Ltd, Tate Gallery, University of London Library, Walker Art Gallery, Wisbech and Fenland Museum.
Whilst it is invidious to single out particular lenders amongst these institutions, it is right to point out that The Dickens House, whilst mounting its own exhibition of the Suzannet

Collection, has denuded itself of a substantial amount of the material usually to be found on view there.

Christopher Firmstone has been very conscious of the development of Dickens's career and of his love of street life, and in designing the exhibition he has related sections devoted to particular aspects of Dickens's life and work to a central thoroughfare, which establishes the general biographical framework. To emphasize the importance of the London scene to Dickens, groups of enlargements from early photographs of places he knew have been hung in the exhibition.

The first draft of the catalogue was prepared by Anthony Burton, Susan Lambert and myself. Although hard-pressed with other duties Mrs Tillotson, Editor of the Clarendon Edition of Dickens and Mrs Madeline House, Joint Editor of the Pilgrim Edition of the Letters of Charles Dickens, have placed their unrivalled knowledge of Dickens and his texts at our disposal, correcting a number of errors and faults of emphasis or judgment. They are not responsible for the defects which remain; but the fact that the text is in places more accurate in fact or in assessment than in previous publications is due to them.

The general literature on Dickens has been a constant source of reference for this compilation. Our debt both to the texts and to the meticulous annotation in the two volumes so far published of the Pilgrim Edition of Dickens's letters requires special mention, but so extensive has been our reliance on published work on Dickens that it seems best to omit the customary bibliography. Edgar Johnson's *Charles Dickens; his Tragedy & Triumph*, Gollancz, 1953, has been a constant source of reference and the extracts from transcripts in *The Speeches of Charles Dickens*, edited by K.J. Fielding, The Clarendon Press, 1960, and *The Letters of Charles Dickens* (The Pilgrim Edition), vols I and II, edited by Madeline House and Graham Storey, The Clarendon Press, 1965, 1969, have been included by kind permission of the Oxford University Press.

GRAHAM REYNOLDS
Keeper of the Department of Prints & Drawings and Paintings

NOTE ON THE CATALOGUE ENTRIES

In the descriptions of paintings, dimensions are given in inches, height before width. 'Oil' implies 'oil on canvas' unless otherwise stated.

In catalogue entries where no ownership is given, the objects described are from the collections of the Victoria and Albert Museum, and their Museum numbers are included in their entries. In the case of items from the Forster Collection and the Dyce Collection the numbers refer to the printed catalogues of the collections: the various catalogues are distinguished by the following abbreviations:

F.MS   Forster Manuscripts

F.P   Forster Paintings, Drawings, Engravings, etc.

F.PAMPH   Forster Pamphlets
These three catalogues are published in one volume: *Science and Art Department of the Committee of Council on Education, South Kensington Museum. Forster Collection. A Catalogue of the Paintings, Manuscripts, Autograph Letters, Pamphlets, etc.* Her Majesty's Stationery Office, 1893.

F.PB   Forster Printed Books. In *Science and Art Department [etc.] Forster Collection. A Catalogue of the Printed Books.* Her Majesty's Stationery Office, 1888.

D.PB   Dyce Printed Books. In *Science and Art Department [etc.] Dyce Collection. A Catalogue of the Printed Books and Manuscripts.* 2 vols. Her Majesty's Stationery Office, 1875.

ILLUSTRATIONS
In the catalogue, plate numbers of objects illustrated follow immediately after the number of the entry.

Catalogue

SECTIONS OF THE CATALOGUE	PAGE
A: Dickens's childhood	1
B: Early life	5
C: Early works	10
D: John Forster	28
E: Dickens's visit to America in 1842	33
F: Novels of the 1840s	36
G: Dickens and the theatre	47
H: Dickens and Christmas	59
I: Social novels	63
J: Dickens as editor	78
K: Dickens at work	85
L: Last novels	92
M: Final years	98
N: Personalia	105
O: Portraits of Dickens	107
P: Dickens's friends	112

PLAN
A plan of the exhibition, showing how these sections are arranged in the hall, will be found at the end of the catalogue

A: Dickens's childhood

Charles Dickens was born on Friday, 7 February 1812 in Mile End, Landport, a district of Portsmouth, where his father was working as a clerk in the Navy Pay Office. The family moved to Chatham in 1817, when Charles was five years old. The five years he spent there was the happiest period of his childhood and he constantly reverts to memories of Chatham, Rochester and the surrounding riverside and country in his writings. This idyllic time came to an end in 1822; his father was recalled to London, and his financial fortunes steadily declined till he was imprisoned for debt in 1824. To raise some money for the household Charles Dickens had been put to work at Warren's Blacking Warehouse and, though this episode only lasted a few months, it left an indelible impression of bitterness and shame on his mind. After he was released from it he set before himself the determination to succeed at whatever he took up, however much it might cost him in time and energy.

A1
Joseph Francis Gilbert (1792–1855)
John Dickens (1785/6–1851)
Photograph (copy) after an oil painting

John Dickens, father of Charles Dickens, was the son of the housekeeper at Crewe Hall, where her husband had formerly been butler. He was appointed clerk in the Navy Pay Office in 1805 and was stationed at Portsmouth when Charles, his second child and first son, was born. The financial difficulties caused by his improvidence led his family into the areas inhabited by the shabby genteel and to his imprisonment for debt. His son incorporated his grandiloquence, financial unreliability and mercurial disposition in the character of Micawber, and wrote later 'the longer I live, the better man I think him'.

The originals of A1 and A3 have been assigned to John W. Gilbert, but no artist of that name is recorded. Joseph Francis Gilbert exhibited landscapes and figure subjects from a Portsmouth address from 1813 to 1816, and is probably the artist intended.

A2
Edwin Roffe (worked 1889–91)
John Dickens
With a remarque of Harry Burnett
Stipple engraving. $6\frac{3}{8} \times 4\frac{1}{2}$
Plate from F.G. Kitton *Charles Dickens by Pen and Pencil*, London, 1890
Lent by the Portsmouth City Museum

Harry Burnett, the crippled son of Fanny, Dickens's sister, died in 1849, the year following his mother's death.

A3
Joseph Francis Gilbert (1792–1855)
Elizabeth Dickens (1789–1863)
Photograph (copy) after an oil painting

Elizabeth Dickens, mother of Charles Dickens, was the daughter of Charles Barrow and Mary Culliford. Shortly after her marriage to John Dickens, Charles Barrow, who held an important position of trust in the Navy Pay Office, absconded to the Continent owing more than £5,000 of public money.

She antagonised her son by wanting him to return to the Blacking Warehouse after his father had arranged for him to leave. 'I never afterwards forgot, I never shall forget, I never can forget, that my mother was warm for my being sent back.' She did not recognise that Mrs Nickleby was drawn from her; 'Mrs Nickleby herself sitting bodily before me . . . once asked whether I really believed there ever was such a woman!'

A4
Edwin Roffe (worked 1889–91)
Elizabeth Dickens
With a remarque from a photograph of her of c.1860
Stipple engraving. $7\frac{1}{2} \times 4\frac{3}{4}$
Plate from F.G. Kitton *Charles Dickens by Pen and Pencil*, London, 1890
Lent by the Portsmouth City Museum

A5
The paternal ancestry of Charles Dickens
Photograph copied from a chart in E. Johnson *Charles Dickens: his Tragedy and Triumph*, London, 1953

A6
The maternal ancestry of Charles Dickens
Photograph copied from a chart in E. Johnson *Charles Dickens: his Tragedy and Triumph*, London, 1953

A7
Daybook of Baptisms at St Mary's Church, Kingston, 1809–12
Photograph

The page shown contains the entry of the baptism of Charles John Huffham, son of John and Elizabeth Dickens, on 4 March 1812. It is reproduced from the register belonging to the Vicar and Churchwardens of St Mary's Church, Kingston, deposited at the Portsmouth City Record Office.

A8 [1]
16 Bayham Street, Camden Town
Photograph copied from an original in the Tyrell Collection, The Dickens House

John Dickens's financial troubles after his recall to London in the winter of 1822/3 forced him to live in this house. Its position is described by Forster: 'Bayham Street was about the poorest part of the London suburbs then, and the house was a mean small tenement with a wretched little back-garden abutting on a squalid court'.

A9
Register of the Marshalsea Prison, 1822–24
Lent by the Public Record Office

The page shown includes a record of the admission of John Dickens, Friday, 20 February 1824.

A10
Letter from Charles Dickens to John Forster [5 March 1839]
L.1595(19)–1938

From the moment he became a successful author Dickens had frequently to pay fresh debts incurred by his father. When in 1839 he found that John Dickens had been borrowing money from his publishers, Chapman and Hall, he determined to settle him and his mother in a remote part of Devonshire. The letter describes the cottage he found for them at Alphington.

A11
Letter from Charles Dickens to John Forster [11 July 1839]
L.1595(13)–1938

Another instance of the exasperation to which his parents drove Dickens. The letter from his mother and his reply, to which he refers, have not survived, so the precise cause of his annoyance is unknown. It is only with difficulty that he has kept his temper and 'struck out sundry "sneezing" [i.e. strongly-worded] passages'.

A12
Charles Dickens's diary entry for 15 June 1841
F.MS.182

Although banished to Alphington, John Dickens did not entirely mend his ways. In March 1841 he was trying to obtain money by circulating promissory notes to be drawn on his son. In anger, Dickens planned to send him abroad with a slightly increased allowance, but in fact he remained at Alphington. In this diary entry Dickens notes, probably in preparation for a letter to his father, the terms on which his mother's allowance is to be paid, until they moved to Blackheath a year or so later.

A13 [2]
George Harley (1791–1871) and Denis Dighton (1792–1827)
Hungerford Stairs, 1822
Lithograph. $10\frac{3}{4} \times 12\frac{1}{2}$
Lent by the Trustees of the British Museum

The blacking warehouse, when Dickens was first put to work in it, 'was the last house on the left-hand side of the way, at old Hungerford Stairs. It was a crazy, tumble-down old house, abutting of course on the river, and literally overrun with rats'.

A14
Warren's Blacking Warehouse
(a) The devices of the rival blacking firms
Reproduced from R. Langton *The Childhood and Youth of Charles Dickens*, 1891, p.75

The blacking warehouse managed by his relative James Lamert in which Dickens worked at the age of 12 for a few months exploited the recipe of Jonathan Warren, and was set up in rivalry to (Robert) 'Warren's Blacking, 30 Strand'. While

Dickens was employed, the warehouse was moved from Hungerford Stairs to Chandos Street, Covent Garden.

(b) Blacking bottle
Lent by The Dickens House

'My work was to cover the pots of paste-blacking; first with a piece of oil paper, and then with a piece of blue paper; to tie them round with a string; and then to clip the paper close and neat, all round, until it looked as smart as a pot of ointment from an apothecary's shop. When a certain number of grosses of pots had attained this pitch of perfection, I was to paste on each a printed label; and then go on again with more pots.'

A15
Seven works from Cooke's Edition of Select Novels:
Cervantes *Don Quixote*
Le Sage *Gil Blas*
Henry Fielding *Tom Jones*
Tobias George Smollett *Peregrine Pickle*, *Humphrey Clinker*
Sir Charles Morrell *Tales of the Genii*
Oliver Goldsmith *Vicar of Wakefield*
Peregrine Pickle, *Tom Jones*, *Gil Blas* lent by the Trustees of the British Museum

In *David Copperfield*, chapter 4, Dickens gives a description of 'the small collection of books in a little room upstairs' in which the hero delighted to browse, and Forster comments 'it is one of the many passages in *Copperfield* which are literally true'. For it is taken from an autobiographical fragment which Dickens wrote for Forster, 'the only change in the fiction being his omission of the name of a cheap series of novelists then in course of publication, by means of which his father had become happily the owner of . . . his small collection of books'. The cheap series was most probably that published by John Cooke (1731–1810): no other contains all the works on Forster's list, which includes, in addition to the titles shown here, *Robinson Crusoe*, *Roderick Random* and the *Arabian Nights*. Though Cooke's Pocket Library first appeared in the final years of the eighteenth century, some volumes at least were reprinted in the second decade of the nineteenth. The ten works in this little library fed Dickens's imagination then and throughout his life, and were the models on which he based his own writing.

A16
Sir John Gilbert, RA (1817–97)
Don Quixote and Sancho Panza
Signed, and dated 1840
Oil. 30 × 25
1835–1900 (Ashbee Bequest)

A17
George Cattermole (1800–68)
Don Quixote in his Study
Water-colour. $11\frac{3}{4} \times 14\frac{3}{4}$
1798–1900 (Ashbee Bequest)

Of *Don Quixote* Dickens wrote 'I was never in Don Quixote's study, where he read his books of chivalry until he rose and hacked at imaginary giants, and then refreshed himself with great draughts of water, yet you couldn't move a book in it without my knowledge or with my consent' ('Nurse's Stories', *The Uncommercial Traveller*). As soon as the first few numbers of the *Pickwick Papers* had been published a comparison was drawn between Mr Pickwick and Sam Weller on the one hand, and Don Quixote and Sancho Panza on the other.

A18
William Simson, RSA (1800–47)
Gil Blas introducing himself to Laura
Signed, and dated 1840
Oil. 36 × 28
F.A.181 (Sheepshanks Gift)

A19
William Mulready, RA (1786–1863)
Burchell and Sophia in the Hayfield
Exhibited at the Royal Academy in 1847
Oil on panel. $24 \times 19\frac{1}{2}$
Lent from a private collection

In 1844 Thackeray claimed that he had promised the editor of *Fraser's Magazine* 'that no pictures taken from "The Vicar of Wakefield" or "Gil Blas" should by any favour or pretence be noticed' in his review of the Royal Academy. *The Vicar of Wakefield* was, by reason of its affecting domestic narrative no less than its robust morality, the most popular of all British novels as a source of subjects for the Victorian genre painters.

Dickens owed the nickname 'Boz' under which he first became famous to this novel. He had called his younger brother, Augustus, Moses 'in honour of the Vicar of Wakefield'. This became corrupted to 'Boses', to 'Bose' and then 'Boz'. When Dickens first signed one of his Sketches, in the *Monthly Magazine* for August 1834, he adopted 'Boz' as his pseudonym.

A20
John Martin (1789–1854)
Sadak in Search of the Waters of Oblivion
Signed, and dated 1812
Oil. 30 × 25
Lent by the Southampton Art Gallery

This picture made Martin's reputation when he exhibited it at the Royal Academy in 1812. Its subject is taken from the *Tales of the Genii*, a collection ostensibly translated from the Persian by 'Sir Charles Morrell, Ambassador to the Great Mogul', but in fact composed by James Ridley. The oriental fantasy of this work and of the *Arabian Nights*, which he also read as a child in Cooke's Edition, left a lasting mark on Dickens and he frequently referred to it. One of his first original compositions as a child was a tragedy *Misnar* founded upon another episode in the *Tales of the Genii*. Dickens met the painter in 1836.

A21
Charles Robert Leslie, RA (1794–1859)
Mrs Grizzle asks Commodore Trunnion's permission to pluck three hairs from his chin
Water-colour. 12 × 17½
F.A.59 (Sheepshanks Gift)

There were three novels by Smollett in Dickens's childhood library, and these were the strongest influence on his earlier work. This illustration to the comic episode in chapter 6 of *Peregrine Pickle* was drawn by Leslie at a meeting of the Sketching Society.

B: Early life

After leaving school at the age of fifteen in 1827 Dickens was employed in a solicitor's office. He disliked this experience of the law, and having mastered shorthand in his spare time he left to become a freelance reporter in Doctors' Commons. By about 1831 he had become a Parliamentary reporter, and he continued with this work, in which he excelled, until November 1836, when the success of *Pickwick Papers* was evident. His first story 'A Dinner at Poplar Walk' was published in the *Monthly Magazine* on 1 December 1833. After the failure of his first love affair with Maria Beadnell in 1833, he became engaged in 1835 to Catherine Hogarth, whom he married the following year.

B 1
Thomas Gurney
Brachygraphy, or an easy and compendious system of shorthand
15th ed. London, 1825
Lent by the University of London Library
(W.J. Carlton Shorthand Collection)

This is the edition in which Dickens studied shorthand whilst working as a solicitor's clerk. In an autobiographical passage in *David Copperfield* he gives this description of the system: 'The changes that were rung upon dots, which in such a position meant such a thing, and in such another position something else entirely different; the wonderful vagaries that were played by circles; the unaccountable consequences that resulted from marks like flies' legs; the tremendous effects of a curve in a wrong place; not only troubled my waking hours, but reappeared before me in my sleep. When I had groped my way, blindly, through these difficulties, and had mastered the alphabet, there then appeared a procession of new horrors, called arbitrary characters; the most despotic characters I have ever known; who insisted, for instance, that a thing like the beginning of a cobweb meant expectation, and that a pen-and-ink sky-rocket stood for disadvantageous. When I had fixed these wretches in my mind, I found that they had driven everything else out of it; then, beginning again, I forgot them; while I was picking them up, I dropped the other fragments of the system; in short, it was almost heart-breaking'.

B 2
The Mirror of Parliament
Issues for 28 February–18 April 1832; 5 July–16 August 1832
Lent by the Trustees of the British Museum

Dickens probably began his career as a Parliamentary reporter in 1831 on being appointed to the staff of the *Mirror of Parliament*. This had recently been founded by his maternal uncle, J.H. Barrow, who described him as 'the best reporter in the Gallery'. He subsequently joined the *True Sun* and then the *Morning Chronicle*.

B 3 [13]
Phiz (Hablôt K. Browne) (1815–82)
Traddles makes a figure in Parliament and I report him
Etching. $4\frac{1}{4} \times 5\frac{1}{2}$

This illustration showing David Copperfield learning to tame 'the savage stenographic mystery' by taking down Traddles's speeches, is a commentary on the autobiographical passage quoted in B 1.

B 4 [14]
Shorthand notes written by Charles Dickens
Lent by Harry Dickens Esq.

These notes were written by Dickens in the late 1850s or early 1860s as part of a course of instruction he was giving in Gurney's system, possibly to his son, Harry, from whom they descended to the present owner. They demonstrate the 'arbitrary characters' described in the quotation at B 1.

B5
David Roberts, RA (1796–1864)
The Palace of Westminster from the River after the Fire of 1834
Oil. $19\frac{1}{8} \times 25\frac{3}{4}$
Lent by the Trustees of the London Museum

The old Houses of Parliament, in the gallery of which Dickens worked as a reporter from c.1831, were burned down on 16 October 1834. The fire was caused by the overheating of a stove when accumulations of old tallysticks were being burnt up. Dickens used this as an illustration of the country's 'all-obstinate adherence to rubbish' in his speech of 27 June 1855 to the newly-formed Administrative Reform Association: 'The sticks were housed at Westminster, and it would naturally occur to any of us unofficial personages that nothing would have been easier than to allow them to be carried away for firewood, by some of the many miserable creatures in that neighbourhood. However, they never had been useful, and official routine could not endure that they ever should be useful, and so the order went forth that they were to [be] privately and confidentially burnt. (*Laughter and cheers.*) It came to pass that they were burnt in a stove in the House of Lords. The stove, overgorged with these preposterous sticks, set fire to the panelling; the panelling set fire to the House of Lords; the House of Lords set fire to the House of Commons; the two houses were reduced to ashes'.

Dickens wrote to David Roberts on 3 January 1850 to thank him for his gift of a painting 'The Simoom in the Desert': 'I shall set it up among my household goods with pride', and in 1851 Roberts painted a scene for *Not So Bad As We Seem* at Dickens's request.

B6 [**9**]
Mrs Janet Barrow (worked 1817–30)
Charles Dickens, 1830
Miniature on ivory. $2\frac{7}{8} \times 2\frac{1}{4}$
Lent by The Dickens House

This is the earliest known portrait of Dickens, painted when he was 18, at about the time he met Maria Beadnell. The artist, formerly Janet Ross, was the wife of Edward Barrow, younger brother of J.H. Barrow and a fellow Parliamentary reporter. Mrs Barrow is said to have suggested traits in the character of Miss La Creevy in *Nicholas Nickleby*. Her work certainly reveals the 'bright salmon flesh-tint' which the friends of the fictional miniaturist consider 'quite a novelty in **art**'.

B7 [**10**]
Mrs Janet Barrow (worked 1817–30)
Frederick Dickens
Miniature on ivory. Circular, diameter $2\frac{1}{4}$
P.6-1937

Frederick William Dickens (1820–68) was John Dickens's second son. He is said to have had the same wearied expression as his sister Letitia, 'the raised eyebrows, small nose and large full lipped mouth'. Dickens obtained for him a clerkship in the Treasury but later he fell into his father's habit of contracting debts and looking to Charles Dickens for help, and this eventually led to their breaking off relations. For the artist, Mrs Barrow, see B6.

B8
Letter from Charles Dickens to Maria Beadnell, 18 March [1833]
(Copy in Maria Beadnell's hand)
Photograph from the original in the Huntington Library

Charles Dickens met Maria Beadnell about May 1830. The intensity of his love for her over three years is, by his own admission, reflected in his account of David Copperfield's love for Dora Spenlow (see B10). The affair went well at first, but her parents began to disapprove, and she ultimately repulsed his affection. This letter is reproduced from a copy presumably made by Maria Beadnell. With it he returned her present. 'Our meetings of late have been little more than so many displays of heartless indifference on the one hand . . . nothing will ever afford me more real delight than to hear that you the object of my first, and my last love, are happy.'

B9
Letter from Charles Dickens to Maria Beadnell [14 May 1833]
Photograph from the original in the Huntington Library

In this letter, one of the last he wrote to Maria Beadnell before the break, he asks her permission to write to Mary Ann Leigh, who had acted as an intermediary, to protest against her duplicity. 'I have been so long used to inward wretchedness, and real, real, misery that it matters little very little to me what others may think of or what becomes of me.'

B10
Phiz (Hablôt K. Browne) (1815–82)
I fall into captivity
Etching. $4\frac{5}{8} \times 4\frac{1}{8}$

Dickens drew the romantic side of his love affair with Maria Beadnell in his account of David Copperfield's courtship of Dora Spenlow. This is the illustration to the first meeting, described in *David Copperfield*, ch. 26. 'All was over in a moment. I had fulfilled my destiny. I was a captive and a slave.'

B11
Mrs H.L. Winter, *née* Maria Beadnell
Photograph

After Dickens broke with Maria Beadnell in May 1833 they did not meet for over twenty years. She was then married to a merchant, Henry Louis Winter. Dickens arranged to meet her in 1855, but was sadly disillusioned, and embodied his impression of her in Flora Finching (*Little Dorrit*, B12).

B12
Phiz (Hablôt K. Browne) (1815–82)
Mr F's Aunt is conducted into retirement
Etching. $4 \times 5\frac{1}{2}$

'Flora, who had been spoiled and artless long ago, was determined to be spoiled and artless now. That was a fatal blow' (*Little Dorrit*, ch. 13). Flora Finching is the second figure from the right in this illustration.

B13
George Hogarth
Photograph
Lent by The Dickens House

George Hogarth (1783–1870) first practised as a lawyer in Scotland, and was a friend of Scott; he then turned to journalism and music criticism. Dickens met him in 1834, when both were on the staff of the *Morning Chronicle*. He wrote an enthusiastic review of *Sketches by Boz*.

B14 [4]
Samuel Laurence (1812–84)
Catherine Dickens
Signed, and dated 1838
Crayon. $19 \times 13\frac{3}{4}$
Lent by Major Sir Charles E. Pym, CBE, DL

Catherine Thomson Hogarth (1815–75), the eldest child of George Hogarth (B13), became engaged to Charles Dickens, apparently in May 1835 and was married to him on 2 April 1836. She is described as 'plump and fresh-coloured; with the large, heavy-lidded blue eyes so much admired by men. The nose was slightly retroussé, the forehead good, mouth small, round and red-lipped, with a genial smiling expression of countenance, notwithstanding the sleepy look of the slow-moving eyes'.

B15
After Daniel Maclise, RA (1806–70)
Catherine Hogarth, later Catherine Dickens
Including a remarque of her from a photograph, 1846
Engraving by Edwin Roffe. $9\frac{3}{8} \times 6\frac{1}{2}$
Plate from F.G. Kitton *Charles Dickens by Pen and Pencil*, London, 1890
Lent by the National Portrait Gallery

B16
Catherine Dickens in later life
Photograph
Lent by The Dickens House

B17
Letter from Charles Dickens to Catherine Hogarth [May 1835]
Lent by the Trustees of the British Museum

After his experience of Maria Beadnell's moods, Dickens was determined not to tolerate 'sudden and uncalled-for coldness' in his fiancée. In this letter, probably written late in the month in which he became engaged to Catherine Hogarth he admonishes her to 'shew me that your love for me, like mine for you, is above the ordinary trickery, and frivolous absurdity which debases the name, and renders it ludicrous'.

B18
Letter from Charles Dickens to Catherine Hogarth [?June 1835]
Lent by the Trustees of the British Museum

Probably written early in their engagement this letter reminds Kate of his 'repeated and solemn assurances of entertaining for you a love which nothing can lessen – an affection which no alteration of time or circumstance can ever abate'.

B19
Charles Dickens to Catherine Hogarth [23 December 1835]
Lent by the Trustees of the British Museum

Excusing himself from going to see her on grounds of work.

B20
Marriage Register of St Luke's Church, Chelsea, February 1835–June 1837
Lent by The Rector and Churchwardens of St Luke's Church, Chelsea

The pages shown contain the entry for the marriage between Charles Dickens and Catherine Hogarth, 2 April 1836.

B21
Phiz (Hablôt K. Browne) (1815–82)
Mary Hogarth (1819–37)
Reproduced from a photograph in The Dickens House of the original oil painting

Mary Scott Hogarth was frequently a guest of Charles Dickens and her elder sister, Catherine, after their marriage. Her sudden death on 7 May 1837 was a great blow to Dickens and he had to suspend work on both *Pickwick Papers* and *Oliver Twist* for a month. This posthumous portrait by Phiz is the only one known; Dickens thought poorly of it.

B22
The Grave of Mary Hogarth at Kensal Green cemetery
Photograph

Dickens composed the epitaph on this tombstone, and for many years desired to be buried in the same grave.

B23
'Lady Maria Clutterbuck' (Catherine Dickens)
What shall we have for Dinner? Satisfactorily answered by numerous Bills of Fare for from two to eighteen persons
New ed. London, Bradbury and Evans, 1852
Lent by the Curators of the Bodleian Library

Catherine Dickens played the part of Lady Maria Clutterbuck in the production of *Used Up* at Rockingham Castle, 1851. She adopted the name for this cookery book, first published later the same year, which she based on the menus for dinner parties at Devonshire Terrace. One reviewer wrote that 'no man could possibly survive the consumption of such frequent toasted cheese', but this was Dickens's favourite ending to a meal.

B24
Life Assurance Proposal Form and Declaration
Facsimile lent by the Sun Life Assurance Company Limited

Early in 1838 Dickens proposed to insure his life with the Sun Life Assurance Society for £1,000. The Board 'seem disposed to think I work too much' and declined the proposal. Later that year the Britannia Life Insurance Company accepted a proposal for insurance for £999.

CHARLES DICKENS'S CHILDREN

Catherine Dickens bore ten children to Charles Dickens between 1837 and 1852. Dora Annie (1850–51) died in infancy. Portraits of the others are shown in this section. Providing for this large family, and the difficulty he experienced in establishing them in life, was a constant anxiety to him.

B25 [5]
George Richmond, RA (1809–96)
Charles Culliford Boz Dickens (1837–96)
Chalk. $23\frac{1}{2} \times 17\frac{3}{4}$
Lent by Dr Margaret Whinney

Charles ('Charley'), the author's eldest son. After some unsuccessful attempts in business he owned and edited *All the Year Round* after his father's death.

B26
Mary Dickens (1838–96) and Kate Dickens (1839–1929) as children
Photograph
Lent by The Dickens House

Mary ('Mamie') Dickens kept house for Dickens in his later years, acting as his hostess, and remained unmarried.

B 27
Marcus Stone (1840–1921)
Kate Macready Dickens (1839–1929)
Dated *Augst/65*
Water-colour. Oval, sight measure $10 \times 7\frac{1}{2}$
Lent by Dr Margaret Whinney

Kate Macready Dickens was the most independent minded and longest lived of Dickens's children. Herself a talented painter, she married the artist, Charles Collins (1828–73), brother of Wilkie Collins, in 1860. A year after his death she married another artist, Charles Edward (Carlo) Perugini (1839–1918). This portrait by Marcus Stone, the illustrator of *Our Mutual Friend*, was painted in 1865, when she was Mrs Collins. It can be seen hanging in Charles Dickens's dining room at Gad's Hill Place in the photograph M 13.

B 28 [7]
After Sir John Everett Millais, P R A (1829–69)
The Black Brunswicker
Engraving. $29\frac{1}{2} \times 20\frac{1}{8}$

Kate Dickens was the model for the girl in the painting, which Millais exhibited at the Royal Academy in 1860. Decorum would not permit the presence of the male model while she was being painted; she stood grasping a lay-figure, and the soldier was painted in a similar way.
The original painting is in the Lady Lever Art Gallery, Port Sunlight.

B 29
Walter Landor Dickens (1841–63)
Photograph
Lent by The Dickens House

Walter Landor joined the East India Company and became Lieutenant during the Indian Mutiny. He died in India without having revisited England.

B 30
Francis Jeffrey Dickens (1844–86) and Henry Fielding Dickens (1849–1933) as children
Photograph
Lent by The Dickens House

Francis Jeffrey ('Chickenstalker'), after a period in the Bengal Mounted Police spent the last years of his life in the Canadian Mounties.

B 31
Alfred d'Orsay Tennyson Dickens (1845–1912)
Photograph
Lent by The Dickens House

Alfred d'Orsay Tennyson emigrated to Australia, where he engaged in farming and business.

B 32
Sydney Smith Haldimand Dickens (1847–72)
Photograph
Lent by The Dickens House

Sydney Smith Haldimand ('The Ocean Spectre') entered the navy as a midshipman.

B 33
Sir Henry Fielding Dickens (1849–1933)
Photograph
Lent by The Dickens House

Henry Fielding was the most successful of Dickens's sons. He was called to the Bar in 1873, became K C and Common Serjeant, and was knighted in 1922.

B 34
Edward Bulwer Lytton Dickens (1852–1920)
Photograph from a painting by Marcus Stone
Lent by The Dickens House

Edward Bulwer Lytton was Dickens's last and favourite child, for whom he invented some of his most fanciful nicknames, such as 'Plornishmaroontigoonter'. He emigrated to Australia in 1868, and was an Australian M P from 1889 to 1894.

B 35
The immediate family of Charles Dickens
Photograph copied from a chart in E. Johnson *Charles Dickens: his Tragedy and Triumph*, London, 1953

C: Early works

Dickens's first attempts at literature took a conventional form: they were short tales and 'sketches' published in magazines and newspapers. In 1836 the publisher Macrone issued a selection of them in book form, with a few additions, as *Sketches by Boz,* first and second series. The unusual talent exhibited in the first series confirmed the publishers Chapman and Hall in their decision to commission Dickens to write a serial story as an accompaniment to etched illustrations by Robert Seymour. This work developed into Dickens's first novel, *The Pickwick Papers,* which brought him immediate fame. For the next year or two he kept on with his journalism, and produced a number of small works: *Sketches of Young Gentlemen,* 1838; *The Memoirs of Grimaldi,* 1838; *The Loving Ballad of Lord Bateman,* 1839; *Sketches of Young Couples,* 1840; and *The Pic Nic Papers,* 1841.

When *Pickwick,* which appeared in monthly parts, was only half finished, Dickens had already begun his second novel, *Oliver Twist.* It was neither a repetition of his first, nor a decline from it, but an equally resounding success in a quite different mood. And in April 1838 a third novel began to appear: *Nicholas Nickleby.* 'All that had given *Pickwick* its vast popularity', wrote John Forster, 'the overflowing mirth, hearty exuberance of humour, and genial kindliness of satire, had here the advantage of a better-laid design, more connected incidents, and greater precision of character.' As Dickens approached the age of thirty, therefore, he had firmly established himself as one of the leading novelists of his time.

SKETCHES BY BOZ

C1

***The Monthly Magazine,* December 1833**
Showing 'A Dinner at Poplar Walk' by Dickens
Lent by London University Library

This is Dickens's first published work. In his Preface (1847) to *Pickwick Papers* (see C40) Dickens recalled how he 'dropped [the manuscript] stealthily one evening at twilight, with fear and trembling, into a dark letter-box, in a dark office, up a dark court in Fleet Street'. The office was that of the *Monthly Magazine,* recently taken over by Captain J.B. Holland, who, having no money to pay his contributors, was willing to publish the work of unknown writers. When Dickens saw his tale in print, 'I walked down to Westminster Hall, and turned into it for half-an-hour, because my eyes were so dimmed with joy and pride, that they could not bear the street, and were not fit to be seen there'. He published eight more tales in the *Monthly Magazine* during 1834 and early 1835.

C2

***The Evening Chronicle,* 21 July 1835**
Showing 'The Streets–Morning' by Dickens
Lent by the Trustees of the British Museum

In the summer of 1834 Dickens obtained a regular post as Parliamentary reporter on the *Morning Chronicle,* and before the year was out had contributed five 'Street Sketches' to that paper. When, in January 1835, its proprietors began a companion paper, the *Evening Chronicle,* Dickens was able to contribute to the latter another series of twenty 'Sketches of London'. As soon as this series was completed he began a new series of 'Scenes and Characters' in *Bell's Life in London.*

It was his 'sketches' of contemporary life, rather than his earliest fiction, that revealed Dickens's talent as writer and observer. Forster remarked that the sketches contained 'unusually truthful observation of a sort of life between the middle class and the low, which, having few attractions for bookish observers, was quite unhackneyed ground'. 'Things are painted literally as they are; and, whatever the picture, whether of every-day vulgar, shabby genteel, or downright low, with neither the condescending air which is affectation nor the too familiar one which is slang.'

C3
The Library of Fiction
Vol. 1. London, Chapman and Hall, 1837
Showing 'The Tuggs's at Ramsgate' by Dickens, with an illustration by Robert Seymour
L.713-1943

This tale marks Dickens's first contact with the publishers Chapman and Hall, and his first collaboration with the artist Robert Seymour (but see C38). The *Library of Fiction*, a monthly publication, was edited by Charles Whitehead, who had previously worked for the *Monthly Magazine* and had there noticed Dickens's stories. He asked Dickens to contribute to the *Library of Fiction* and Dickens agreed. It was because of the contact thus made that Dickens was asked, shortly afterwards, to work with Seymour on what came to be *Pickwick Papers*. 'The Tuggs's at Ramsgate' was included in the 1839 edition of *Sketches by Boz*.

C4
Pierce Egan
Life in London; or the Day and Night Scenes of Jerry Hawthorn ... and ... Corinthian Tom
London, Sherwood, Neely and Jones, 1821
Showing a hand-coloured aquatint by I.R. and G. Cruikshank: 'Tom, Jerry and Logic making the most of an Evening at Vauxhall'
29.V.1875

Dickens's originality lay not in the choice of the subject matter for his sketches, but in his treatment of it. There had been many books about London life: the favourite in the generation before Dickens's was Pierce Egan's *Life in London:* 'Tom and Jerry were as popular twenty years since', wrote Thackeray in 1840, 'as Mr. Pickwick and Sam Weller now are'. Like Tom and Jerry, Dickens visited the famous pleasure-gardens at Vauxhall, though he saw them in the cold light of day and in their decline. George Cruikshank, who had helped to illustrate Tom and Jerry, provided an illustration for Dickens also (see C18).

C5
'An Amateur'
Real Life in London; or, the Rambles and Adventures of Bob Tallyho ... and ... the Hon Tom Dashall
Vol. 2. London, Jones & Co, 1822
Showing a hand-coloured aquatint:
'Tom and Bob taking a stroll down Drury Lane at five in the Morning'
L.413-1943

The sensitive and highly individual tone of Dickens's sketches was very different from the tone of Pierce Egan and his followers, who certainly exhibited 'the condescending air which is affectation' and 'the too familiar one which is slang'. The incident in the plate shown here is described thus:

'... they were suddenly attracted by a female purveyor for the stomach, who was serving out her tea, coffee, and saloop, from a boiling cauldron, and handing with due complaisance to her customers bread and butter, which was as eagerly swallowed and devoured by two dustmen, who appeared to relish their delicate meal with as much of appetite and *goût*, as the pampered palate of a City alderman would a plate of turtle. The figure of the Lady ... struck *Bob* at first view as having something matronly and kind about it.

"These persons", said *Tom*, "are really useful in their vocation; and while they provide a wholesome beverage for the industrious, are rather deserving of approbation than censure or molestation: the latter, however, they are frequently subjected to; for the *lads of lark*, in their moments of revelry, think lightly of such poor people's stock in trade, and consider it a prime *spree* to upset the whole concern..."'

For *Sketches by Boz* Cruikshank illustrated a similar scene (see C17): one of the best of his etchings for Dickens, it is as different in atmosphere from the earlier aquatint, as Dickens's sketch is different in tone from the words of Bob and Tom.

C6
Sketches by Boz: illustrative of Every-day Life, and Every-day People. The Second Series
2nd ed. London, John Macrone, 1837
F.PB.2447

In 1835 Harrison Ainsworth introduced Dickens to his first publisher John Macrone, who offered to bring out in book form a collection of the sketches and tales which were establishing the reputation of the young author. Dickens gladly agreed. George Cruikshank, firmly established as the foremost comic draughtsman of the time, was enlisted as illustrator, and work began on the book in October 1835. At first intended for the Christmas trade, it was eventually published, with the title *Sketches by Boz*, on 8 February 1836. It was very successful: a second series of *Sketches by Boz* was issued by Macrone in December 1836. It was in this volume (here displayed) that Dickens's first published piece (see C1) was reprinted, with a new title: 'Mr. Minns and his Cousin'.

C7
Sketches by Boz illustrative of Every-day Life and Every-day People
New ed. London, Chapman and Hall, 1839
F.PB.2446

Dickens had sold the copyright of *Sketches by Boz* to Macrone, and in May 1836 signed a contract to write a 3-volume novel for him. He had already begun to write *Pickwick* for Chapman and Hall, and in a few months would begin to feel the full force of its success. In August 1836, however, he undertook to write a novel for a third publisher, Richard Bentley, and shortly afterwards agreed to edit the new *Bentley's Miscellany*. By the summer of 1837 it was clear that he would not be able to keep to all his contracts, and Macrone, wishing to make the best of what he already had, decided to re-issue the *Sketches* in parts (see C10) similar to the *Pickwick* parts. Dickens was strongly opposed to this but could only prevent it by inducing Chapman and Hall to buy back from Macrone the copyright of the *Sketches*. Macrone, however, drove such a hard bargain that Chapman and Hall were themselves obliged to re-issue the *Sketches* in parts in order to offset the cost of buying the copyright. Hence the new edition of the *Sketches* in 1837–39, in pink-covered parts easily distinguished from *Pickwick*'s green covers, with illustrations, re-engraved, by Cruikshank, and a considerably revised text.

C8
James Grant
Sketches in London
London, W.S. Orr & Co, 1838
Showing an etching by Phiz: 'Out-door Relief'
12.xi.74

If there were many writers before Dickens who sketched life in London, there were also many after him. James Grant's *Sketches in London* – a rather ill-digested mixture of anecdote and statistics – can hardly be called an imitation of Dickens, but is obviously intended to take advantage of the fashion for 'sketches'. It was illustrated by Phiz, and in his two plates for the chapter on workhouses, he has clearly been inspired by certain of Cruikshank's plates for *Sketches by Boz* (see C20) and *Oliver Twist*.

C9 [**16**]
Anonymous
George Cruikshank (1792–1878), wearing theatrical costume
C.1836
Oil. $17 \times 10\frac{3}{4}$
Lent by the National Portrait Gallery

In 1835, when George Cruikshank was suggested by Macrone as the illustrator for Dickens's first book *Sketches by Boz*, the artist was at the peak of his career; his pre-eminence in the field of book illustration was so unchallenged, that his name on a title-page alone was enough to guarantee a good sale. The professional collaboration of Cruikshank and Dickens was shorter than is often realized, for Cruikshank only illustrated two major works by Dickens: *Sketches by Boz* and *Oliver Twist*. However, as the artist later claimed, he set the style for Dickens's other illustrators, one of whom, Seymour, had, at the outset of his etching career, even imitated Cruikshank's name with the pseudonym 'Shortshanks'.

Dickens, who, before they met claimed that 'no one appreciates' Cruikshank's talents 'so highly as myself', always retained a high opinion of the artist's work. Shortly before his death he told Luke Fildes, the illustrator of *Edwin Drood*, 'I want you to make a drawing as good as Cruikshank's "Fagin in the Condemned Cell"'. The break in their relationship was not due, therefore, to the novelist's dissatisfaction and their association on a social basis lasted much longer. They shared an early ambition to act; Cruikshank had participated in Dickens's family theatricals and in 1847 and 1848 he played small parts in the benefits for Hunt and Knowles (see Section G). In spite of his enthusiasm, and his ability as a mimic, Cruikshank was not a good actor. Dickens complained to Forster: 'In spite of all the trouble he gives me, I am sorry for him, he is so evidently hurt by his own sense of not doing well'. Their friendship was irretrievably impaired only in 1850, as a result of a battle in print provoked by Cruikshank's uncompromising attitudes on temperance. In subsequent years, as Dickens's fame spread, the formerly 'illustrious George' was supplanted in his profession by younger artists. Cruikshank's growing delusions perhaps further embittered his later attitude to Dickens; on hearing of Dickens's death, he exclaimed triumphantly 'one of our greatest enemies gone'.

ILLUSTRATIONS TO *SKETCHES BY BOZ* BY GEORGE CRUIKSHANK (1792–1878)

George Cruikshank illustrated Macrone's collected edition of *Sketches by Boz* with 28 small etchings. These, with the exception of 'The Free and Easy', were redrawn and enlarged, and 13 additional subjects etched, for Chapman and Hall's 'New Edition, Complete'. The small plates were etched on copper afterwards coated with steel, two subjects to a plate; the larger plates with single illustrations, on solid steel. Cruikshank transferred the drawn designs to the plate by means of a detailed tracing. This was placed upon the prepared plate, and both the plate and tracing were laid between damp paper and passed through the printer's press. By this process the black lead outline was transferred to the etching ground.

The artist himself chose the incident for illustration from each story – a freedom which Dickens when more confident did not give to this or any other illustrator again. The author who, in launching his 'pilot balloon' had been 'naturally desirous to secure some well-known individual, who had frequently contributed to the success, though his [George Cruikshank's] well-earned reputation rendered it impossible for him ever to have shared the hazard, of similar undertakings', was aware of his debt to the popular artist.

C 10
(a) **Wrapper design for Macrone's proposed monthly issue of *Sketches by Boz* in 1837**
Signed in pencil *Geo Cruikshank*
Lithographed by L. Schönberg. $8\frac{1}{4} \times 4\frac{7}{8}$
9794

(b) **Proof of the wrapper for Chapman and Hall's edition of *Sketches by Boz* in monthly parts, 1837–39**
Signed in pencil *Geo Cruikshank* and inscribed *First Proof*
Lettered *GCk* and *J. Jackson Sc*
Engraved on wood by John Jackson. $8\frac{1}{8} \times 4\frac{3}{4}$
9726.A.1
(see note to C 7)

C 11
Sketches and suggestions for illustrations to *Sketches by Boz*
Inscribed with a list of abbreviated titles
Signed in ink at a later date *George Cruikshank* and inscribed *Some of these suggestions to Chas. Dickens & which he wrote to in the second part of Sketches by Boz*, and *For Sketches by Boz*
Pencil. $10\frac{1}{2} \times 8\frac{1}{2}$
9995.Q

The inscriptions in ink were added many years after the sketches were drawn to add substance to Cruikshank's claim, expressed for the first time five months after Dickens's death, that the 'great part' of the Second Series of the *Sketches by Boz* was written from his 'hints and suggestions'.

The two sketches in the lower left-hand corner were used for the illustration to 'The Streets, Morning' (see C 17); the sketch above these for an unetched illustration to 'The River', and that to the right, below the centre, for the illustration to 'Scotland Yard'.

C 12
Proof on India paper of the etching for the illustration to 'The Tuggs's at Ramsgate' for Chapman and Hall's edition of *Sketches by Boz*
Signed *George Cruikshank*. $4\frac{3}{8} \times 3\frac{5}{8}$
9407.31

Cruikshank's composition for the illustration is based, in reverse, on Seymour's illustration of the same incident, which accompanied the story when it was first published in the *Library of Fiction* (see C 3).

C 13 [21]
(a) **Studies and a drawing in pencil on one sheet**, (b) **tracing** and (c) **proof of the etching for the illustration to 'The Bloomsbury Christening' for Macrone's edition of *Sketches by Boz***
(a) inscribed with the title. (c) Signed *George Cruikshank*
$6\frac{1}{4} \times 6$; $3\frac{1}{4} \times 3$
9725G, 9725AG, 9726.4

C14
Five pencil and wash studies and a proof of the etching for the illustration to 'The Last Cabdriver' for Macrone's edition of *Sketches by Boz*
One signed *Geo Cruikshank* and the etching *George Cruikshank*. Inscribed variously *Sketches by Boz*, *The first omnibus cad* and *The Last Cabman*
Various sizes
(a) to (e) lent by the Trustees of the British Museum. (f) 9726.13

These studies display the progress of the artist's work on the illustration from his first thoughts through to the final etched version. The illustration gives an example of the artist's accuracy and attention to detail; the cab depicted was an obsolete form of cabriolet with the driver seated over the right wheel.

C15
(a) **Drawing in pencil and** (b) **worked proof of the etching for the illustration to 'Seven Dials' for Macrone's edition of** *Sketches by Boz*
(a) inscribed with an alternative title *Fight of the Amazons* (b) signed *Geog Cruikshank*
$3\frac{1}{2} \times 3$; $3\frac{7}{8} \times 3$
(a) Lent by the Trustees of the British Museum
(b) 9726.9

(c) **Drawings in pencil and** (d) **proof of the etching for the illustration to 'Watkins Tottle' for Macrone's edition of** *Sketches by Boz*
(d) signed *George Cruikshank*
$3\frac{1}{4} \times 3\frac{3}{8}$; $3\frac{3}{8} \times 2\frac{3}{4}$
9725.I, 9726.5

(e) **Drawing in pencil and** (f) **proof of the etching for the illustration to 'Sentiment' for Macrone's edition of** *Sketches by Boz*
(e) inscribed with titles. (f) signed *George Cruikshank*
$4\frac{1}{2} \times 3\frac{3}{4}$; $3\frac{1}{8} \times 3$
9725.P, 9726.8

C16
(a) **Preliminary drawing in pencil, and unrelated sketches and** (b) **proof of the etching for the illustration to 'Hackney Coach Stands' for Macrone's edition of** *Sketches by Boz*
(b) signed *George Cruikshank*
$6\frac{1}{4} \times 4$; $3\frac{3}{8} \times 2\frac{7}{8}$
(a) Lent by the Trustees of the British Museum
(b) 9726.2

(c) **Drawing in pencil,** (d) **tracing and** (e) **India proof of the etching for the illustration to 'Hackney Coach Stands' for Chapman and Hall's edition of** *Sketches by Boz*
(c) inscribed with the title. (d) and (e) signed *George Cruikshank*
$5\frac{1}{2} \times 4\frac{3}{4}$; $4\frac{3}{8} \times 3\frac{1}{2}$
9725.F, 9725A.F, 9407.10

C17
(a) **Drawing in pencil,** (b) **tracing and** (c) **worked proof of the etching for the illustration to 'The Streets, Morning' for Macrone's edition of** *Sketches by Boz*
(a) inscribed with an alternative title *Covent Garden Market* and *Streets Morning*. (c) signed *George Cruikshank*
$5\frac{3}{4} \times 4$; $4 \times 3\frac{1}{4}$
(a) Lent by the Trustees of the British Museum.
(b) and (c) 10025.A and 10024.1

(d) **Study,** (e) **drawing in pencil and** (f) **India proof of the etching for the illustration to 'The Streets, Morning' for Chapman and Hall's edition of** *Sketches by Boz*
(d) inscribed in ink *Sketches by Boz*. (e) in pencil *The Streets – Morning*. (f) signed *George Cruikshank*
6×4; $4\frac{5}{8} \times 3\frac{3}{4}$; $4\frac{5}{8} \times 3\frac{3}{4}$
10023.G.2, 10023.G, 9407.6
(see note to C5)

C18
(a) **Drawing in pencil for the illustration to 'Vauxhall Gardens by Day' for Chapman and Hall's edition of** *Sketches by Boz*
(b) **Touched proof of the etching for the same subject for Macrone's edition**
(a) inscribed with titles and notes. (b) signed *Georg* [sic] *Cruikshank*
$6\frac{1}{4} \times 3\frac{7}{8}$; $5 \times 3\frac{1}{8}$
9725.R, 9726.10
(see note to C4)

(c) **Drawing in pencil for the illustration to 'London Recreations' for Chapman and Hall's edition of** *Sketches by Boz*
Inscribed with title
$4\frac{1}{8} \times 3\frac{7}{8}$
9725.D

(d) **Drawing in pencil for the illustration to 'Greenwich Fair' for Chapman and Hall's edition of** *Sketches by Boz*
Signed *Geo Cruikshank*. Inscribed with title
6×4
9725.H

C19
Four illustrations drawn especially for Chapman and Hall's edition of *Sketches by Boz*

(a) **Drawing in pencil and sepia wash for the illustration to 'Public Dinners'**
Inscribed with title
6 × 4
9917

The two stewards with official wands, helping to direct a procession of indigent orphans, are portraits of Dickens and Cruikshank.

(b) **Drawing in pencil and sepia wash for the illustration to 'Early Coaches'**
Inscribed with title, and, partly erased *I am ready Mr Boz but more time I beg*
6 × 3¾
9920

The young man paying his booking fee is a portrait of Dickens; in the etching his pseudonym Boz is faintly traced on the trunk on the counter.
The erased inscription is an example of one of Cruikshank's not infrequent complaints that the busy author, whose commitments were growing daily, did not send him the manuscript on time.

(c) **Drawing in pencil for the illustration to 'The Broker's Man'**
Inscribed with titles and *large*
4¾ × 3¾
10023.E

(d) **Drawing in pencil for the illustration to 'Our Next-Door Neighbours'**
Inscribed *Sketches by Boz*. Signed in ink *Geo Cruikshank* and inscribed *Next-Door Neighbours*
6 × 4
10023.F

C20 [22]
(a) **Drawing in pencil for the illustration to 'The Parish Engine' for Chapman and Hall's edition of *Sketches by Boz***
Inscribed with titles and notes
5¾ × 4⅜
10023.A

This illustration was a new subject drawn especially for Chapman and Hall's edition of the *Sketches*. The parish engine is an accurate drawing of the kind of fire extinguisher then in use.

(b) **Drawing in pencil and proof of the etching for the illustration to the 'Election for Beadle' for Macrone's edition of *Sketches by Boz***
Inscribed with title
7 × 3¾
9725.A, 9726.1

SKETCHES OF YOUNG GENTLEMEN

C21
'Quiz' (Rev. Edward Caswall)
Sketches of Young Ladies
London, Chapman and Hall, 1837
Lent by Bedford College, University of London

This lightly satirical work, with etched illustrations by Phiz, was published by Chapman and Hall in 1837, when Phiz had just risen to fame as the illustrator of *Pickwick*. Dickens, in his companion volume, *Sketches of Young Gentlemen*, presents himself as the ladies' champion against the 'malice prepense and ... wickedness aforethought' of Quiz.

C22
Sketches of Young Gentlemen
5th ed. London, Chapman and Hall, 1838
F.PB.2449

Of this book (designed as a companion to C21, and also illustrated by Phiz) and of *Sunday under Three Heads* Dickens remarked in 1838: 'I wrote [them] sub rosâ as the fancy struck me, and they are not generally known to be mine'. That they brought a useful addition to his income is shown by an entry in his 1838 diary (see C23).

C23
Dickens's diary (*The Law and Commercial Daily Remembrancer*) for 1838
F.MS.182

Under 8 January 1838 is the entry:

'I began the Sketches of Young Gentlemen to-day. One hundred and twenty five pounds for such a little book without my name to it, is pretty well. This and the "Sunday" by the bye, are the only two things I have not done as Boz.'

C24
The Fly, 3 February 1838
Showing a lithograph by W. Clerk: 'Sketches from Life. A nice young man, for a small party'.

Dickens was not the only author to try to supply the obvious companion piece to *Sketches of Young Ladies*. The publisher William Kidd brought out a *Sketches of Young Gentlemen*, by 'Quiz, Jun.' with illustrations by Cruikshank. And a week before Dickens's *Young Gentlemen* appeared, the magazine the *Fly* took up the motif in its Picture Gallery.

MEMOIRS OF JOSEPH GRIMALDI

C25
Charles Dickens, *ed.*
Memoirs of Joseph Grimaldi
2 vols. London, Richard Bentley, 1838
F.PB.2426

The publisher Richard Bentley, for whom Dickens was writing *Oliver Twist* in 1837–38, had acquired from Thomas Egerton Wilks a poorly edited manuscript version of the autobiographical memoirs of Grimaldi, the celebrated clown, who died in 1837. Bentley engaged Dickens to revise the manuscript for publication. 'My Dear Sir', Dickens wrote to him in early December 1837, 'I am getting on with Grimaldi, and I think am bringing the points out as well as it is possible to do from Mr. Wilks's dreary twaddle.'

C26
Draft of a letter from Dickens to the Sub-Editor of Bentley's Miscellany [March 1838]
F.MS.172

Dickens was stung by a comment made by a reviewer of the *Memoirs of Joseph Grimaldi* in the *Athenaeum*, 3 March 1838: 'We should almost venture the belief that Mr. Dickens had never seen Grimaldi on the stage'. He drafted a letter, in the end not published, in which he protested that he had – in earliest childhood – seen Grimaldi act, but that in any case 'I never heard it established as a sound position before, that to write a biography of a man . . . it is essential that you should have known him'.

C27
Letter from Dickens to Forster [? late March 1838]
Enlarged photograph
F.MS.172

Forster tells us that Dickens wrote this note at the end of the first week in which *Grimaldi* was on sale. Its quick success evidently surprised him; and not many more than 1700 copies were sold altogether, since out of an edition of 3000 Bentley still had 920 left when, on 25 June 1840 after he had severed his connection with Dickens, he wrote to William Jerdan to offer terms on which he would relinquish his interest in the book (see C59).

ILLUSTRATIONS TO THE
MEMOIRS OF JOSEPH GRIMALDI
BY GEORGE CRUIKSHANK (1792–1878)

In 1850 Dickens claimed that the *Memoirs* were published 'chiefly to please Cruikshank'. Although he was not proud of his own contribution the novelist acknowledged that 'the good right hand of George Cruikshank had seldom been better exercised'. Cruikshank's illustrations were reviewed with enthusiasm. The *Athenaeum* found the artist's sketches 'Capital: full of character, spirit and fun. *He* must have seen Joe'. Indeed he had; Cruikshank had belonged to 'The Crib', a club presided over by Grimaldi and had drawn his portrait as early as 1815 for the heading of a song Grimaldi had popularized. He also sketched him during performances in the 1820s.

C28
Two sheets of sketches, containing suggestions for all the illustrations to the Memoirs of Joseph Grimaldi
Inscribed with notes
Pencil. 9×7; $7\frac{3}{8} \times 8\frac{1}{2}$
9537a and b

C29
(a) Drawing in pencil (b) tracing and (c) India proof of the etching for the illustration 'Master Joe's Unexpected Visit to the Pit' to the Memoirs of Joseph Grimaldi
Each signed *George Cruikshank*. (c) signed additionally in pencil and inscribed *first proof*
$5\frac{1}{8} \times 3\frac{1}{4}$; $4\frac{1}{2} \times 3\frac{1}{4}$
9703.A, 9704.A, 9538.1

C30
(a) **Drawing in pencil**, (b) **tracing** and (c) **India proof of the etching for the illustration 'Master Joey Going to Visit his Godpapa' to the** *Memoirs of Joseph Grimaldi*
(b) and (c) signed *George Cruikshank*. (a) inscribed with notes and the title *Little Joe going to visit his Godpapa*
$6 \times 3\frac{3}{8}; 4\frac{1}{4} \times 3\frac{1}{4}$
9703.B, 9704.B, 9538.2

(d) **Drawing in pencil**, (e) **tracing** and (f) **India proof of the etching for the illustration 'A Bit of Pantomime off Stage' to the** *Memoirs of Joseph Grimaldi*
(e) and (f) signed *George Cruikshank*
$5\frac{1}{2} \times 3; 4 \times 3\frac{1}{4}$
9703.C, 9704.C, 9538.3

C31
(a) **Drawing in pencil**, (b) **tracing** and (c) **India proof of the etching for the illustration 'The Barber's Shop' to the** *Memoirs of Joseph Grimaldi*
(b) signed in ink, (c) signed *George Cruikshank*
$6 \times 4; 4 \times 3\frac{1}{8}$
9703.K, 9704.J, 9538.11

The drawing includes a small study for the figure of Grimaldi in 'The Last Song'.

(d) **Drawing in pencil**, (e) **tracing** and (f) **India proof of the etching for the illustration 'The Last Song' to the** *Memoirs of Joseph Grimaldi*
(f) signed *George Cruikshank*
$4\frac{1}{8} \times 3\frac{1}{8}; 4\frac{1}{4} \times 3\frac{1}{4}$
9703.L, 9704.K, 9538.12

An earlier version of this etching has the main design surrounded by a border, considered so grotesque, that it was cancelled in subsequent editions.

OTHER MINOR WORKS

C32
Manuscript of *Sketches of Young Couples*
[1839]
F.MS.154

After concluding *Nickleby* in Sept. 1839, Dickens tried unsuccessfully to make progress with *Barnaby Rudge*, due to be delivered to Richard Bentley on 1 January 1840. Disinclined to work on *Barnaby*, however, he found time to write another volume of *Sketches*, published anonymously in the same format as *Sketches of Young Gentlemen*.

C33
Sketches of Young Couples
London, Chapman and Hall, 1840
L.585-1918

Mr and Mrs Chirrup, the 'Nice Little Couple', are said to be based on William Hall and his wife. Hall and his partner Edward Chapman were Dickens's publishers.

C34
Charles Dickens, *ed.*
Pic Nic Papers. By Various Hands
3 vols. London, Henry Colburn, 1841
F.PB.2442

Dickens had parted with his first publisher Macrone on rather bad terms (see C7). But when Macrone died suddenly in September 1837, leaving a widow and children, Dickens and several other authors and artists (including Forster, Ainsworth, Cruikshank and Browne) joined to produce these commemorative volumes. Dickens wrote 'The Lamplighter's Story' (see G10), undertook the editing and saw the book into print. The profits, amounting to £300, were given to Mrs Macrone.

C35
George Cruikshank (1792–1878)
(a) **Study and** (b) **drawing in pencil and wash, and** (c) **India proof of the etching for the illustration 'The Philosopher's Stone' to 'The Lamplighter's Story' which was published as a frontispiece to** *Pic Nic Papers,* **1841**
(a) and (b) signed. (b) inscribed *The Philosopher's Stone* (c) inscribed and signed in pencil *first proof Geo Cruikshank*. Signed *George Cruikshank fec*
$7 \times 4; 7 \times 3\frac{1}{2}; 4 \times 3\frac{1}{4}$
(a) and (b) lent by the Trustees of the British Museum. (c) 9388.1

C36
George Cruikshank (1792–1878)
Eleven proofs of the etchings and text, and the music for *The Loving Ballad of Lord Bateman*, 1839
Each inscribed with a variant of *Designed Etched & Published by George Cruikshank, 1839*
Each $3\frac{1}{2} \times 3\frac{1}{4}$
9441.1–12

The little book *The Loving Ballad of Lord Bateman*, 1839, was the last collaboration of Dickens and Cruikshank. Cruikshank had heard a cockney version of this traditional ballad sung outside a public house, and repeated it to Dickens. Dickens touched it up and added some facetious notes for the published version, which Cruikshank illustrated with a series of jaunty etchings, over which Dickens was unusually enthusiastic. 'You never did anything like those etchings — never.' Henry Burnett noted down the tune hastily, intending to make a fair copy, but Cruikshank felt the crudely-written notes would add to the humour of the piece.

Thackeray also designed illustrations for this ballad, but they were not published in his lifetime.

PICKWICK PAPERS

C37
Robert Seymour (1798–1836)
Four Sketches by Seymour
Plates from a series of 180 caricatures published by R. Carlyle, London 1834–35
Each lettered with title, publisher's name and address and dates, etc.
Lithographs. Average size of sheets $6 \times 5\frac{1}{2}$
No. 5 vol. 3. 'In it or trying the Middle'
No. 19 vol. 3. 'Hunting may be sport, but I'm bless'd if it's pleasure'
No. 19 vol. 4. 'Shooting from a bank'
No. 21 vol. 4. 'Have you caught anything, Sir?'
E.1192-5-1963

The first illustrator of *Pickwick Papers* was Robert Seymour (1798–1836). The son of a decayed gentleman, he was apprenticed in his youth to a pattern drawer, but aspired to 'the higher style of art'. At the house of his uncle Thomas Holmes (whose daughter he married in 1827) he formed an acquaintance with the painter Joseph Severn. By 1822 he had established himself as an illustrator, and in the following five years contributed wood-engraved designs to a large number of books.

After the bankruptcy of his first publisher, he worked, now in etching and lithography, for Thomas McLean.

In the early 1830s his series of 'Sketches' began to appear. They depict the adventures and misadventures of cockney sportsmen, a theme particularly congenial to Seymour. He designed caricatures for the magazine *Figaro in London*, from 1831 to 1834 and 1835–36. He died by his own hand in April 1836.

C38
Robert Seymour
Seymour's Comic Album; or Museum of Entertainment
London, William Kidd [1834]
Lent by the Trustees of the British Museum

Over a year before he collaborated with Dickens on *Pickwick Papers*, the artist Robert Seymour had illustrated a story by Dickens, unaware of the identity of its author. Dickens's tale 'The Bloomsbury Christening' had appeared, unsigned, in the *Monthly Magazine* in April 1834, and a few pages from it were reprinted, along with other borrowed pieces, in *Seymour's Comic Album*. This little book, made up of comic extracts illustrated by Seymour, appeared late in 1834, obviously intended for the Christmas trade. The illustration shows an omnibus 'cad' disputing with Mr Nicodemus Dumps, who, carried past his stop, has declined to pay his fare.

C39
Enlarged photographs of letters in the *Athenaeum*
(a) **Letter from Robert Seymour, junior, 24 March 1866**
(b) **Letter from Dickens, 31 March 1866**

After his death, Seymour's wife and son claimed that he had been the originator of *Pickwick*. His plan had been to produce a set of comic designs dealing with a club of sporting characters. He proposed the plan to his publisher McLean, who did not undertake it, and to William Spooner, for whom he was illustrating *The Book of Christmas*. Spooner suggested that letterpress should accompany the plates and offered to publish the work, but after some delays Seymour offered it instead to Chapman and Hall. They took it up, and, looking for a writer for the letterpress, found Dickens. It was obviously intended at first that Dickens should write to Seymour's suggestions, but he soon made himself the dominant member of the partnership.

C40
Two sheets of the proof of Dickens's Preface to the 1847 edition of *Pickwick Papers*
F.MS.170

Here Dickens gives his version of the origin of Pickwick. The heart of the matter is what Edgar Johnson calls 'one of those bare little sentences that history makes famous when time has invested their flatness with pregnancy. "I thought", he said simply, "of Mr. Pickwick." ' It will be seen that the sentence was not quite so impressively simple until Dickens had made a small alteration in the proof. The Preface also contains an interesting comment on the method of publication in monthly parts: 'My friends told me it was a low, cheap form of publication, by which I should ruin all my rising hopes'.

C41
Robert Seymour
A Search after the Comfortable, being the Adventures of a Little Gentleman of Small Fortune
London, Thomas McLean, 1829
Etchings, coloured by hand. Open at Plate 1.
$9\frac{7}{8} \times 13\frac{3}{4}$
E.5286-1904

Seymour's very first idea, according to J.C. Hotten's memoir (1867), was to cast his work on a sporting club in the form of 'a pictorial novel, in six plates, each plate consisting of about five subjects'. In this form he had produced *The Heiress*, 1830, and *A Search after the Comfortable*, 1829.

C42 [23]
Thomas K. Hervey
The Book of Christmas
London, William Spooner, 1837
Showing an etched illustration by Robert Seymour: 'Enjoying Christmas'
23.vi.1868

Pickwick, we are told (see C39), was originally drawn as a thin man, but changed at the suggestion of Edward Chapman, Dickens's publisher. However this may be, there is no doubt that the character of a fat, bespectacled man occurs frequently in Seymour's etchings (compare C41). He is at his most Dickensian in the plate shown here in *The Book of Christmas*, first published c.1835.

C43
The Athenaeum, 26 March 1836
Showing the first advertisement for *Pickwick Papers*

The book turned out to be rather different from the publisher's description of it in the advertisement: the description, while borrowing phrases from Dickens's first chapter, still reflects something of Seymour's plan. Below the advertisement for *Pickwick* is one for the *Library of Fiction*, to which Dickens also contributed (see C3).

C44
The Posthumous Papers of the Pickwick Club. Number II
London, Chapman and Hall, May 1836
Lent by The Dickens House

Pickwick virtually inaugurated a new method of publishing fiction. Most novels of the 1830s were published in three volumes. It was not uncommon, however, for illustrated works, in which the plates were more important than the words, to be published in monthly parts; and this was the form in which Chapman and Hall chose to publish *Pickwick*. In this work the normal balance between artist and writer was soon shifted, partly because of Dickens's assertiveness, and partly because on Seymour's death he was succeeded by the young, retiring and biddable Hablôt K. Browne. It was Dickens's text therefore, and not the illustrations, which formed the essence of this work, and which secured its immense popularity. Because the book came out in monthly parts, Dickens was able to sense his rising popularity unusually keenly and enjoy a close and protracted relationship with his audience. Anxious to preserve this, he published all his other novels serially, in one way or another. Monthly parts had the added advantage that they were much more widely and cheaply saleable than three-volume novels. Each monthly number of *Pickwick*, once Phiz had settled to his task, contained 32 pages and two plates, and had a green cover by Seymour, which depicts cockney sportsmen.

C45
The Posthumous Papers of the Pickwick Club
London, Chapman and Hall, 1837
F.PB.2443

When the novel had appeared in twenty parts (in fact nineteen, as the last was a double number) monthly from April 1836 to November 1837, it was published complete in one volume.

C46
The Posthumous Papers of the Pickwick Club
Philadelphia, Carey, Lea and Blanchard, 1838
F.PB.2444

Before the establishment of international copyright laws, American publishers were accustomed to reprint books published in England without offering payment or seeking permission. On 14 June 1837, however, the firm of Carey, Lea and Blanchard wrote to Dickens to announce that, having published twelve parts of *Pickwick* in America, they had instructed their English agent to pay Dickens £25, and wished to make an arrangement with him to publish his forthcoming works. The Philadelphia edition of *Pickwick* was illustrated by 'Sam Weller, jr.' (T.H. Onwhyn) and 'Alfred Crowquill' (A.H. Forrester). The copy shown here was presented to Forster by Dickens.

C47
T. Young
The Star of Cambridge leaving the Belle Sauvage, Ludgate Hill
Lettered with the title
Lithograph. $16\frac{1}{2} \times 17$
Lent by the Trustees of the British Museum

According to Sam, Tony Weller's headquarters in London was at the Belle Sauvage. He gave this inn as his 'Parish' when trying to take out a marriage licence.

C48
C.B. Newhouse (worked c.1820–c.1845)
The sleepy Gate-Keeper
Plate II from the *Roadster's Album*, 1845
Inscribed with the title and *C.B. Newhouse Delt. London, Published Jany. 2nd. 1845, by Messrs. Fores, 41, Piccadilly*
Etching and aquatint, coloured by hand. $8\frac{1}{2} \times 12\frac{1}{2}$
E.418-1946

This print shows a Bath to London coach, such as Dickens came to know well in his reporting days. Professor Kathleen Tillotson has noticed in *Pickwick* 'one curious and unique feature: the consistent relevance of the numbers to the time of year in which they appeared, so that, for example, the cricket match falls in the June number... The law terms are observed, and when, after the trial [of Bardell v. Pickwick], Mr. Pickwick is told that "they can issue execution just two months hence", the necessary interval is occupied with the visit to Bath in the next two numbers'.

ILLUSTRATIONS TO *PICKWICK PAPERS*

C49
Robert William Buss (1804–75)
(a) **The Cricket Match**
Inscribed *Drawn & Etch'd by R.W. Buss. Page 69*
Etching. $4\frac{1}{2} \times 3\frac{1}{2}$
Lent by Major Sir Charles E. Pym, CBE, DL

(b) **The Fat Boy Awake on This Occasion Only**
Inscribed *Drawn & Etch'd RW Buss Page 74*
Etching. $5 \times 3\frac{1}{2}$
Lent by the Trustees of the British Museum

After Seymour's death, Buss was recommended to Chapman and Hall as his successor by John Jackson the engraver of the *Pickwick* cover. He accepted, although lacking experience in etching, and did a trial plate from a subject in *Pickwick* No. II, 'Mr Pickwick at the Review', which in spite of its deficiencies Chapman and Hall approved. He then made the two drawings for the illustrations exhibited, but this time had the biting-in done by a professional etcher. They appeared in the third part; the artist prepared two more subjects, but the publishers, convinced of his unsuitability, had meanwhile engaged H.K. Browne. In October 1836 Phiz replaced Buss's two illustrations, both of which are displayed, with two new designs, retaining the subject of the 'Arbour Scene' but replacing 'The Cricket Match' with 'Mr. Wardle and His Friends under the influence of the salmon'.

Earlier Buss had illustrated the story 'A Little Talk about Spring and the Sweeps' by Dickens when it was published in the *Library of Fiction*, (June 1836) with a design engraved on wood by John Jackson. The story was republished under the title 'The First of May' in *Sketches by Boz*, 1839, with an etched illustration by George Cruikshank, depicting an entirely different incident.

C50
F.W. Pailthorpe (worked c.1870 – past 1899)
Hablôt K. Browne ('Phiz') (1815–82)
Signed with initials *F.W.P.*
Inscribed with facsimile signature of the sitter *Yours truly H. K. Browne (Phiz)*
Etching on India paper. $8\frac{3}{4} \times 5\frac{5}{8}$
L.2734-1969

Unlike Cruikshank, Hablôt K. Browne was unknown when he was first employed to illustrate the work of Dickens; his introduction to the author, in his twenty-first year, was the beginning of his successful career. He had studied under the Findens, one of the best engraving firms of the day, and in 1832 won the silver Isis medal for the best illustration of an historical subject, and another awarded by the Society of Arts for an etching of John Gilpin. Nevertheless, he was humble enough to change his pseudonym 'Nemo', with which he signed his first two illustrations to *Pickwick Papers*, to Phiz 'to harmonise ... better with Dickens's Boz'.

Before illustrating *Pickwick*, Phiz had contributed designs to several publications, including the *Library of Fiction*, which was issued by the same publishers as *Pickwick*. He had illustrated, with a title page and three wood-cuts, a pamphlet *Sunday Under Three Heads*, which bore a dedication dated June 1836, and was written by Dickens under the pseudonym Timothy Sparks. Their partnership lasted for 23 years, resulting in over 400 illustrations to 10 major novels.

Phiz began illustrating *Pickwick Papers* at a crucial moment in its history. The publishers, disappointed by the sales, had even wondered whether to close the enterprise altogether. From the moment Dickens introduced the character of Samuel Weller into the fourth number, which included Phiz's illustration showing him brushing his boots in the courtyard of the White Hart Inn, the sales went up at an amazing pace, eventually reaching the astonishing record of 40,000 per issue.

Phiz seldom saw the manuscript before drawing the illustrations. He was visited regularly by the author who reviewed any work that was in hand and gave him verbal descriptions of the next two scenes for illustration. Each scene was drawn straight on to the plate so that the design appeared in reverse when printed. His fellow student Robert Young assisted on the technical side when Browne was short of time. Seymour's original illustrations had been etched on steel plates, which were hard on the surface, but very soft underneath. When Phiz had established himself as Seymour's successor he made duplicates of all his predecessor's plates. From the tenth part, Phiz etched each part in duplicate immediately, which accounts for the variations observable in different copies of the first issues.

C51
Phiz (Hablôt K. Browne) (1815–82)
Drawing for the illustration 'The discovery of Jingle in the Fleet' to *Pickwick Papers*
Pencil and wash
Lent by the Comtesse de Suzannet

C52
Phiz (Hablôt K. Browne) (1815–82)
(a) **Drawing for the illustration 'Mr. Winkle soothes the refractory steed' to the Household Edition of *Pickwick Papers***
Signed *Phiz*
Pen and ink and wash. $3\frac{5}{8} \times 5\frac{1}{2}$

(b) **Drawing for the illustration 'First appearance of Mr. Samuel Weller' to the Household Edition of *Pickwick Papers***
Pen and ink and wash. $4\frac{1}{8} \times 5\frac{5}{8}$

(c) **Drawing for the illustration 'Mr. Solomon Pell, assisted by a Select Committee of Coachmen, arranges the Affairs of the elder Mr. Weller' to the Household Edition of *Pickwick Papers***
Signed *Phiz*
Pen and ink and wash. $4\frac{1}{2} \times 5\frac{1}{2}$

(d) **Study for the figure of Mr Weller Senior**
Signed *HKB*. Inscribed *study for Mr Weller Senr. (Pickwick)*
Pencil. $5\frac{1}{4} \times 5\frac{1}{2}$
Lent by the Trustees of the British Museum

In appearance, Tony Weller was one of Phiz's stock figures. The same obese individual had already appeared in an illustration to the story 'John Smith' by E. Mayhew, *Library of Fiction*, 1836.

After Dickens's death, Phiz, although his right hand was paralysed, redrew the original illustrations to *Pickwick Papers*, for incorporation in Chapman and Hall's Household Edition of Dickens's works.

C53 [frontispiece, 25]
Phiz (Hablôt K. Browne) (1815–82)
Illustrations to *Pickwick Papers*
Each signed *Phiz*
Etchings. Average size $5 \times 4\frac{1}{2}$
(a) 'First appearance of Mr. Samuel Weller'
(b) 'The unexpected breaking up of the seminary for young ladies'
(c) 'Mr. Weller Attacks the Executive of Ipswich'
(d) 'Christmas Eve at Mr Wardle's'
(e) 'The Valentine'

OLIVER TWIST

See also Section K

C54

Letter from Dickens to Forster, [? 14 June 1837]

F.MS.172

Throughout the writing of *Oliver Twist*, Dickens's relations with its publisher, Richard Bentley, were deteriorating. For he had entered into various agreements with Bentley, on terms which seemed unfavourable, now that he had achieved fame with *Pickwick*. In particular, he had agreed not only to edit *Bentley's Miscellany* and to write *Oliver Twist* for it, but to produce two more novels for Bentley within a comparatively short period. He sought the advice of Forster, and in this letter to him confesses to the unsatisfactory nature of his contract with Bentley. Dickens and Forster exerted pressure on Bentley, who made unwilling concessions while trying to hold Dickens to his legal obligations. Strained relations and excessive work caused Dickens to withhold an instalment of *Oliver Twist* from the *Miscellany* in October 1837.

C55

Letter from Richard Bentley to John Forster, [3 November 1838]

On permanent loan from the Executors of John Forster

The last instalment of *Oliver Twist* appeared in April 1839, but Dickens had finished writing by the end of October 1838 because the complete novel was to be published in three volumes in 1838. Readers who had followed the story in the *Miscellany* and wished to know the outcome of it before April 1839 might be expected to obtain the three-volume edition. It was at first intended to publish the complete novel in September, but Dickens, busy with *Nickleby*, did not manage to finish writing until the following month. Bentley was then forced to 'prodigious exertion' in printing the novel as quickly as possible. In the scribbled note shown here he asks Forster to return proofs before leaving London to join Dickens in Liverpool. Forster sat up until four in the morning labouring at the task.

C56

Draft of a letter from Dickens to Cruikshank, [9 November 1838]

F.MS.172

In order to have *Oliver Twist* ready for publication in three volumes late in 1838, Cruikshank, as well as Dickens, had to work hard. He finished the illustrations in time, but when Dickens, returning to London on 8 November from a tour in Wales and the Midlands, saw the plates in the third volume, he was greatly dissatisfied with some of them. After considering the matter he decided that only one plate, now known as the 'Fireside Plate', was irredeemably unsatisfactory, and wrote to Cruikshank to ask him to design another. The book was already on sale, but in later copies the 'Church Plate' was substituted for the offensive design (see C68).

C57

George Cruikshank

The Artist and the Author. A statement of facts

London, Bell and Daldy [1872]

12.iv.1929

After Dickens's death, Cruikshank claimed to have been the originator of *Oliver Twist*. This claim was refuted by Forster in the first volume of his *Life of Dickens*, 1871, but repeated by Cruikshank in a letter to *The Times*, 20 December 1871. Forster considered that he had disposed of the matter when in his second volume (1872) he printed a facsimile of the letter from Dickens to Cruikshank shown at C56, in which there is no doubt who is master. But Cruikshank, smarting under a deep sense of injury, published in 1872 a pamphlet entitled *The Artist and the Author*, in which he repeated both his claim to have originated *Oliver Twist* and similar claims he had made in respect of several of Harrison Ainsworth's novels.

C58

Letter from Dickens to Forster [26 January 1839]

F.MS.172

By the beginning of 1839, Dickens had obtained considerable concessions from his publisher Richard Bentley. *Oliver Twist* was now regarded as one of the two novels which Dickens owed Bentley, and it was agreed that the other, *Barnaby Rudge*, should be published in the *Miscellany* and not separately. But still Dickens was unable to supply *Barnaby Rudge* at the agreed date, and with Forster's support, he asked for a postponement of six months. Bentley replied in what Dickens took to be a 'style of offensive impertinence', and so Dickens threatened to break off all his agreements with Bentley forthwith. He sent his letter of repudiation to Forster for approval, with the covering note shown here. After negotiations between Dickens's solicitors and Bentley's, new agreements were drawn up, under which Dickens resigned from the editorship of the *Miscellany*, and the delivery date of *Barnaby Rudge* was postponed until 1 January 1840.

C59
Letter from Richard Bentley to William Jerdan, 25 June 1840
On permanent loan from the Executors of John Forster

In December 1839, with the delivery date of *Barnaby Rudge* imminent, Bentley had begun to advertise the book. Dickens, however, had written only a chapter or two. His antagonism towards Bentley had grown into a resentful rancour, and he was determined to free himself from his contracts. 'War to the knife and with no quarter on either side, has commenced with the Burlington Street Brigand', he wrote on 17 December. Bentley, finding that the law, though on his side, could not force Dickens to write *Barnaby Rudge*, agreed to come to a settlement. He was represented in negotiations by William Jerdan, editor of the *Literary Gazette*, while Forster represented Dickens. The copyright, the etched plates for the illustrations, and the stock of *Oliver Twist* were sold to Dickens, and similar arrangements, outlined by Bentley in the letter shown here, were made with the *Memoirs of Grimaldi*. In these transactions Dickens was financed by Chapman and Hall, with whom he now began a long and satisfactory relationship.

ILLUSTRATIONS TO *OLIVER TWIST* BY GEORGE CRUIKSHANK (1792–1878)

Although it was Bentley rather than Dickens who asked Cruikshank to illustrate the *Miscellany*, there is no sign that the novelist was anything but pleased with the illustrations until November 1838 (see C56). The subjects for illustration were usually selected by Dickens in consultation with Cruikshank. Sometimes Dickens indicated a subject on the manuscript, as in the case of 'Oliver's escape from being bound apprentice to the sweep'; or sometimes as in the case of 'Mr. Bumble and Mrs. Claypole taking tea', he supplied the artist with a detailed précis of the incident to be depicted. When Dickens left London on 29 October 1838 to tour Wales and the Midlands he gave the artist a list of the final six subjects. Cruikshank omitted one, 'The Interview between Rose and Nancy' (see C67.b), and substituted a subject of his own choice 'Sikes attempting to destroy his dog'. The artist sometimes suggested a variety of titles for an illustration, from which the author made his choice.

Although Bradbury and Evans seem to have considered asking another artist to design a cover for their new issue of *Oliver Twist* in parts in 1846, they finally asked Cruikshank. For this edition the worn plates were rebitten and touched up probably by an engraver named Findlay, with a resulting loss of detail and a distinct darkening of the background (see C62, 66).

C60
(a) **'Oliver introduced to the Respectable Old Gentleman'**
Signed *George Cruikshank*. Inscribed *Original Sketch*
Water-colour. $4 \times 3\frac{1}{4}$
Lent by the Trustees of the British Museum

During the 1860s Cruikshank redrew in colour many of his earlier illustrations for Dickens and other authors. He made a complete set of the illustrations to *Oliver Twist* for his friend and patron F.W. Cosens.

(b) **Study in pen and ink for the illustration 'Oliver's reception by Fagin and the boys' to *Oliver Twist***
Signed *Geo Cruikshank* and inscribed *Oliver Twist* and in pencil *Oliver's reception by Fagin & the boys*
$4\frac{1}{4} \times 3\frac{3}{8}$
9995.L

This study shows the importance Cruikshank attached to the dispersal of light and dark areas to evoke the required atmosphere.

Tracings for the illustrations (c) **'Oliver asking for more'**, (d) **'Oliver Plucks up a spirit'**, (e) **'Monks and the Jew'**
Each signed, (e) in ink. (c) and (d) inscribed *Oliver Twist*
$4\frac{3}{4} \times 3\frac{3}{8}$; $4\frac{1}{2} \times 3\frac{1}{4}$; $4\frac{3}{4} \times 3\frac{3}{4}$
9797.A, 9797.B, 9995.P

C61
(a) **Pencil sketch and** (b) **proof of the etching for the illustration 'Oliver recovering from the fever' to *Oliver Twist***
(a) inscribed *Oliver Twist. Vignette for title page, Don Quixote* (b) signed *George Cruikshank*
$8 \times 4\frac{1}{2}$; $4\frac{1}{2} \times 3\frac{5}{8}$
9995.M, 9996.5

This etching was not retouched for the 1846 edition. In the lower right corner of the drawing there is a sketch for the frontispiece to *Rambles in the Footsteps of Don Quixote* by H.D. Inglis, which the artist was also illustrating in 1837.

(c) **Tracing and** (d) **proof of the etching for the 1846 edition of the illustration 'Oliver claimed by his affectionate friends' to** *Oliver Twist*
Both signed *George Cruikshank*
$4\frac{3}{4} \times 3\frac{3}{4}$
9797.C, 9996.6

c62 [20]
(a) **Preliminary sketch in pen and ink,** (b) **tracing,** (c) **proof of the etching for the first edition,** (d) **proof of the etching for the 1846 edition of the illustration 'The Burglary' to** *Oliver Twist*
(a) inscribed in pencil *Oliver Twist – The Burglary*.
(c) and (d) signed *George Cruikshank*
(a) $3\frac{7}{8} \times 3\frac{1}{8}$; (c) $4\frac{1}{4} \times 3\frac{3}{4}$
9995.N, 9797.D, 9996.2, 9996.3

This sketch shows Cruikshank exploring abstract and purely linear means to give the spectator Oliver's sense of shock. The difference between the early proof of the etching and the proof pulled after Findlay had retouched the plate is particularly clear in this illustration.

c63 [18]
(a) **Drawing in pencil and** (b) **proof of the etching for the 1846 edition of the illustration 'Mr. Claypole as he appeared when his master was out' to** *Oliver Twist*
(a) inscribed *Dr. Dickins* [sic] '*title wanted – will any of these do? Yours G. Ck. Mr. Claypole astonishing Mr. Bumble and "the native"? Mr. Claypole indulging. Mr. Claypole as he appeared when his master was out.*' and with other notes
(b) signed *George Cruikshank*
$4\frac{1}{4} \times 3\frac{3}{4}$; $4\frac{1}{8} \times 3\frac{3}{4}$
9995.H, 9996.I

c64 [19]
(a) **Drawing and studies in pen and ink and pencil for the illustration 'Mr. Bumble degraded in the eyes of the paupers' to** *Oliver Twist*
Inscribed *Oliver Twist*, and by Dickens *Mr. Bumble degraded in* (*presence*, deleted) *the eyes of the Paupers*
$7\frac{1}{2} \times 6\frac{1}{2}$
9995.I

(b) **Pencil study and drawing on one sheet, and** (c) **tracing for the illustration 'Mr. Bumble and Mrs. Corney taking tea' to** *Oliver Twist*
(c) inscribed with titles
9995.F, 9797.E

c65
(a) **Preliminary study in pencil,** (b) **drawing in pencil,** (c) **tracing and** (d) **proof of the etching for the 1846 edition of the illustration 'Oliver waited on by the Bow Street Runners' to** *Oliver Twist*
(a) signed in ink *Geo Cruikshank*. (d) signed *George Cruikshank*. (b) inscribed with title and *All these as done in the etchings*
$3\frac{1}{2} \times 6\frac{1}{2}$; $4\frac{3}{4} \times 5\frac{1}{2}$; $4\frac{5}{8} \times 3\frac{5}{8}$
9995.O, 9995.G, 9797.F, 9996.4

c66
Four proofs of the etchings for the 1846 edition of the illustrations to *Oliver Twist*
(a), (b) and (d) signed *George Cruikshank*. (c) signed *Geog Cruikshank*
Average size $4\frac{1}{2} \times 3\frac{5}{8}$
(a) 'The evidence destroyed'
(b) 'Mr. Fagin and his pupil recovering Nancy'
(c) 'The Jew & Morris Bolter begin to understand each other'
(d) 'The last Chance'
9996.10, 9996.8, 9996.7, 9996.9

c67 [17]
(a) **Pencil sketch for the illustration 'Fagin in the Condemned Cell' to** *Oliver Twist*
Signed in ink *Geo Cruikshank* and inscribed *Fagin in the condemned cell*
$5 \times 6\frac{7}{8}$
9995.K

Cruikshank identified himself to a remarkable degree with his image of Fagin in the condemned cell. His earliest account of the inspiration of this plate was given to Horace Mayhew. One morning after the artist had begun to despair of creating a graphic equivalent of Dickens's gripping 'out and outer', Cruikshank said he sat up in bed with his hand covering his chin, his fingertips between his lips, his whole attitude expressive of disappointment and despair. He saw his face in the cheval glass opposite him, and exclaimed 'That's it, that's just the expression I want'. Though he modified the story later, Cruikshank did not deny that he fixed the peculiarly effective pose of Fagin by studying himself in a mirror.

This sketch is either a very early idea for the plate 'Fagin in the Condemned Cell' or a drawing for the cover for the issue of *Oliver Twist* in parts, by Bradbury and Evans in 1846

(b) **Studies for the illustration 'Fagin in the Condemned Cell' and other incidents in the story of *Oliver Twist***
Inscribed in pencil with notes and titles. Signed and inscribed in ink, at a later date, *George Cruikshank First Idea & Sketch for Fagin in the condemned cell*
Pencil and pen and ink. $7\frac{1}{2} \times 9$
9995.J

Cruikshank's inscription, claiming that this was his first sketch for Fagin, was almost certainly added long after the drawing was made – compare the different styles of handwriting – and is probably contemporary with his claim to have invented the characters of *Oliver Twist*. In pose, the Fagin figures are closer to that used on the part cover, designed in 1846, than to that in the illustration.

The possibility that the sketches were made for the part cover is strengthened by the confining border around the smaller complete study, the inscription *wood-cut*, and the presence of other small sketches, different in subject but similar in format to the scenes represented on the cover design. These sketches are related to the illustrations: 'The evidence destroyed', 'The Jew and Morris Bolter begin to understand each other' and 'The Interview between Rose and Nancy'. The latter was a subject suggested by Dickens, but never illustrated by Cruikshank.

(c) **Three studies on one sheet in pen and ink and pencil for 'Bill Sikes in the condemned Cell'**
Signed *George Cruikshank*. Inscribed in ink *Bill Sickes* [sic] *in the condemned cell*
$6\frac{3}{4} \times 8\frac{1}{2}$
Lent by the Trustees of the British Museum

As far as is known Dickens never considered putting Bill Sikes in the condemned cell. One can only suppose that at one stage, Cruikshank believed that this was how the story would come to its close.

C68
(a) **Drawing in pencil and** (b) **proof of the etching touched with sepia for the rejected illustration 'Rose Maylie and Oliver' to *Oliver Twist***
(a) inscribed with titles and *rejected plate*.
(b) signed *George Cruikshank*. Lettered *London, Published by Richard Bentley 1838*
6×6; $4\frac{1}{2} \times 3\frac{5}{8}$
9995.D, 9996.11

In spite of Dickens's letter (see C56), Cruikshank appears to have tried to make the illustration acceptable to the author, by adding strengthening shadows to the plate.

C69
John Wykeham Archer (1808–64)
Old Houses in Jacob's Island, Bermondsey. 1855
Water-colour. $9\frac{1}{8} \times 14\frac{3}{4}$
Lent by the Trustees of the British Museum

Jacob's Island was the scene of Bill Sikes's death. In the Preface to the Cheap Edition of *Oliver Twist*, 1850, Dickens once again denounced the conditions of this slum quarter, in reply to Sir Peter Laurie's claim that Jacob's Island 'only existed in a work of fiction, written by Mr. Charles Dickens ten years ago'.

C70
Toy theatre, with a scene from the *Juvenile Drama* version of *Oliver Twist*
The cut-out characters and scenery lent by Pollock's Toy Museum; the toy theatre, E.244-1924

This toy theatre is based upon the Britannia Theatre, Hoxton, which is described by Dickens in 'Two Views of a Cheap Theatre' (*Uncommercial Traveller*, ch. 4). The scenery and characters for the *Juvenile Drama* were accompanied by a text based on Almar's version (see C71).

C71
Playbill for a performance of *Oliver Twist* at the Surrey Theatre, 21 December 1838

The success of *Oliver Twist* is shown by the number of dramatic versions which were produced. Three were playing at London theatres by December 1838. This bill relates to the dramatisation by George Almar, the text of which was also the basis for the version in the *Juvenile Drama*.

NICHOLAS NICKLEBY

C72
The Life and Adventures of Nicholas Nickleby
London, Chapman and Hall, 1839
F.PB.2437

C73
The Life and Adventures of Nicholas Nickleby. Number XII
London, Chapman and Hall, March 1839
Lent by The Dickens House

Nicholas Nickleby, like *Pickwick Papers*, was published in monthly parts. At a banquet to celebrate the completion of the book Sir David Wilkie made a speech, Forster tells us, 'all about the reality of Dickens's genius, and how there had been nothing like him issuing his novels part by part since Richardson issued his novels volume by volume, and how in both cases people talked about the characters as if they were next-door neighbours or friends, and how as many letters were written to the author of *Nickleby* to implore him not to kill poor Smike as had been sent by young ladies to the author of *Clarissa* to "save Lovelace's soul alive"'.

C74
Dickens's diary (*The Law and Commercial Daily Remembrancer*) for 1839
F.MS.182

The entries for the fortnight before 19 September are, for the most part, the single word 'Work'. Under Friday, 20 September comes:

'Finished Nickleby this day at 2 o'Clock.... Thank God that I have lived to get through it happily.'

C75
The New Work by the Author of 'The Pickwick Papers'.... Proclamation
London, Chapman and Hall, 1838
F.PAMPH.72

Both *Pickwick Papers* and *Oliver Twist* were pirated and plagiarized. In this publicity leaflet Dickens defies his imitators to set to work on *Nickleby*.

The 'Board of Trade' referred to in the final paragraph is the premises of Chapman and Hall at 186 Strand, where at the end of each month, the latest monthly part of the current novel by Dickens was put on sale.

C76
A sheet of the manuscript of Dickens's Preface to the 1848 edition of *Nicholas Nickleby*
F.MS. 170

'This story was begun', writes Dickens, 'within a few months after the publication of the completed Pickwick Papers. There were, then, a good many cheap Yorkshire schools in existence. There are very few now.'

He goes on to explain why it was that he made 'Yorkshire schools' the object of a satirical attack in this novel.

C77
An advertisement for Shaw's Bowes Academy, near Greta Bridge, Yorkshire
Lent by The Dickens House

Dickens and Browne, under assumed names and on the pretext of looking for a school for the son of a widowed friend, visited William Shaw (?1783–1850) the owner of Bowes Academy on 2 February 1838, during their tour of Yorkshire schools. In the past, Shaw had been sued by the parents of two children who had gone blind through infection and gross neglect; he had been convicted and had paid damages of £500, but continued to run the school. The schoolmaster was suspicious of his visitors and let them see very little; nevertheless, as a result of what he saw there and in other schools, Dickens felt justified in writing to Mrs S.C. Hall on his return: 'Depend upon it that the rascalities of those Yorkshire schoolmasters *cannot* easily be exaggerated, and that I have kept down the strong truth and thrown as much comicality over it as I could, rather than disgust and weary the reader with its fouler aspects'.

ILLUSTRATIONS TO *NICHOLAS NICKLEBY* BY HABLÔT K. BROWNE (PHIZ) (1815–82)

Phiz supplied two illustrations to each part. Since the publishers expected as great a circulation as *Pickwick Papers* had enjoyed, two plates of each subject were made at the outset, in order to avoid the confusion of having to make new plates later. In fact the sales for *Nickleby* were higher than anticipated, and many of the plates were etched in triplicate; some were reproduced as many as four times.

A time-table drawn up by Browne shows that he usually expected to receive the copy for the first subject by the 11th of the month, and would send a sketch to Dickens on the 13th. This would be returned, with instructions for the second subject on the 14th, and a sketch of the second subject would go to the author on the 15th, being returned the next day. The plates were generally finished ten days later. The titles of the plates were not etched, but engraved, probably by a professional engraver, after the etchings were finished.

c78
(a) Drawing in pencil and (b) etching for the illustration 'The Yorkshire Schoolmaster at The Saracen's Head' to *Nicholas Nickleby*
(a) Lent by the Comtesse de Suzannet

Although in his 1839 Preface to *Nicholas Nickleby* Dickens stated that Squeers was 'the representative of a class, and not an individual', it has been recognised generally that he was based directly on William Shaw (see c77). Phiz said that his etching was 'not unlike' a particular master, but gave no name. Shaw was the only schoolmaster in the district with one eye – or, as a former pupil recalled, 'a slight scale covering the pupil of one of his eyes'.

The drawing was changed considerably before it was transferred to the plate. In the sketch, Squeers's young protégé is not sitting on his trunk but on the seat of the settle; he is much less hunched up and looks less frightened than in the final illustration.

c79
(a) Drawing in pencil and wash and (b) etching for the illustration 'Kate Nickleby sitting to Miss La Creevy' to *Nicholas Nickleby*
Inscribed in ink with the title, possibly by Dickens. And by the artist in pencil partly obscured
[   ] *you have the goodness to send* [   ]
(*either home or C & H*) *early* [   ] — H.K.B
Lent by the Comtesse de Suzannet

(see note to B6)

c80
Five pencil sketches for the Cheeryble Brothers
Signed variously *Phiz* and *HKB*. One inscribed *Cherrible* [sic] *Bros*
Various sizes
Lent by the Trustees of the British Museum

The artist is searching for exactly the right expression for the Cheeryble Brothers, the benefactors and employers of Nicholas Nickleby. The originals of these benevolent characters were William and Daniel Grant, cotton-spinners and calico-printers near Manchester.

c81
(a) Steel plate and (b) an impression from it for the illustration 'Nicholas Instructs Smike in the Art of Acting' to *Nicholas Nickleby*
Signed *Phiz*
$4\frac{1}{8} \times 4$
Lent by The Dickens House

This plate was etched in triplicate.

c82
Five illustrations to *Nicholas Nickleby*
Each Signed *Phiz* and lettered with the title of the plate.
Etchings. Average size $4\frac{1}{2} \times 4\frac{1}{4}$
(a) 'The internal economy of Dotheboys Hall'
(b) 'The Professional Gentlemen at Madame Mantalini's'
(c) 'Mr. Linkinwater intimates his approval of Nicholas'
(d) 'Mysterious appearance of the Gentleman in small clothes'
(e) 'Great excitement of Miss Kenwigs at the hairdresser's shop'

Dickens gave the following instructions to Browne for the illustration of Miss Kenwigs at the hairdresser: '– A hairdresser's shop at night – not a dashing one, but a barber's, Morleena Kenwig[s] on a tall chair having her hair dressed by an underbred attendant with his hair parted down the middle, and frizzed up into curls at the sides. Another customer, who is being shaved, has just turned his head in the direction of Miss Kenwigs, and she and Newman Noggs (who has brought her there, and has been whiling away the time with an old newspaper), recognise, with manifestations of surprise, and Morleena with emotion, Mr. Lillyvick, the collector. Mr. Lillyvick's bristly beard expresses great neglect of his person, and he looks very grim and in the utmost despondency –'. These instructions must have been amplified further, as they make no mention of the coal-heaver in the doorway, described in the text.

c83 [75]
No. 1 Devonshire Terrace
Photograph of a wood-engraving after Daniel Maclise

Dickens moved to this house in December 1839 and lived there till 1851, when he moved to Tavistock House.

D: John Forster

EARLY FRIENDSHIP

What first impressed many of his contemporaries about Forster, it seems, was his assertive temperament. Even when he was in 'a tip top state of amiability' he could give Dickens cause to lament: 'I think I never heard him *half so loud*(!)' Though often exasperating, and the subject of many jokes, he was the staunchest of friends, not only keeping the affection of his early professional associates, Chitty and Elwin, but forming close and constant friendships with such men as Lamb, Leigh Hunt, Landor, Macready, Bulwer, Carlyle, and above all Dickens.

D1
Thomas Warrington (exhibited 1829–31) and Daniel Maclise, RA (1806–70)
John Forster, 1830
Oil. 30 × 20
P.35–1935

Forster was born in 1812 in Newcastle and educated at the Grammar School there, evincing an eager interest in literature and the theatre. With the help of an uncle he was sent in 1828 to London University, and studied law at the Inner Temple. By the early 1830s he was writing for newspapers and magazines, and journalism gradually gained ground over his legal studies.

D2
***The Examiner*, 28 February 1836**
Open at a review of *Sketches by Boz*
F.PB.2914

Forster wrote for a time for the newspaper the *True Sun*, founded in 1832, for which Dickens also briefly worked as a parliamentary reporter. It was while Dickens was leading a reporters' strike that he first attracted Forster's notice. Before the two men actually met, Forster had extended his knowledge of Dickens by reviewing *Sketches by Boz*, *Pickwick* and *The Village Coquettes* in the *Examiner* (28 February, 4 September and 11 December 1836).

D3
Photograph of Kensal Lodge and Kensal Manor House
Reproduced in S.M. Ellis *William Harrison Ainsworth and His Friends*, London, 1910

Ainsworth was living in Kensal Lodge (the further house in the photograph) in 1836, and it was probably here that Dickens and Forster were first introduced to each other in the winter of that year. From 1841 to '53 Ainsworth lived in Kensal Manor House, the larger building in the foreground.

D4
Letter from Dickens to Forster [?2 March 1837]
F.MS.172

This letter is the earliest that survives from Dickens to Forster. It records, Forster tells us in his *Life*, one of several attempts by each party to visit the other, which were defeated by circumstances.

D5
Letter from Dickens to Forster [?11 Jan 1838]
F.MS.172

In the late 1830s and early 1840s Dickens was working at intense pressure, and sought relaxation in equally intense physical exercise. Many notes survive in which he calls on Forster to accompany him on rides and walks; here he suggests 'a good brisk walk over Hampstead Heath'.

D6 [28]
A facetious account, written by Dickens, of Forster making an ascent in a balloon. 17 June 1838
L.1595(25)–1938

In 1838 and 1839 Dickens and his family spent the summer out of town, taking cottages at Twickenham in the first year and at Petersham in the second. Forster and other friends were often present, relaxing and making merry with Dickens. At Petersham there was 'much athletic competition, from the more difficult forms of which I in general modestly retired', Forster recalled, and at Twickenham 'we had ... a balloon club for the children, of which I appear to have been elected president on condition of supplying the balloons'. Several playful documents written by Dickens remain to evoke the high spirits of that time.

D7 [**27**]
Daniel Maclise, RA (1806–70)
John Forster: two sketches
Each signed and dated *D. Maclise R.A. Friday 22d May: 1840*
Pen. $3 \times 3\frac{1}{4}$; $3\frac{3}{4} \times 4\frac{3}{8}$
F.P.69

D8
Richard Doyle (1824–83)

(a) **John Forster**
Pen. $5 \times 2\frac{3}{4}$

(b) **Charles Dickens and John Forster**
Pen. $2\frac{5}{8} \times 2\frac{3}{8}$

(c) **Charles Dickens, John Forster and Douglas Jerrold**
Pen. $3\frac{7}{8} \times 3\frac{1}{4}$
Lent by the Trustees of the British Museum

D9
Anonymous
Dickens, Maclise, Stanfield and Forster in a carriage, on their tour of Cornwall.
Caricature. Pen and ink. $4\frac{3}{4} \times 8\frac{3}{4}$
F.P.110

In autumn 1842, after Dickens had returned from his first visit to America, he went on a week's tour in Cornwall with Forster, Stanfield and Maclise. Forster mentions that the tour was 'celebrated ... by Thackeray in one of his pen-and-ink pleasantries': this unsigned sketch may well be by Thackeray (cf. D23).

D10 [**49**]
Clarkson Stanfield, RA (1793/4–1867)
The Logan Rock, Cornwall climbed by Charles Dickens, John Forster, Daniel Maclise and the Artist
Water- and body-colour on brown paper. $10 \times 6\frac{7}{8}$
F.P.93

Forster was particularly lively on the Cornish tour; many years later, in a letter (D11), Maclise recalled his exploits on the Logan Rock.

D11
Letter from Maclise to Forster, 13 October 1868
F.MS.385

Maclise wrote:
'... As to your clambering in itself Don't I know you of old – need I mention the Logan Stone – you perched on the giddy top, me rocking it on its pivot while to look down –
Thought shrinks from all that lies concealed
below.
But there was the sea lapping into such solitary rocky nooks that if one caught sight of the bright flap of a mermaids tail it would only appear the appropriate figure of the scene. And don't I see you again sitting on the tip top stone of the cradle turret high up over the topmost battlements of the Castle of St Michaels Mount your legs dependent over the side and not a ledge projection or coign of vantage "twixt you & the depths below" ...'

PROFESSIONAL COLLABORATION

The great value of Forster's friendship lay in the steady and skilful help – both practical and critical – that he was able to give with the most important activity of Dickens's life, his writing. Moreover Forster's business sense made him an invaluable ally in negotiations with publishers.

D12
Letter from Dickens to Forster [?26 May 1837]
F.MS.172

D13
Letter from Dickens to Forster [?12 October 1837]
F.MS.172

These two letters demonstrate Forster's establishment as Dickens's most trusted adviser on his own work. From late 1837 'there was nothing written by him ... which I did not see before the world did, either in manuscript or proofs', and from this time, perhaps from the very moment marked by the second letter, Forster was accustomed to help Dickens in the labour of proof correcting.

D14
Photograph of 58 Lincoln's Inn Fields

D15 [29]
Edward Mathew Ward, RA (1816–79) and
Ebenezer Newman Downard (exhibited 1849–89)
John Forster in his study
C.1850
Inscribed on a label on the back of the stretcher
*John Forster in his study – painted by – Ward R. A.
for himself: bought by Mr. Forster – Finished later
by Mr. Downard*
Oil. 25 × 30
P.74-1935

While helping and advising Dickens, Forster was working hard at his own career as a critic, historian and biographer. Too busy to spend much time in the British Museum Reading Room he now began to build up his own fine library in his rooms at 58 Lincoln's Inn Fields, where he moved in 1834, and where he is no doubt seen in E.M. Ward's portrait. By 1840 he had laid claim on the English Republic as the special subject of his historical studies, contributing to Lardner's *Cabinet Cyclopaedia* (1836–39) several lives of the statesmen of the Commonwealth, which appeared in a collected edition in 1840.

D16
Letter from Dickens to Forster [29 August 1838]
L.1595(10)-1938

D17
***The Examiner*, 2 September 1838**
Showing a review of 'Refutation of the Misstatements . . . in Mr. Lockhart's Life of . . . Scott'
F.PB.2914

During most of the 1840s Forster devoted himself to journalism, being chief critic of literature and drama, and, from 1847, editor of the *Examiner*. From time to time he secured a contribution from Dickens. This early review is the first of three by Dickens, taking Lockhart's side in the Lockhart/Ballantyne controversy.

D18
Corrected proofs of an article by Forster on 'The inventor of the power-loom'
L.354-1916

D19
***Household Words*, 9 July 1853**
Showing the article 'The Power-Loom'
F.PB.4285

In 1850 Dickens began his own magazine, for which Forster occasionally wrote. In his marginal note on this proof, Forster has asked the printer's reader to check a fact for him.

D20
John Forster
The Life and Adventures of Oliver Goldsmith
London, Bradbury and Evans, and Chapman and Hall, 1848
F.PB.3151

D21
John Forster
Manuscript of a dedicatory sonnet to Dickens, prefixed to Forster's *Life . . . of . . . Goldsmith*, dated 12 October 1847
F.MS.203

D22
Letter from Dickens to Forster, 22 April 1848
F.MS.172

In 1848 Forster followed his volumes on the statesmen of the Commonwealth with a *Life of Goldsmith*, which he dedicated to Dickens. Dickens sent him a long letter of critical and appreciative comment, writing in the final paragraph:

'. . . I desire no better for my fame when my personal dustyness shall be past the controul of my love of order, than such a biographer and such a critic. And again I say, most solemnly, that Literature in England has never had, and probably never will have, such a champion as you are, in right of this book.'

D23
Enlarged photograph of caricatures by W.M. Thackeray
Reproduced in the *Dickensian*, 1926, p.204

These caricatures were drawn on the back of an undated letter from Thackeray to Clarkson Stanfield. In the bottom right-hand corner stands the solid figure of Forster, and in the bottom left-hand corner the daintier figure of Dickens with loose, copious hair.

D 24
Enlarged photograph of a letter from Dickens to Forster, 8 January 1845
As printed in Forster's *Life*

This letter testifies to the warmth of Dickens's regard for Forster.

THE MIDDLE YEARS

From the 1850s Dickens and Forster were less constantly in touch. This was partly due to changes in Forster's life: in 1855 he became the Secretary of the Lunacy Commission, giving up journalism to devote himself to exacting public service, and in 1856 he married Eliza Colburn, widow of the publisher Henry Colburn. It was also partly due to Dickens's absorption in public readings, of which Forster always disapproved. But when Dickens's marriage broke up in 1858 Forster rallied to him loyally (see the letter from Forster to Landseer at M9); and, if in the last decade of Dickens's life they were slightly less in sympathy than in earlier years, their friendship continued unbroken to the end.

D 25
The Posthumous Papers of the Pickwick Club
Library edition. London, Chapman and Hall, and Bradbury and Evans, 1858
Showing an inserted sheet with an inscription by Dickens
Another copy
F.PB.2400

The printed dedication of the Library edition of Dickens's works, and even more, the inscription in the copy he presented to Forster, bear witness to the strength of the twenty-year-old friendship.

D 26
After William Powell Frith, RA (1819–1909)
Charles Dickens
Signed by the engraver in pencil *Thos Oldham Barlow*. India proof before letters.
Mixed mezzotint. $25\frac{1}{8} \times 18\frac{7}{8}$
24195

D 27
Letter from Forster to Frith, 8 April 1859
L.186–1922

D 28
Letter from Forster to Frith, 6 May 1859
L.186–1922

It was in the difficult period after Dickens had separated from his wife that Frith completed a portrait which had been commissioned by Forster in 1854 (see O 10). With an understandable burst of proprietary feeling, Forster at first refused to allow it to be engraved, but eventually was persuaded.

FORSTER'S LATER LIFE

Forster's later middle age was cheered by the faithful support of his wife. Himself fretted by illness, he outlived all but one of his close relations, and undertook three substantial acts of piety in memory of intimate friends who died before him. After Landor's death in 1864, Forster prepared an edition of his works and a biography; when the Rev. Alexander Dyce died in 1869 the third edition of his Shakespeare remained to be seen through the press by Forster. And the *Life of Dickens* occupied Forster from 1870 to 1874.

D 29
Sir William Boxall, RA (1800–79)
Mrs John Forster, née Eliza Ann Crosbie
Signed in ink on a label on the back *W. Boxall A.R.A. No 1 (?)*
Oil on panel. $24 \times 18\frac{1}{4}$
P.36–1935

D 30
Photograph of Forster's house in Palace Gate, Kensington
Photograph Collection

D 31
Forster's library at his house in Palace Gate
Photograph of a drawing by John Watkins
F.P.140

After his marriage, Forster moved from Lincoln's Inn Fields, first to Montagu Square, and in 1863 to a grander house in South Kensington, where his library was installed in a stately room.

D 32
Forster in late middle age
Carte de visite photograph by Elliott & Fry
Photograph Collection

D 33
A notebook compiled by Forster: 'Manuscripts, Letters, Deeds, Papers, Pamphlets, & Matters Miscellaneous. February 1864. Palace Gate House'
On permanent loan from the Executors of John Forster

Once settled in his new house, Forster began to sort his immense correspondence with hundreds of his contemporaries, and to list it in a small account book. On the right-hand page displayed, he records a packet of Dickens's letters.
'4. *Dickens* – (with family letters and Georgina, CD – brothers – and boys & Girls –) also letters *very private* – Examine bound vols to destroy letters – same as to Macready –'

It is clear from this that Forster had begun to destroy the confidential parts of his correspondence; after his death his executors destroyed much more. All his letters from Dickens, save for a small number from the early years, must have been lost in this way, or else must have disappeared with the manuscript of the *Life of Dickens*, to which many of them were attached. Dickens bequeathed to his 'dear and trusty friend John Forster' all the surviving manuscripts of his works still in his possession at his death. These were treasured by Forster, who left them to the nation with the rest of his collection of books, manuscripts, paintings and drawings.

D 34
John Forster
Life of Charles Dickens
3 vols. London, Chapman and Hall, 1873–74
F.PB.3142

The *Life* is Forster's last tribute to Dickens and remains a classic of English biography. Forster died in 1876, and it is appropriate to quote Bulwer-Lytton's tribute to him: 'A most sterling man, with an intellect at once massive and delicate. Few indeed have his strong practical sense and sound judgement... He has a rare capacity for affection which embraces many friendships without loss of depth or warmth in one'.

E: Dickens's visit to America in 1842

After finishing *Barnaby Rudge* Dickens resolved to pay a visit to America. He embarked with his wife on the steamship 'Britannia' on 4 January 1842. Owing to an exceptionally bad crossing they did not reach Boston till 22 January; they spent a fortnight there. Their subsequent itinerary included Hartford, New York (for three weeks), Philadelphia, Washington, Richmond, St Louis, Buffalo and the Niagara Falls. After a visit to Montreal the party returned to New York, re-embarking for England on 12 June.

Dickens was attracted by the ideals of American republicanism, democracy and freedom, but became somewhat disillusioned by his direct experience of the country. He aroused hostility by his public advocacy of International Copyright, and by his denunciation of slavery. The letters he wrote home to Forster, his own note-book (no longer extant), pages from the 1842 Report of the Perkins Institution for the Blind, and passages quoted verbatim from Weld's *American Slavery as It Is* (E6) formed the basis of *American Notes*. He reserved his more pungent satire for the fictional account of Martin Chuzzlewit's visit to America.

E1
American Notes for General Circulation
2 vols in one. London, Chapman and Hall, 1842
F.PB.2408

The passage describing the people waiting in the anteroom to the President's office was taken by Dickens virtually verbatim from his letter to Albany Fonblanque (E3), which he had borrowed.

E2
Manuscript of *American Notes for General Circulation* [1842]. Vol. B
F.MS.156

The final paragraph of his description of Niagara Falls is based on passages in Dickens's letter to Henry Austin (E4), which he had borrowed.

E3
Letter from Charles Dickens to Albany Fonblanque written from Washington, 12 March 1842
Photograph from the original in the New York Public Library (Berg Collection)

Dickens used much of this letter in *American Notes* but omitted the paragraph describing the President's 'spit box' and his conversation with him.

E4
Letter from Charles Dickens to Henry Austin written from Niagara Falls, 1 May 1842
Facsimile, reproduced from *A Reference Catalogue of British and Foreign Autographs and Manuscripts*, edited by Thomas J. Wise, part III, 1894

This letter contains the passages which Dickens drew on for his description of Niagara Falls in *American Notes* (E2).

E5
John Forster
Life of Charles Dickens
Vol. II. Leipzig, Tauchnitz, 1872
F.PB.3145
Open at the printed text of the letter written by Dickens to Forster from Niagara Falls, 26 April 1842

Forster remarks how much he often prefers the 'first fresh version' of Dickens's letters from America to the passages 'strengthened by rhetorical additions' for *American Notes*. A striking example is provided by this letter, in which he simply says of standing in the basin of the Horse-shoe-fall 'It would be hard for a man to stand nearer God than he does there'. In *American Notes* he attaches this feeling to the moment when he was standing on Table Rock and elaborates it to: 'Then, when I felt how near to my Creator I was standing, the first effect, and the enduring one – instant and lasting – of the tremendous spectacle, was Peace. Peace of Mind, tranquillity, calm recollections of the Dead, great thoughts of Eternal Rest and Happiness;

nothing of gloom or terror. Niagara was at once stamped upon my heart, an Image of Beauty; to remain there, changeless and indelible, until its pulses cease to beat, for ever'.

E6
Anonymous [T.D. Weld]
American Slavery as It Is: Testimony of a Thousand Witnesses
New York, 1839
Lent by the Trustees of the British Museum

Dickens quoted from these advertisements in *American Notes*, chapter 17, 'Slavery,' without acknowledgement.

E7 [30]
The Extra Boz Herald, 15 February 1842
F.MS.176

This describes the Boz Ball held in Dickens's honour in New York, 14 February 1842.

E8
Playbill for performance of *A Roland for an Oliver* at the Queen's Theatre, Montreal, 25 May 1842
F.MS.180

Dickens met Lord Mulgrave on the passage out and promised him that he would take part in private theatricals with officers of the garrison and in the presence of the Governor-General on his return through Canada. This is the bill for the first performance, with the actors' names written in by Dickens. His comment to Forster 'But only think of Kate playing! and playing devilish well, I assure you!' is reinforced by the eight exclamation marks he has put after her name.

E9 [6]
Daniel Maclise, RA (1806–70)
The four elder children of Charles Dickens
Pencil and wash. Diameter 21
Lent by Cedric C. Dickens Esq.

Drawn by Maclise at Mrs Dickens's request when her accompanying Dickens to America, leaving the children in Macready's care, had been settled. She took and displayed it throughout their travels.

The children are, from left to right: Katey, Walter, Charley and Mamie. Mamie is saying 'Bid a good hea' Katy', to her sister, who is playing with Strutt's *Antiquities*. The bird is probably Grip's successor, the 'older and more gifted raven', which was discovered at a village public house in Yorkshire.

E10 [33]
Clarkson Stanfield, RA (1793–1867)
The S.S. Britannia at Liverpool embarking Charles Dickens
Water-colour. $3\frac{1}{2} \times 5\frac{1}{4}$
Lent by Captain Peter Dickens

It was in this ship that Charles Dickens sailed to America. In one of the most stormy passages in the experience of the crew, the passage took eighteen days. The watercolour was engraved by T. Bolton for the Cheap Edition of *American Notes*, 1850.

E11 [34]
Thomas Creswick, RA (1811–69)
Mount Tom, and the Connecticut River
Oil on panel. 7×10
580 – 1882 (Jones Bequest)

After leaving Worcester, Dickens joined the Connecticut River at Springfield, just below the point seen in this painting. 'The Connecticut River is a fine stream; and the banks in summertime are, I have no doubt, beautiful.' So far as is known, Creswick was never in America. He elaborated this oil painting from a sketch by W.H. Bartlett: it was then engraved as an illustration to *American Scenery; or Land, Lake and River* by N.P. Willis, vol. II, London, 1840, facing p.27 (see E13, 14).

E12 [32]
After John Haviland (1792–1852)
Eastern Penitentiary, Philadelphia
Photograph of an engraving by Cephas Grier Childs after a drawing by the architect
Lent by the Historical Society of Pennsylvania

Dickens visited the prisons in every American town where it was possible to do so, comparing American methods unfavourably with those in London's Coldbath Fields and Tothill Fields. The famous experimental Eastern Penitentiary, run on a system of solitary confinement, seemed to him 'wonderfully kept, but a most dreadful, fearful place'.

E13
After W.H. Bartlett (1809–94)
Washington, from the President's House
Engraving. $5 \times 7\frac{1}{4}$

This engraving made by H. Wallis as an illustration to *American Scenery; or Land, Lake and River* by N.P. Willis, vol. II, London, 1840, facing p.49, shows the capital city as it was two or three years before Dickens's visit.

E14 [35]
After W.H. Bartlett (1809–94)
Niagara Falls, from the Ferry
Engraving. $4\frac{3}{4} \times 7$

Engraved by J. Cousen as an illustration to *American Scenery; or Land, Lake, and River* by N.P. Willis, vol. I, London, 1840, facing p.4

E15 [31]
John Warner Barber (1798–1885) and O'Brien
The Tontine Hotel, New Haven, Connecticut
Lettered *Drawn & Engraved by O'Brien & J.W. Barber. New Haven Post Office, 1825–1835*
Colour wood-engraving. $6\frac{7}{8} \times 9\frac{1}{2}$
Lent by Professor Gordon S. Haight

This print is from an edition of *Connecticut Historical Collections, containing a general collection of interesting facts . . . relating to the history and antiquities of every town in Connecticut, with geographical descriptions*, written and illustrated by J.W. Barber, New Haven, 1837.

After leaving Hartford on 11 February Dickens travelled by rail to New Haven. There he stayed the night at the Tontine Hotel ('the best inn') before taking the steamboat the next day for New York. His reception here was as enthusiastic as elsewhere, and the choir of Yale College turned out to serenade him as he was trying to sleep. As Dickens joined the steamboat for New York the next day, souvenir-hunters tore pieces of fur from his great-coat.

E16
(a) **High Water Cairo 1844**

(b) **View of Cairo 1856**

Photographs reproduced from (a) W.G. Wilkins *Charles Dickens in America*, 1911, plate facing p.214; (b) *Lloyd's Steamboat Directory*, Cincinnati, 1856

Cairo, at the junction of the Ohio and Mississippi Rivers, had been 'vaunted in England as a mine of Golden Hope'. Dickens found it 'a hotbed of disease, an ugly sepulchre, a grave uncheered by any gleam of promise' and drew on it for his description of Eden in *Martin Chuzzlewit*.

E17
Map of Dickens's travels in America 1842

F: Novels of the 1840s

At the beginning of the 1840s, Dickens's fame seemed secure. By now the serial publication of his first three novels had accustomed him to intimate and continuous contact with his audience, and in 1840 he began a weekly magazine, *Master Humphrey's Clock*, through which he might further enjoy that contact. Dickens intended the magazine to be a miscellany, but it was not successful in this form, and he therefore made it a vehicle for the serialization of two further novels: *The Old Curiosity Shop* and *Barnaby Rudge*. In 1842 Dickens visited America (see Section E); when in 1843 the sales of his new novel *Martin Chuzzlewit* were hanging fire he was able to stimulate them, by using in the novel some of his memories of America. In 1844–45 he was living abroad, and *Pictures from Italy* is a record of his observations at this time.

Dickens's later novels betray an increasing sense of unease with contemporary society, first perceptible, perhaps, in *Dombey and Son* (1846–48), shown in Section I. But unease is not prominent in his subsequent novel *David Copperfield* (1849–50), which, with its considerable autobiographical element, may stand here as a kind of summing-up of Dickens's early life.

THE OLD CURIOSITY SHOP

F1
Manuscript of *The Old Curiosity Shop* [1840–41]. Vol. IIB
F.MS.153

The manuscript is open at the description of the death of Little Nell. Although there were many contemporary readers who, for various reasons, declined to surrender themselves to the pathos of Little Nell's death, that event was certainly intended by Dickens to be affecting, and several of his friends were deeply grieved and edified by it.

F2
Letter from Dickens to Forster, 17 January 1841
F.MS.153

Forster had written to Dickens: 'I had felt this death of dear little Nell as a kind of discipline of feeling and emotion which would do me lasting good . . . You and I have sometimes had hasty differences . . . but certain am I, that if, at any time hereafter, a word or tone that might possibly give you pain should threaten to rise to my throat, I'd gulp it down in the memory of Nell'.

Dickens was equally emotional:

'When I first began (on your valued suggestion) to keep my thoughts upon this ending of the tale, I resolved to try and do something which might be read by people about whom Death had been, with a softened feeling, and with consolation. . .'

F3
***Master Humphrey's Clock*. Vol. I**
London, Chapman and Hall, 1840
The volume contains also the first part of Volume II, comprising the conclusion of *The Old Curiosity Shop*
F.PB.2434

The illustration shows the death bed of Little Nell. In a letter to the artist, the author described in detail the scene to be represented (see F6). However, he was not satisfied with Cattermole's first design for this subject: 'I cannot tell you how obliged I am to you for altering the child, or how much I hope that my wish in that respect didn't go *greatly* against the grain'. Exactly what changes were made is not known.

F4

(a) **Enlarged photograph of an entry for 22 January 1841 in** *Macready's Reminiscences, and selections from his diaries and letters*
Ed. Sir F. Pollock, vol. 11, 1875, pp. 169–70

(b) **Portrait of Macready**

What Macready saw is shown at F3. He later wrote to Dickens: 'You have crowned all that you have ever done in the power, the truth, the beauty and the deep moral of this exquisite picture – but my God – how cruel after all! – It is true that we must be taught in all things through endurance – and the best charity is clear and bright through every lesson you teach. – I have had thoughts and visions of angelic forms and pictures of the last sad truth of our being here, in constant succession through the night. – I cannot banish the images you have placed before us'.

F5

(a) **Enlarged photograph from** *The Dickensian*, **1918, p.96**

(b) **Portrait of Lord Jeffrey**

Lord Jeffrey enjoys abiding fame as the *Edinburgh Review* critic who trounced Wordsworth, dismissing *The Excursion* as 'a tissue of moral and devotional ravings' and criticizing, among other things, Wordsworth's 'unlucky habit of debasing pathos with vulgarity'. Yet he had an exceedingly tender and sensitive nature and wept at the deaths of both Little Nell and Paul Dombey.

F6

Letter from Dickens to George Cattermole, [? 22 December 1840]
Lent by Mr Roger W. Barrett

In this exceptionally interesting letter Dickens proposes two subjects for illustration.
'Dr. George
The child lying dead in the little sleeping room which is behind the oaken screen. It is winter time, so there are no flowers; but upon her breast, and pillow, and about her bed, there may be slips of holly, and berries, and such free green things. – Window overgrown with ivy –. The little boy who had that talk with her about angels, *may* be by the bedside, if you like it so, but I think it will be quieter and more peaceful if she is quite alone. I want it to express the most beautiful repose and tranquillity, and to have something of a happy look, if death can.

2nd.
The child has been buried *inside* the church, and the old man who cannot be made to understand that she is dead, repairs to the grave every day, and sits there all day long, waiting for her arrival, to begin another journey. His staff and knapsack, her little bonnet and basket, &c lie beside him. "She'll come tomorrow" he says when it gets dark, and goes sorrowfully home. I think an hour-glass running out, would help the notion. – Perhaps *her* little things upon his knee, or in his hands –

I am breaking my heart over this story, and cannot bear to finish it.
 Love to Missis
 Ever & always heartily
  CD'

The engraving of the first subject is shown in the first edition at F3. The engraving of the second subject follows a few pages later in the book. Dickens also commissioned from Cattermole a water-colour of the same subject (F8).

F7
George Cattermole (1800–68)
Little Nell's Home
Signed with the monogram *GC* and dated *1840*
Water-colour. 15 × 20
Lent by The Dickens House

F8 [45]
George Cattermole (1800–68)
The Grave of Little Nell
Water-colour. 15 × 20
F.P. 53

Dickens commissioned Cattermole to paint these two water-colours based on illustrations to the *Old Curiosity Shop*; he felt that they expressed the mood of the story 'to the gratification of my inmost heart'.

F9 [44]
Robert Braithwaite Martineau (1826–69)
Kit's Writing Lesson
Exhibited at the Royal Academy in 1852
Oil. 21 × 28
Lent by the Tate Gallery

This painting, Martineau's first exhibited work, illustrates the penultimate paragraph of chapter 3 in *The Old Curiosity Shop*: 'He tucked up his sleeves and squared his elbows and put his face close to the book and squinted horribly at the lines ... he began to wallow in blots, and to daub himself to the roots of his hair'.

F10
William Holman Hunt (1827–1910)
Little Nell and her Grandfather
Signed and dated *W. Hunt, June, 1845*
Oil. 30 × 25
Lent by Sheffield City Art Galleries

This painting illustrates a passage in the *Old Curiosity Shop*, chapter 15, which describes how Little Nell and her grandfather, having left London in order to escape the clutches of Mr Quilp, look back at the city from Highgate Hill.

Holman Hunt painted this picture three years before the foundation of the Pre-Raphaelite Brotherhood; at that time he had never met the novelist. In 1860 he was best man at the marriage between Charles Collins, a former member of the Brotherhood, and Kate, Dickens's daughter. The same year he consulted Dickens about the price of 'The Finding of the Saviour in the Temple', and he agreed that 5,500 guineas was a fair price for it.

F11
Sir William Quiller Orchardson, RA (1835–1910)
Little Nell and her Grandfather in the Wood
Indistinctly signed
Oil. $22\frac{3}{8} \times 18\frac{1}{8}$
Lent by Sheffield City Art Galleries

H.O. Gray in *The Life of Sir William Quiller Orchardson*, RA, 1930, lists two paintings of Little Nell by this artist, dating one to 1855 and one to 1863. On the grounds of style, as well as title, the present picture would appear to be the later one.

BARNABY RUDGE

F12
Mr. Macrone's Select List of New Works and New Editions
London, 3, St. James's Square, December 1836
Lent by Miss Susan Lambert

Barnaby Rudge should have been Dickens's first published novel, for he agreed to deliver it (its original title being *Gabriel Vardon, the Locksmith of London*) to his first publisher Macrone on 30 November 1836; and Macrone was hopefully advertising it in the catalogue shown here in December 1836. But by this time *Pickwick* had begun, and the terms of Dickens's contract with Macrone seemed unrealistic. Eventually released from this contract, he offered *Barnaby Rudge* in fulfilment of a contract made with Richard Bentley. But once again he was unable to deliver the manuscript of the work to time, and after protracted wranglings, he broke with Bentley. He resumed the hardly begun novel in 1841, for publication in *Master Humphrey's Clock*.

F13
Manuscript of *Barnaby Rudge* [1841]. Vol.IIB
F.MS.155

F14
Barnaby Rudge
London, Chapman and Hall, 1841
Lent by A.P. Burton Esq.

Master Humphrey's Clock, almost alone among Dickens's works, was illustrated with 'woodcuts dropped into the text and no separate plates'. In the manuscript of *Barnaby Rudge* may be found instructions from Dickens to his printer concerning the placing of the woodcuts on the page. These instructions show that he took a careful interest in the illustration of his work.

At the climax of the novel, Newgate Prison is sacked by a mob. As he leaves the scene Barnaby Rudge observes the rioters glutting themselves on wine which flows into the streets from the burning premises of a vintner. It was 'a sight not easily to be erased', writes Dickens, 'even from his remembrance, so long as he had life'. The scene is described in two paragraphs. Then (after the second line on the page of manuscript displayed) Dickens inserts an instruction to the printer: 'Printer – cut here.' Accordingly, Phiz's remarkable woodcut appears at this point in the printed text, and fixes the scene in the reader's mind. Aptly, the text continues: 'With all he saw in this last glance fixed indelibly upon his mind, Barnaby hurried from the city'.

F15
Manuscript of *Barnaby Rudge* [1841]. Vol.IIA
F.MS.155

F16
***Master Humphrey's Clock*. Vol.III**
London, Chapman and Hall, 1841
Includes the latter part of *Barnaby Rudge*
F.PB.2433

Passages in this and the preceding chapter have been underlined in red in the manuscript possibly in order to indicate to the artist suitable moments for illustration. The woodcut showing Barnaby's first meeting with Lord George Gordon occurs in the printed text at a point marked in the manuscript with underlinings.

F17
Letter from Dickens to John Landseer, 5 November 1841
L.1316–1962

John Landseer, father of the painter, had seen the Gordon riots at first hand, and wrote to Dickens about his descriptions of them in *Barnaby Rudge*. In particular, he evidently mentioned that John Wilkes had been active as a magistrate in suppressing the riots. Dickens writes:

'... Now, if I had talked about Wilkes, it would have been necessary for me to glance at his career and previous position (for in that, lies the singularity you speak of) – and if I had stopped to do that, I should have stopped the riots which must go on to the end headlong, pell mell, or they lose their effect. I therefore resolved to defer that point, with some others of equal curiosity and interest, until the appearance of another edition would afford me an opportunity of relating them in *Notes*, where they would not stem the current of the Tale, or embarrass the action.

I need not tell you who are so well acquainted with "art" in all its forms, that in the description of such scenes, a broad, bold, hurried effect must be produced, or the reader instead of being forced and driven along by imaginary crouds will find himself dawdling very uncomfortably through the town, and greatly wondering what may be the matter. In this kind of work the object is, – not to tell everything, but to select the striking points, and beat them into the page with a sledge-hammer. And herein lies the difficulty. No man in the crowd who was pressed and trodden here and there, saw Wilkes'.

F18 [43]
William Powell Frith, RA (1819–1909)
Dolly Varden
Oil. 21½ × 17½
F.P.8

This represents the second type in a series of paintings which Frith made of Dolly Varden. The original version was completed by 31 January 1842, and this is a replica painted later the same year for Frank Stone, who gave it to John Forster. Dickens saw this painting in Stone's home and his pleasure in Frith's interpretation of his heroine led him to commission the 'Dolly Varden, looking back at her

Lover', 1843, now in the collection of Baron Burton, and a companion piece of Kate Nickleby. Both of these are seen in the photograph of the dining-room at Gad's Hill (M13).

ILLUSTRATIONS TO *THE OLD CURIOSITY SHOP* AND *BARNABY RUDGE* BY GEORGE CATTERMOLE (1800–68) AND HABLÔT K. BROWNE (PHIZ) (1815–82)

The illustrations to *The Old Curiosity Shop* and *Barnaby Rudge*, the two novels published in *Master Humphrey's Clock* (see Section J) differ in nature from those in Dickens's other major works. Not only were they illustrated by more than one artist, but the designs were engraved on wood and 'dropped into the text' rather than etched on separate plates. This technique, which allowed the illustrations to be printed along with the text, was favoured by various cheap magazines. However, although Dickens was planning a periodical when he chose this method of illustration, the inherent financial advantage was not the main attraction. He considered it an 'improvement' upon the separate plates. By inserting the wood-engravings at strategic points in the text, the author tightened the relationship between the written and visual image. The illustrations strengthen, by contrast or emotional enforcement, the impact of the words.

With two exceptions (see F20a and e) the illustrations were drawn by two artists: Hablôt K. Browne, now established as Dickens's principal illustrator, and George Cattermole, a personal friend of the novelist and a distant relative by marriage. Browne, whose true identity was disclosed for the first time when *Master Humphrey* appeared in volume form, designed most of the figure pieces and violent scenes, while Cattermole drew the romantic and architectural subjects. At the outset, until Cattermole became familiar with the technique, Browne also transferred the older artist's designs to the block. The illustrations were engraved by E. Landells, C. Gray, S. Williams (see F20a) and Vasey.

Dickens and Cattermole (playfully named by the author Kittenmoles) were warm friends. After Cattermole's death, Dickens organized a fund to alleviate the distress of his wife and children. The novelist was very appreciative of the artist's illustrations for *The Old Curiosity Shop*: 'I have deeply felt your hearty and most invaluable co-operation in the beautiful illustrations you have made for the last story . . . I look at them with a pleasure I cannot describe to you in words – and . . . it is impossible for me to say how sensible I am of your earnest and friendly aid. Believe me that this is *the very first time* any designs for what I have written have touched and moved me, and caused me to feel that they expressed the idea I had in my mind. I am most sincerely and affectionately grateful to you, and am full of pleasure and delight'.

F 19
Phiz (Hablôt K. Browne) (1815–82)
Four illustrations portraying Quilp in different scenes in The Old Curiosity Shop, 1840–41
Wood-engravings

(a) 'Quilp and his Wife'
Lettered *Vasey* and *H.B.*
$2 \times 2\frac{1}{2}$

This illustration appears as a tail piece to chapter 4, accompanying the following description of Quilp's behaviour: '"Now, Mrs. Quilp", he said; "I feel in a smoking humour, and shall probably blaze away all night. But sit where you are, if you please, in case I want you." . . . Mr. Quilp went on smoking and drinking in the same position and staring listlessly out of the window with the dog-like smile always on his face, save when Mrs. Quilp made some involuntary movement of restlessness or fatigue; and then it expanded into a grin of delight'.

(b) 'Quilp and his dog'
Lettered *E. Landells*
$3\frac{1}{2} \times 4\frac{1}{2}$

'. . . The dwarf remained upon his back in perfect safety, taunting the dog with hideous faces, and triumphing over him in his inability to advance another inch, though there were not a couple of feet between them.' Chapter 21.

(c) 'Quilp at the window'
Lettered *HKB* and *C. Gray*
$3\frac{1}{4} \times 4\frac{1}{2}$

'And what a leer there was upon the face! It was from the open window of a tavern that it looked out; and the dwarf had so spread himself over it, with his elbows on the window-sill and his head resting on both his hands, that what between his attitude and his being swollen with suppressed laughter, he looked puffed and bloated into twice his usual breadth.' Chapter 60.

(d) 'Quilp's corpse'
Lettered *Landells* and *HKB*
$3\frac{1}{4} \times 4\frac{1}{2}$

Browne produced a particularly forceful image to accompany Dickens's description of the death of the villainous dwarf. The river 'toyed and sported with its ghastly freight, now bruising it against the slimy piles, now hiding it in mud or long rank grass now dragging it heavily over rough stones and gravel . . . until, tired of the ugly plaything, it flung it on a swamp . . . and left it there to bleach'. Chapter 67.

The placing of the engraving immediately before the new chapter heightens the contrast with the 'lighted rooms, bright fires, cheerful faces, the music of glad voices, words of love and welcome . . .' which await Kit in its opening sentence, and intensifies the desperate brutality of the scene illustrated.

F 20
Five illustrations to The Old Curiosity Shop 1840–41
Wood-engravings

(a) Samuel Williams (1788–1853)
'Nell in bed'
Lettered *Williams. Del. et. Sc.*
$3\frac{1}{8} \times 4\frac{1}{2}$

It was Chapman rather than Dickens who asked Williams to contribute this, the second illustration to *The Old Curiosity Shop*. The story of Little Nell had not as yet developed into a full scale novel; it was probably thought desirable to have a second illustrator with experience in antiquarian subjects working on the periodical. In spite of the merit of this illustration, which Thomas Hood described as an 'Allegory' in his congratulatory review of *Master Humphrey's Clock* in the *Athenaeum*, 7 November 1840, Williams did not draw any other illustrations for Dickens.

(b) George Cattermole (1800–68)
'Nell and the Old Man looking back at London.' Chapter 15
Lettered *Landells Sc*
$3\frac{1}{2} \times 4\frac{3}{4}$

(c) Phiz (Hablôt K. Browne) (1815–82)
'Nell and the wax works.' Chapter 28
Lettered *E. Landells* and *HB*
$3\frac{1}{2} \times 4\frac{1}{2}$

(d) Phiz (Hablôt K. Browne) (1815–82)
'Kit working in the garden.' Chapter 40
Lettered *E. Landells* and *HKB*
$3\frac{3}{4} \times 4\frac{1}{2}$

(e) Daniel Maclise, RA (1806–70)
'Nell and the Sexton.' Chapter 55
Lettered *Landells*
$4\frac{1}{2} \times 3\frac{3}{4}$

It was originally Dickens's intention that Maclise should supply a number of illustrations for *Master Humphrey's Clock*. In fact he only contributed this one, which Dickens felt to be particularly suitable for him: 'a little design embodying the bells above and the wall below, and the old sexton and the child'.

F21
George Cattermole (1800–68)
Two illustrations to *Barnaby Rudge*, 1841
Wood-engravings

(a) 'The Maypole Inn.' Headpiece to chapter 1
Lettered *Landell*
$3\frac{3}{8} \times 4\frac{1}{2}$

Dickens was particularly pleased with this, the first illustration to *Barnaby Rudge*. 'Words cannot say how good it is. I can't bear the thought of it being cut, and should like to frame and glaze it in statu quo for ever and ever.'

(b) 'The Murderer Arrested.' Tailpiece to chapter 56
Lettered *Landells*
$3\frac{5}{8} \times 4\frac{1}{2}$

Cattermole gave Dickens the following explanation of this design: 'I cannot hope that you will make much out of this accompanying scratch. I suppose the spectator to be placed upon the roof of one of the wings of the Warren house and towards him are rushing——and Mr. Haredale as they issue from a small door in the tower whereunto is attached (as part & parcel of the same) the bell-turret: a small closet through which they pass to the roof has been dismantled or rather thrown down and ruined by the fire and the other spoilers: on the grass below is rooted Solomon Daisy in an ecstasy of wonder &c. &c. beyond are clouds of smoke a passing over and amongst many tall trees and all about overhead their tenants the frightened rooks are flying and cawing like mad . . .'.

F22
Phiz (Hablôt K. Browne) (1815–82)
Six illustrations to *Barnaby Rudge*, 1841
Wood-engravings

(a) 'Barnaby's phantom-haunted dreams.'
Tailpiece to chapter 7
Lettered *HKB* and *Landells*
$2\frac{1}{4} \times 4\frac{1}{2}$

(b) 'Hugh accosts Dolly Varden.' Illustration to chapter 21
Lettered *Gray sc.* and *HKB*
$4\frac{1}{2} \times 3\frac{1}{4}$

(c) 'Joe bids Dolly good-bye.' Headpiece to chapter 31
Lettered *Gray sc.* and in reverse *HKB*
$3\frac{1}{2} \times 4\frac{1}{2}$

(d) 'Lord George ordering Barnaby to join the mob.' Illustration to chapter 48
Lettered *C. Gray* and *HKB*
$3\frac{3}{8} \times 4\frac{1}{2}$

(e) 'The rioters at Moorfields.' Illustration to chapter 66
Lettered *HKB* and *E. Landells*
$4 \times 4\frac{1}{2}$

(f) 'Barnaby in the condemned cell.' Illustration to chapter 76
Lettered *HKB* and *C. Gray*
$3\frac{1}{4} \times 4\frac{3}{8}$

Before Grip the raven had been introduced into the story, Dickens wrote to Cattermole: 'I want to know whether you *feel* Ravens in general, and would fancy Barnaby's raven in particular. Barnaby being an idiot my notion is to have him always in company with a pet raven who is immeasureably more knowing than himself. To this end, I have been studying my bird, and think I could make a very queer character of him. Should you like the subject where this raven makes His first appearance'. Evidently the idea of depicting the raven did not appeal to Cattermole; all six illustrations in which the bird figures were drawn by Browne. Grip's first appearance was in the headpiece to chapter 6.

F23 [47]
Letter from Dickens to Daniel Maclise, 12 March 1841
Covering note from Maclise to Forster with a sketch of the apotheosis of the raven
F.MS.175

Dickens, like the hero of *Barnaby Rudge*, kept a raven as a pet. In 1841 it died. For its successor see E9.

'My dear Maclise.
 You will be greatly shocked and grieved to hear that the Raven is no more.
 He expired to-day at a few minutes after Twelve o'Clock at noon. He had been ailing (as I told you t'other night) for a few days. . . .
 I am not wholly free from suspicions of poison. . . .
 I have directed a post mortem examination. . . .
 I could wish, if you can take the trouble, that you would inclose this to Forster when you have read it. I cannot discharge the painful task of communication more than once. . . .
 . . . The children seem rather glad of it. He bit their ancles. But that was play –'

MARTIN CHUZZLEWIT

F24
Manuscript of *Martin Chuzzlewit* [1843-44]. Vol. IIB
F.MS.157

The manuscript is open at the portentous moment when Betsey Prig says to Mrs Gamp: 'Bother Mrs. Harris . . . I don't believe there's no sich a person!'

F25
Sheet from the corrected proofs of *Martin Chuzzlewit* [1843-44]
F.MS.170

F26
***The Life and Adventures of Martin Chuzzlewit.* Number XIII**
London, Chapman and Hall, Jan. 1844
Lent by The Dickens House

F27
The Life and Adventures of Martin Chuzzlewit
London, Chapman and Hall, 1844
F.PB.2432

In the second paragraph on p.59, Dickens uses the simile of 'the shadow of the church-spire moving round the church-yard as on a vast dial-plate', which Longfellow, in a letter to Forster (F 28) claims as his own.

F28
Letter from Longfellow to Forster, 28 February 1843
F.MS.366

'I was wrong in saying that the Acadia brought us nothing; it brought in Chuzzlewit No. 3. The story opens with great freshness and vigor. The Autumn Evening – the strong-minded lady (a kind of oboë-accompaniment in the family concert) Tom Pinch's journey to Salisbury – and the arrival of the new pupil – together with the great, moral Pecksniff, are all as *the Reviewers would say*, in Boz's *happiest vein*. The figure of speech about the shadow of the church-spire moving round the church-yard as on a vast dial-plate, I claim as my own; see Preface to Ballads. p.XI. – a very good figure notwithstanding.'

F29
Henry Wadsworth Longfellow
Ballads and other Poems
4th ed. Cambridge [Massachusetts], John Owen, 1842
F.PB.*5465

Longfellow, in a letter to Forster (F 28), draws attention to a passage in the Preface to his *Ballads*, 1842: 'daily the shadow of the church spire, with its long tapering finger, counts the tombs, representing a dial-plate of human life'. This, he suggests, may have inspired a similar image in *Martin Chuzzlewit*.

F30
Henry Behnes Burlowe (1802-37)
Samuel Carter Hall (1800-89)
Dated 1834
Marble bust. 32 × 21
Bethnal Green Museum

S.C. Hall, writer and editor, moved in the literary circles which Dickens joined in the late

1830s. On the publication of *Sketches by Boz*, Hall reviewed them favourably in the *New Monthly Magazine*.

According to *Blackwood's Magazine*, 'Pecksniff owed much of his celebrity, we believe, to his remarkable likeness to the late Sir Robert Peel'. But the *American Publishers' Circular* for 27 June 1857, in announcing that S.C. Hall was to visit the United States to deliver a series of lectures, asserted that: 'Mr. Hall is supposed to be the actual, veritable Pecksniff of *Martin Chuzzlewit*. For a time, and by a few, it was supposed that the late Sir Robert Peel was the original of the character; but the impression faded off, and Mr. Samuel Carter Hall is universally confessed to be the man. The artist "Phiz" has even hit off, in *his* Pecksniff, a strong personal resemblance to Mr. Hall, – an unmistakable resemblance, indeed. So did Dickens point him out, showing him in his family, surrounded by portraits and busts of himself' (see F 31a).

Burlowe was the brother of the sculptor, William Behnes. He took the name at S.C. Hall's suggestion to avoid confusion over their work, and to disassociate himself in the public's mind from the irregular life led by his brother.

F31 [24]
Phiz (Hablôt K. Browne) (1815–82)
Five drawings for illustrations to *Martin Chuzzlewit*, 1843–44

(a) 'Meekness of Mr. Pecksniff and his charming daughters'
Pencil. $5\frac{1}{2} \times 4\frac{3}{8}$

(b) 'Pleasant little family party at Mr. Pecksniff's'
Inscribed by Dickens with the title of the plate and *Pinch starts homeward with the new Pupil*
Pencil. $5\frac{1}{4} \times 4\frac{1}{2}$

(c) 'Mr. Jonas Chuzzlewit entertains his cousins'
Pencil and wash. $5\frac{1}{4} \times 4\frac{3}{4}$

(d) 'Mr. Pecksniff renounces the deceiver'
Pencil and wash. $5\frac{1}{2} \times 4\frac{1}{4}$

(e) 'The Nuptials of Miss Pecksniff receive a temporary check'
Inscribed with the title of the plate and a note
Pencil and wash. $5 \times 4\frac{3}{4}$
Lent by the Trustees of the British Museum

Phiz was the sole illustrator of *Martin Chuzzlewit*. He designed, as was usual for Dickens's novels, two plates for each of the nineteen parts and a frontispiece.

F32
Phiz (Hablôt K. Browne) (1815–82)
Four illustrations to *Martin Chuzzlewit*, 1843–44
Each signed *Phiz*, and lettered with the title of the plate
Etchings. $5\frac{1}{2} \times 4\frac{1}{2}; 5 \times 3\frac{7}{8}; 5\frac{1}{4} \times 4\frac{1}{2}; 4\frac{5}{8} \times 4\frac{1}{4}$

(a) 'Mr. Tapley succeeds in finding a "jolly" subject for contemplation'

(b) 'The Thriving City of Eden, as it appeared on paper'

(c) 'The Thriving City of Eden, as it appeared in fact'

Dickens sent the artist long and detailed instructions for this illustration, to which the artist replied: 'I can't get all this perspective in, unless you will allow of a long subject – something less than a mile!' For the relationship of Eden to Cairo see E16.

(d) 'Mrs. Gamp propoges a toast'

PICTURES FROM ITALY

F33
John Forster
Life of Charles Dickens
Library edition. Vol.1. London, Chapman and Hall, 1876
F.PB.3143

During the period from July 1844 to June 1845, which Dickens spent abroad, he wrote regularly to Forster, giving an account of his movements. His letters to Forster have now disappeared, but, when Forster wrote his *Life of Dickens*, he still possessed them and drew upon them. At the beginning of chapter 6 of Book IV he paraphrases Dickens's first letter from Ferrara, giving its date. In 1846 Dickens used this letter as the basis for his own account of the incident in the story of his travels, published in part in the *Daily News* and subsequently as a book (see F34 and F35).

F34
Manuscript of *Travelling Letters... No. VII. In Genoa, and out of it*
F.MS.159

When he returned to England, Dickens borrowed from Forster and other friends the letters he had written to them from abroad, and had them copied by an amanuensis so that he could work them up into his own account of his travels. On the page displayed, the spidery hand is that of the amanuensis, and the blacker writing is Dickens's. The passage here copied is obviously from Dickens's 'first letter from Ferrara' referred to by Forster in his *Life*, Book VI, ch. 6 (see F33). Dickens has corrected it for publication as part of the seventh of eight *Travelling Letters*, published in the *Daily News* between 21 January and 11 March 1846. It is interesting to see that he removes personal details. He has crossed out the words: 'I left my disconsolate wife (who is now living, shut up in her palace like a Baron's lady in the time of the Crusades) on Wednesday afternoon last, at 5 oClock: when I . . .'.

F35
Pictures from Italy
London, Bradbury and Evans, 1846
F.PB.2445

After the *Travelling Letters* had appeared in the *Daily News*, Dickens worked over them still further before publishing them in book form with more than as much additional matter as *Pictures from Italy*. The beginning of the chapter 'To Parma, Modena, and Bologna' in the book corresponds to the passage in the seventh *Travelling Letter* of which the manuscript is shown at F34. In comparison with the manuscript, the text of the book shows several revisions.

F36
Samuel Palmer (1805–81)
Four illustrations to *Pictures from Italy*, 1846
(a), (b) and (c) lettered with the title of the illustration
Wood-engravings. $1\frac{5}{8} \times 3$; $5\frac{1}{4} \times 3$; $2\frac{5}{8} \times 3$; $5\frac{1}{4} \times 3$

(a) 'The Street of the Tombs: Pompeii'
E.792–1924

(b) 'The Villa d'Este at Tivoli from the Cypress Avenue'
E.3896–1920

(c) 'The Colosseum of Rome'
E.3897–1920

(d) Illustrative border depicting a vineyard
E.3898–1920

Samuel Palmer and the novelist were never on terms of intimacy, although the artist's son recalled that he was an insatiable reader of Dickens.

F37
Samuel Palmer (1805–81)
The Villa d'Este, Tivoli
Painted in 1837
Water-colour. $10\frac{3}{4} \times 14\frac{3}{4}$
P.29–1919

After his marriage in 1837, Palmer lived in Italy for two years. Nine years later he used this view of the façade of the Villa d'Este and the cypress avenue, seen from a slightly different angle, as the basis for his illustration of the same subject to *Pictures from Italy*.

F37A
Samuel Palmer (1805–81)
The Street of the Tombs, Pompeii
Painted in 1838
Water-colour. $11\frac{1}{2} \times 16\frac{5}{8}$
P.28–1919

Palmer illustrated the Street of the Tombs in *Pictures from Italy*. In this painting he depicts the same subject from a slightly different viewpoint – from a mound a few paces more distant.

DAVID COPPERFIELD

F38
**Manuscript of *David Copperfield*
[1849–50]. Vol.IA**
F.MS.161

About one third of the way down the page, Mr Micawber delivers his celebrated advice: 'Annual income twenty pounds. . . .'

F39
**Corrected proofs of *David Copperfield*
[1849–50]. Vol.II**
F.PB.2421

One of the portions of the novel over which Dickens laboured with special care was chapter 50, in which Mr Peggotty at last succeeds in finding Little Em'ly, who has fled to London after her seduction by Steerforth. There are many corrections in the manuscript, and even in page-proof Dickens continued to make substantial changes in this chapter, notably in the timing of Mr Peggotty's appearance on the scene.

F40
The Personal History, Adventures, Experience and Observation of David Copperfield the younger, of Blunderstone Rookery
In parts. London, Bradbury and Evans, 1849–50
D.PB.3053

F41
The Personal History of David Copperfield
London, Bradbury and Evans, 1850
F.PB.2420

F42
George Lethbridge Sandars (1774–1846)
Lord Byron (1788–1829)
C.1809
Oil on canvas. $42\frac{1}{2} \times 35$
Lent by Her Majesty The Queen

Steerforth is perhaps the most Byronic of Dickens's characters, and this painting of the poet by the seashore may suggest something of the glamour of Little Em'ly's seducer at Yarmouth.

F43
Phiz (Hablôt K. Browne) (1815–82)
Four illustrations to *David Copperfield*, 1850
Each signed *Phiz* and lettered with the title of the plate
Etchings. $4 \times 6\frac{1}{2}$; $4 \times 5\frac{1}{2}$; $4 \times 5\frac{1}{2}$; $4 \times 5\frac{1}{8}$

(a) 'Steerforth and Mr. Mell'

(b) 'We arrive unexpectedly at Mr. Peggotty's fireside'

(c) 'Mr. Micawber delivers some valedictory remarks'

(d) 'Our Housekeeping'

F44 [50]
William Powell Frith, RA (1819–1909)
Life at the Seaside (Ramsgate Sands)
Exhibited at the Royal Academy 1854
Oil. 30×60
Lent by Her Majesty The Queen

Dickens shared the Victorians' enthusiasm for the seaside. As early as 1836 he wrote 'The Tuggs's at Ramsgate' (*Library of Fiction*, C3). His own preference was for Broadstairs, a few miles away on the Kent coast, which he visited regularly from 1836 till 1851. He describes one of his visits in his letter to Felton, 1 September 1843: 'In a bay-window in a one-pair sits, from nine o'clock to one, a gentleman with rather long hair and no neck-cloth, who writes and grins as if he thought he were very funny indeed. His name is Boz'. He gives a more detailed description of Broadstairs in 'Our Watering Place', *Household Words*, 2 August 1851.

'Life at the Seaside' was Frith's first important attempt to paint a panorama of modern life, and he devoted over two years to its composition. As might be expected a number of the episodes he has introduced have parallels in Dickens's 'The Tuggs's at Ramsgate' and 'Our Watering Place'; for instance, the Punch-and-Judy show, the Menagerie, the minstrels, the portable chairs, the ladies knitting or reading, and the old man with a telescope.

F45
Frank Stone, ARA (1800–59)
The duet 'andante con moto'
Signed *F. Stone*
Exhibited at the Royal Academy, 1849
Oil. $33\frac{1}{4} \times 44$
Lent by Mrs Patrick Gibson

One of the characters in the group has been said to be Dickens; however, this is not so. Marcus Stone, the artist's son, recalled that his brother sat for the head of one of the figures and that 'the seated "jeune premier" was painted from Alfred Tennyson, and the white woolly animal in the foreground was Dickens's little dog Timber'.

F46
George Cattermole (1800–68)
Sintram and his Companions
Water-colour. $12\frac{1}{4} \times 8$
Lent by Mrs S.A. Radcliffe

This illustration to a tale by La Motte Fouqué was one of three water-colours by Cattermole sold at the dispersal of the contents of Gad's Hill on 9 July 1870 (Lot 7).

F47
Angus Fletcher (1799–1862)
Villa Bagnerello, Albaro, Genoa
Pencil. $4\frac{3}{8} \times 7\frac{1}{2}$
F.MS.181.1

When the Dickenses visited Italy in 1844, Angus Fletcher, who was living near Genoa, rented an expensive and unpicturesque house for them at Albaro, although the magnificent Palazzo Doria, only six miles outside Genoa, had been offered to him at a quarter the price. The Villa di Bella Vista, which the novelist called the Villa Bagnerello after its owner, at once impressed Dickens with its likeness to a pink jail. 'The most perfectly lonely, rusty, stagnant, staggerer of a domain that you can possibly imagine ... with a stable so full of vermin and swarmers ... that I always expect to see the carriage going out bodily, with legions of industrious fleas harnessed to and drawing it off on their own account.'

G: Dickens and the theatre

Dickens had a pronounced gift for dramatic self-expression. Charles Kent suggested that he was unconsciously portraying himself at the time of 'his buoyant youth' in his description of Nicholas Nickleby: 'There's genteel comedy in your walk and manner, juvenile tragedy in your eye, and touch-and-go farce in your laugh'. While he was earning a poor living as a shorthand writer at Doctors' Commons, Dickens seriously considered the theatre as a profession. 'I went to some theatre every night, with a very few exceptions, for at least three years: really studying the bills first, and going to where there was the best acting: and always to see Mathews whenever he played. I practised immensely ... often four, five, six hours a day ...' Eventually he secured an audition at Covent Garden before George Bartley and Charles Kemble, at which he was to perform a piece by Mathews. 'I was laid up when the day came, with a terrible bad cold and an inflammation of the face.' He therefore cancelled the audition intending to try again in the next season. By that time, however, his first success as a journalist had distracted his mind from acting. 'See how near I may have been to another sort of life.'

G1

Four souvenir accounts of Charles Mathews's 'At Homes', published by John Duncombe, with hand-coloured frontispieces showing Mathews in character
Mr. Mathews' Memorandum-Book [1825]
Mathews' Home Circuit [1827]
Mr. Mathews' Spring Meeting [1829]
Mr. Mathews' Comic Annual for 1831
Enthoven Collection

Charles Mathews the elder (1776–1835) established himself as one of the most popular comic actors on the English stage as the nineteenth century began. Although he played nearly four hundred parts during his career, he began to feel deprived of opportunities in legitimate comedy by 1818. He was conscious of being 'laid upon the shelf: but I was too fond of my profession and public applause to lie quietly there', and therefore presented his first 'At Home', in which he offered 'a whole evening's entertainment by my own individual exertions'. This collection of solo comic sketches, designed to exploit his gift for mimicry, and involving quick changes of costume and even ventriloquism, 'excited continual peals of laughter from the beginning to the end'. The At Homes, in which Frederick Yates often shared, became almost annual events, and Dickens attended some of the later ones.

G2

Richard James Lane (1800–72)
George Bartley (1782–1858) in character as Colonel Detonator, playing with Drinkwater Meadows (1799–1869) as Sir Jacob Lukewarm in *The Original*
Signed with monogram
Lithograph. $7\frac{3}{8} \times 10$
Enthoven Collection

George Bartley was stage-manager at Covent Garden from 1829 till 1843. Dickens wrote to him about March 1832 telling him that he knew three or four successive years of Mathews's *At Homes* and asking for an audition. *The Original* was an interlude in one act by John Maddison Morton (1811–91), first performed at the Theatre Royal, Covent Garden, 13 November 1837.

DRAMATIST

A few years later Dickens again applied his talents to the theatre, this time as playwright. Three of his pieces reached the stage, in 1836–37, with modest success. A fourth piece, written in 1838, was not considered worthy of performance, and his thoughts were again distracted from the theatre by the success of his other writings. By now, with *Pickwick* complete and *Oliver Twist* in progress, Dickens was fully launched on his career as a novelist.

G3
The Strange Gentleman; a comic burletta, in two acts. By 'Boz'
London, Chapman and Hall, 1837
With an etched frontispiece by Phiz
F.PB.6974/3

G4
After James Warren Childe (1780–1862)
John Pritt Harley (1786–1858) as the Strange Gentleman
Dated 23 January 1837
Aquatint and stipple; engraved by R. Easton and hand-coloured. Cut to $15 \times 10\frac{3}{4}$
Enthoven Collection

G5
John Leech (1817–64)
J.P. Harley as the Strange Gentleman
Stipple engraving; hand-coloured. Plate size $8\frac{7}{8} \times 5\frac{1}{4}$
Enthoven Collection

The Strange Gentleman, which Dickens adapted from his tale 'The great Winglebury duel', was the first of his dramatic pieces to be performed. It was played for the first time on 29 September 1836 at the St James's Theatre, with John Pritt Harley, the principal comedian of the St James's company, in the leading part. The *Morning Post* considered that 'it is calculated to sustain the reputation [Boz] has already gained for smartness and graphic humour. His forte is in the ludicrous, a personal peculiarity or an absurd foible he hits off with the touch of an artist. To the delineation of character, however, or the sustaining of a witty dialogue by its intrinsic humour or its faithful observance of nature we think him inadequate. The piece bore marks of this'.

G6
Songs, choruses and concerted pieces in the operatic burletta of the Village Coquettes
London, Bradbury and Evans, 1837
F.PB.2455

G7
The Village Coquettes. A comic opera in two acts. The words by Charles Dickens, the music by John Hullah
Rustic Edition. Reconstructed for the Dickens Fellowship
[Duplicated sheets.] London (1934)
Enthoven Collection

G8
Playbill for *The Village Coquettes* at the St James's Theatre, 14 April 1837
F.MS.180

When *The Strange Gentleman* came on the stage in September 1836, Dickens had already been working for a year on an operetta *The Village Coquettes* which was performed also at the St James's Theatre, from 6 to 24 December 1836, and occasionally in the following spring. The music was provided by John Hullah (1812–84), a young composer whom Dickens probably met through his sister Fanny, and the principal part was taken by the celebrated tenor John Braham (1774?–1856), who was also manager of the St James's Theatre. At the end of the first night Dickens broke with convention by appearing on stage to take a bow. Forster, covering the performance for the *Examiner* and as yet unacquainted with 'Boz', wrote that he 'left the audience in perfect consternation that he neither resembled the portraits of Pickwick, Snodgrass, Winkle, nor Tupman'.

G9
Playbill for *Is She His Wife?* and other burlettas at the St James's Theatre, 6 and 7 March 1837
Enthoven Collection

On this bill there is no reference to the author of *Is She His Wife?*, but on a bill for a performance of 13 March 1837, a benefit for Harley, the name of the author is given as 'Boz'. A unique copy of the first edition of this play (c.1837) was destroyed by fire in 1879. A reprint made probably in 1872 is now hardly less scarce. 'The Plot', noted *The Times* of 8 March 1837, 'bordered on the dangerous, but it was so dexterously and delicately managed that its success was decided.'

G10
Manuscript of *The Lamplighter* [1838]
F.MS.152

This farce was written for Macready, who recorded in his *Journal* for 1838:
'December 11. Dickens came with Forster and read his farce. There was manifest disappointment; it went flatly, a few ready laughs, but generally an even smile, broken in upon by the horse-laugh of Forster, the most indiscreet friend that ever allied himself to any person. He has goaded Dickens to write this farce, and now (without testing its chances of success) would drive it upon the stage. Defend me from my friends! It was agreed that it

should be put into rehearsal, and, when nearly ready, should be seen and judged of by Dickens! I cannot sufficiently condemn the officious folly of this marplot, Forster, who embroils his friends in difficulties and distress in this most determined manner. It is quite too bad.

December 12. A long discussion on Dickens's farce; called in for their opinion Messrs. Bartley and Harley. The result was that Forster decided on withdrawing the farce.'

The farce survived only in this manuscript (which is not in Dickens's handwriting) until 1879, when a printed version appeared, edited by R.H. Shepherd. Dickens adapted it as 'The Lamplighter's Story' for *The Pic Nic Papers*, 1841.

AMATEUR THEATRICALS

Dickens's plays are his least successful works – perhaps, it has been suggested, because the dramatic form does not permit the expression of the author's personality, which is vividly present in both Dickens's journalism and his fiction. He never again seriously tried to write plays. But he did preserve his enthusiasm for acting. A family performance of his play *O'Thello* (of which only a few pages survive) had taken place in 1833 and in the same year he organized a more ambitious performance of J.H. Payne's opera *Clari*. In 1842 while on his first American tour he took part in a charity performance by the Coldstream Guards of three plays at the Queen's Theatre, Montreal. As stage manager, he found himself directing the whole operation with immense vigour and enjoyment. 'The *furor* has come strong upon me again, and I begin to be once more of opinion that nature intended me for the lessee of a national theatre, and that pen, ink and paper have spoiled a manager.' (See E8.)

Two years later, stimulated after giving a reading of *The Chimes* to a small audience of friends, he resolved to organize some amateur theatricals of his own. Returning from his spell of residence in Italy, 'he flung himself with the passionate fulness of his nature' into gathering a cast and choosing a play. On 20 September 1845, Ben Jonson's *Every Man in his Humour* was played to a private audience at Miss Kelly's Theatre, 'with a success that outran the wildest expectation', as Forster recalled, 'and turned our little enterprise into one of the small sensations of the day'. A public performance for charity was given at the St James's Theatre on 15 November, and at the conclusion Forster announced that the amateurs proposed to get up another play for Miss Kelly's benefit. Fletcher's *Elder Brother* was eventually chosen, and performed at Miss Kelly's Theatre on 3 January 1846. Theatricals were then laid by until the following year, when *Every Man in his Humour* was taken on tour to Manchester and Liverpool for the benefit of Leigh Hunt.

G 11
Playbill for *Every Man in his Humour* at Miss Kelly's Theatre, 20 September 1845
With sketches by Daniel Maclise of Dickens as Bobadil and Forster as Kitely
F.MS.180

G 12
St James's Theatre – The Amateurs
Cuttings, with engravings after Kenny Meadows of six actors in character, from the *Illustrated London News*, 22 and 29 November 1845
Enthoven Collection

G 13 [37]
After Charles Robert Leslie, RA (1794–1859)
Charles Dickens as Captain Bobadil in *Every Man in his Humour*
Lithograph by Thomas Maguire. 14 × 17
24621

The painting was exhibited at the Royal Academy in 1846. Dickens was much admired in the part of Captain Bobadil. But Mrs Carlyle commented: 'poor little Dickens, all painted in black and red, and affecting the voice of a man of six feet, would have been unrecognizable for the mother that bore him'. And Forster cautiously suggested that 'though Dickens had the title to be called a born comedian . . . his strength was rather in the vividness and variety of his assumptions, than in the completeness, finish or ideality he could give to any part of them. It is expressed exactly by what he says of his youthful preference for the representations of the elder Mathews'.

G 14
Letter from Robert Bell to Forster, 25 September 1845
F.MS.7

'. . . Dickens, who seems to me to execute with felicity everything he attempts, was glorious in Bobadil. He literally floated in braggadocio. His air of supreme conceit & frothy pomp in the earlier scenes came out with prodigious force in [contrast with the subsequent humiliation . . .]'

Robert Bell (1800–67), the Irish journalist, belonged to the literary circle of Forster and Dickens.

G 15 [39]
Daniel Maclise, RA (1806–70)
Scene from Ben Jonson's *Every Man in his Humour* with portrait of Forster as Kitely
Oil. $25 \times 20\frac{3}{4}$
F.P.20

The painting was exhibited at the Royal Academy in 1848.

G 16
Three notes from William Charles Macready to Forster
Undated
F.MS.388

Forster, taking great pains over his part in the theatricals, consulted Macready about his costume.

G 17
Letter from Bryan Waller Procter to Forster [25 September 1845]
F.MS.7/8–9

'. . . I think that by adding a beard you make the lower part of your face too large & burly. This & the fact of your hair being thin towards the crown of the head gives you too *monastic* an appearance (you understand me) – & this is all increased by the loose sort of robe or dress which you wear. Could you not abandon the beard & wear a *moustache* only? or would this be incorrect? I am sure that this would look better – the more especially if you added something to your hair. [I dare not utter the word wig.] . . .' Procter was a lifelong friend of Dickens and Forster.

G 18
Daniel Maclise, RA (1806–70)
Sketch, supposedly of the costume worn by Forster as Kitely
Pen. 9×7
F.MS.7

G 19
Ben Jonson
Every Man in his Humour
(Cumberland's British Theatre No. 69.) London, G.H. Davidson, n.d.
L.350–1916

An acting copy signed and lightly annotated by Forster.

G 20
Ben Jonson
Every Man in his Humour
London, John Cumberland, n.d.
F.PB.4695

An interleaved acting copy signed by Forster on the flyleaf with the date 'August 1st. 1845'. It contains a detailed analysis of the part of Kitely.

G 21
John Fletcher
The Elder Brother
N.p., n.d. Printed copy lacking title-page
L.352–1916

Interleaved, with annotations and a cast list by Forster.

G 22
Miss Kelly
Cutting, with a wood-engraved portrait, from the *Illustrated London News*, 3 January 1846
Enthoven Collection

This account of Miss Kelly (1790–1882) was prompted by the benefit performance of *The Elder Brother* given for her on 3 January 1846.

G 23
Sir Edward Bulwer-Lytton
Address written for the occasion of the Amateur Performance at Liverpool, on Wednesday, July 28 1847, for the benefit of Mr. Leigh Hunt
London, Bradbury and Evans (1847)
F.PAMPH.141/13

The pamphlet includes cast lists. Forster spoke the address, and for the Manchester benefit performance for Leigh Hunt, Dickens spoke a prologue by T.N. Talfourd.

'SPLENDID STROLLING'

The next venture of the amateurs also had a benevolent purpose. In 1847 Shakespeare's birthplace at Stratford-upon-Avon had been offered for sale, and had been purchased as a memorial by a London and Stratford Shakespeare Committee. Dickens and his amateurs then decided to raise funds for the endowment of a perpetual curatorship of the house, to be held in the first instance by the aging dramatist James Sheridan Knowles (1784–1862). *Every Man in his Humour* was again to be performed in alternation with another play. Several plays were considered and rehearsed, including Jonson's *The Alchemist*, Jerrold's *Rent Day* and Bulwer-Lytton's *Money*. The play chosen was *The Merry Wives of Windsor*. After opening in May 1848 at the Haymarket Theatre the amateurs went on tour to Manchester, Birmingham, Edinburgh and Glasgow.

G24
Henry Wallis (1830–1916)
Shakespeare's house, Stratford-upon-Avon
Interior, showing the stairs leading to the bedroom where he was born
Oil. $25\frac{3}{4} \times 19\frac{1}{2}$
F.P.38

The dog, heron, etc. were added by Sir Edwin Landseer.

G25
F.W. Fairholt
The Home of Shakespeare illustrated and described
London, Chapman and Hall, 1847
D.PB.3654

G25A
Enlarged photograph of engraving of Shakespeare's birthplace
From the *Illustrated London News*, 18 September 1847

G26
Ben Jonson
The Alchemist
Printed copy extracted from *The Works of Ben Jonson with a Memoir . . . by Barry Cornwall* [i.e. B.W. Procter]. London, Edward Moxon, 1838
F.PB.139/10

The play was rehearsed in late 1847 or early 1848. This copy is marked by Forster, who played Face.

G27
Manuscript copy of Ben Jonson *The Alchemist*, dated 1847
F.PB.139/11

G28
Manuscript abstract of the part of Face in *The Alchemist*, with a cast list attached
F.PB.139/9

Dickens played Sir Epicure Mammon, and Forster thought this part 'as good as anything he had done'.

G29
Douglas Jerrold
The Rent Day
London, John Duncombe, n.d.
F.PB.139/2

G30
Manuscript abstract of the part of Evelyn in Lytton's *Money*
F.PB.139/6

The Rent Day and *Money* were rehearsed in early 1848 but did not reach performance.

G31
Playbill for Shakespeare's *The Merry Wives of Windsor* at the Theatre Royal, Haymarket, 15 May 1848
Enthoven Collection

The playbill announces the opening night of the new play performed by the amateurs in aid of the fund for the endowment of a perpetual curatorship of Shakespeare's house.

G32
William Shakespeare
The Merry Wives of Windsor
N.p., n.d. Printed copy lacking title-page
F.PB.139/I

This copy is marked by Forster, who played Ford. Dickens took the part of Justice Shallow.

G33
Letter from Daniel Maclise to Forster [?May 1848]
F.MS.385

The drawing shows Mark Lemon (1809–70) as Falstaff 'in his Robe de Chambre'. Dickens and Lemon were acquainted by 1843; later they were both to be found at convivial evenings at the home of George Cattermole. Lemon became one of the staunchest of the amateurs, and Dickens relied on him especially for comic parts.

G34
Mr. Mark Lemon as Falstaff
Engraving after John Tenniel (1820–1914) from the *Illustrated London News*, 17 October 1868
Enthoven Collection

G35
Photograph of Mark Lemon as Falstaff (c.1868)
Enthoven Collection

Lemon was very well suited in temperament and physique to his part in *The Merry Wives*; twenty years after the amateur performances, he returned to the part, making it the basis of a solo entertainment, *Falstaff*, which he performed successfully at the Gallery of Illustration.

G36
Mary Cowden Clarke as Mistress Quickly in *The Merry Wives of Windsor*
Photograph of a water-colour painting by William Havell (1782–1857)
Enthoven Collection

Mary Cowden Clarke (1809–98), the authoress, published her *Concordance to Shakespeare* in 1844–45. She had taken part in amateur productions of Sheridan's *The Rivals* in 1847–48, which led to an introduction through Leigh Hunt to Dickens.

G37
Poster for Ben Jonson's *Every Man in his Humour* at the Theatre Royal, Haymarket, 17 May 1848
Enthoven Collection

G38
Playbill for the same performance as G37
Enthoven Collection

Every Man in his Humour was the second play in the amateurs' 1848 repertoire.

COUNTRY-HOUSE THEATRICALS

After the amateurs had energetically ended their tour in Glasgow on 19 July 1848 with the performance of a new play, *Used Up* by Boucicault, they did not meet again for two years. Dickens meanwhile was involved in an evening of impromptu theatricals in November 1849, while visiting his friends the Hon. Richard and Mrs Watson at Rockingham Castle, Northamptonshire. Another of the guests was Miss Mary Boyle, like Dickens an enthusiastic amateur actor; together they acted the scene from *Nicholas Nickleby* in which Mrs Nickleby is wooed by the mad gentleman. Impressed by Miss Boyle's talent, Dickens enrolled her in the amateur troupe, which reassembled in 1850 at the invitation of Bulwer-Lytton to perform *Every Man in His Humour* at Knebworth, his Hertfordshire country house. In the following January there were amateur theatricals at Rockingham again, more ambitious than those of 1849. Though the amateur troupe was not involved, Dickens took part, playing once more opposite Mary Boyle. She became a faithful friend of his, regularly providing buttonholes for his public readings: 'flowers have fallen in my path wherever I have trod' he wrote to her in acknowledgement (10 September 1858).

G39
Playbill for a performance of amateur theatricals at Rockingham Castle, 13 January 1851
Lent by Mrs J.E. Egerton

'Picture to yourself', Dickens wrote to Forster, in a parody of the style of Henry Colman, the American writer, 'a large old castle, approached by an ancient keep, portcullis, etc., filled with company, waited on by six-and-twenty servants;

the slops (and wine-glasses) continually being emptied; and my clothes (with myself in them) always being carried off to all sorts of places; and you will have a faint idea of the mansion in which I am at present staying.' He was writing on the day after the impromptu theatricals.

G40
Frederick William Hulme (1816–84)
Knebworth, Hertfordshire
Lithotint. $9\frac{3}{4} \times 12\frac{3}{4}$
From S.C. Hall, *The Baronial Halls . . . of England*
London, Chapman and Hall, 1847

G41, G41A
Invitations to private theatricals at Knebworth, 18 and 19 November 1850
G41 lent by Lady Cobbold, G41A: F.MS.7

Three performances of *Every Man in His Humour* were given at Knebworth on 18, 19 and 20 November. 'All the circumstances and surroundings were very brilliant', Forster recalled.

G42
Manuscript of the Epilogue by F.P. Delmé Radcliffe, written for the performances of *Every Man in His Humour* at Knebworth, 18–20 November 1850
F.MS.7

Mr Delmé Radcliffe (1804–75), a neighbour of Lytton's, was a gentleman jockey and steeplechase rider, a yachtsman and fisherman, and master of the Hertfordshire hounds, 1834–39. Various members of the theatrical party are mentioned in his prologue: the lines on Dickens come low on the left-hand page.

'Amongst that party there are pretty pickings
But say can newspaper describe Charles Dickens?
Author & Actor – Manager – the Soul
Of all who read or hear him! on the whole
A very 'Household Word'!'

G43 [36]
Augustus Egg, RA (1816–63)
Charles Dickens as Sir Charles Coldstream in *Used Up*
Oil. $23\frac{1}{2} \times 19\frac{1}{4}$
Lent by The Dickens House

Dickens acted four times in *Used Up*: besides the Rockingham production, there were performances by the amateur company in Glasgow on 19 July 1848, and in Manchester and Liverpool on 1 and 3 September 1852. In these Egg also acted, and this picture, if it represents an actual production at all, probably represents one of these performances in which the part of the maid, shown with Dickens, was taken in 1848 by Anne Romer and in 1852 by Mrs Henry Compton. At Rockingham the maid was played by Mary Boyle.

THE GUILD OF LITERATURE & ART

From the proceeds of their performances the amateurs had already been able to assist Leigh Hunt and Sheridan Knowles. In 1850 plans were made to put such benevolent activity on an organized footing. The connection just established with Lytton was turned to advantage: he was to write a five-act comedy for the amateurs, and the money gained from a series of public performances of it was to be used as the basic capital of a charitable body 'the Guild of Literature and Art.' The Guild was to have two functions: to encourage and assist artists and writers to take out life insurance policies; and from its own funds (which were to be sustained by amateur theatrical performances) to grant pensions to needy members, and to endow an Institute where some of them might reside in return for light duties.

The play written by Lytton was *Not So Bad As We Seem*, and its first performance was given on 16 May 1851, in the presence of Queen Victoria and the Prince Consort, at Devonshire House, the London home of the Duke of Devonshire, who took a great interest in the Guild from its beginning. Public performances followed in the Hanover Square Rooms in June and July, and between 10 November 1851 and 30 August 1852 performances were given in the provinces.

G44
Daniel Maclise, RA (1806–70)
Edward George Earle Lytton Bulwer-Lytton, First Baron Lytton (1803–73)
Ink. $4\frac{1}{2} \times 5\frac{1}{2}$
F.P.88

Bulwer-Lytton and Dickens first met at Kensal Lodge in 1836. Lytton, who was a Member of Parliament while Dickens was working as a reporter in the House of Commons, praised *Pickwick Papers*, but they did not become intimate until some years later. The friendship established during the theatricals was maintained. When

Dickens was visiting Knebworth in 1861 he showed Lytton the proofs of the last chapters of *Great Expectations*, in which Pip was to have lost Estella and to have realized that his love had always been hopeless. Lytton was so distressed at this that he persuaded Dickens to alter the story, giving it a happier ending than he had originally intended.

G 45
Sir Edward Bulwer-Lytton
Manuscript of *Not So Bad As We Seem* [1851]
F.MS.374

The manuscript of the play in Lytton's handwriting.

G 46
Enlarged photograph of an engraving of the amateur performance at Devonshire House, 16 May 1851
From the *Illustrated London News*, 24 May 1851

Joseph Paxton, fresh from his triumph as architect of the Great Exhibition, directed the construction of a stage in the drawing-room of Devonshire House. It was ingeniously designed so that not a single nail was hammered into either the walls or the floor of the room. The scenery was painted free of charge by Clarkson Stanfield, David Roberts, Thomas Grieve, William Telbin, John Absolon and Louis Haghe.

When the amateurs went on tour they took their stage and scenery with them, and erected it in halls or concert rooms instead of hiring theatres. Dickens was full of praise for the 'good temper and cheerfulness' of their carpenters. 'I mean to give them a supper at Liverpool, and address them in a neat and appropriate speech.'

G 47
Sir Edward Bulwer-Lytton
Not So Bad As We Seem ... as first performed at Devonshire House, in the presence of Her Majesty and his Royal Highness the Prince Albert
London, Published for the Guild of Literature and Art by Chapman and Hall, 1851
F.PB.6968

With a pencil drawing, perhaps by Maclise, inserted.

G 48 [40]
After Edward Mathew Ward, RA (1816–79)
Admission ticket to amateur dramatic performances organized by the Guild of Literature and Art, 1851
Etched by Thomas O. Barlow
Size of plate 8 × 10
F.MS.181

The admission ticket depicts the conditions which the Guild of Literature and Art hoped to improve. On the right the author Daniel Defoe returns to his disappointed wife and child after Edmund Curll the bookseller has refused to publish his novel *Robinson Crusoe*. On the left the artist Richard Wilson surreptitiously takes a completed painting to a pawnshop.
The original drawing by E.M. Ward belonged to Dickens and was included in the sale of his collection on 9 July 1870.

G 49
Playbill for Sir Edward Bulwer-Lytton's *Not So Bad As We Seem* at the Hanover Square Rooms, 3 June 1851
Enthoven Collection

This performance was cancelled, since inadequate publicity had failed to attract a sufficiently large audience. The first performance at the Hanover Square Rooms was on 18 June.

G 50
Enlarged photograph of an advertisement for the amateur company's performance at the Hanover Square Rooms, 18 June 1851
From the *Athenaeum*, 14 June 1851

It will be observed that Thackeray's readings were a counter-attraction to the theatricals. The play was not one of the amateurs' more successful choices, and Dickens's performance as Lord Wilmot was criticized as 'too rigid, hard, and quarter-deck-like'. After the first performance, however, a farce was added to the bill, *Mr. Nightingale's Diary*, written by Mark Lemon, and much adapted by Dickens. With his elastic physical energy and his readiness to 'gag', Dickens had always made the amateurs' farces brilliant affairs: 'I have seen people laugh', he wrote 'until they have hung over the front of the boxes like ripe fruit'. In *Mr. Nightingale's Diary* he excelled himself, taking six parts (one female), with a succession of quick changes.

HOME THEATRICALS

In 1851 Dickens and his family moved from Devonshire Terrace to Tavistock House, and there, in the back room on the first floor, Dickens set up 'the smallest theatre in the world' for the benefit of his children, two of whom had reached their teens. For several years plays were staged on Twelfth Night, which was Charley's birthday. The children alone performed Albert Smith's *Guy Fawkes* in 1852, and in the following year Robert Brough's *William Tell*. In the two subsequent years, Dickens and other grown-ups participated, and in the summer of 1855 Dickens used the theatre to put on a new play by Wilkie Collins. Eighteen months later another play by Collins was undertaken as the New Year's theatricals of 1857. Further performances of this in the summer, as a memorial to Douglas Jerrold, were the last of Dickens's amateur theatricals.

G 51
Sir Edward Bulwer-Lytton
Not So Bad As We Seem
N.p., n.d. Printed copy, imperfect
F.PB.139/5

This copy has been marked, and the cast list annotated, by Forster.

G 52
Manuscript abstract of the part of Hardman in *Not So Bad As We Seem*
F.PB.139/4

Hardman was the part played by Forster.

G 53
Manuscript of a draft statement of thanks, in Dickens's handwriting, from the amateurs to their audiences and committee at Manchester, during the Guild of Literature and Art tour [1852]
F.PB.2205/32(135)

The tour took the amateurs to Bath, Bristol, Reading, Manchester, Liverpool, Shrewsbury, Birmingham, Nottingham, Derby, Newcastle, Sunderland and Sheffield. Dickens always engaged the whole of the largest hotel in the town for the troupe, and they lived convivially, taking supper together after the performance and playing boisterous games.

G 54
Enlarged photograph of an engraving of the Institute of the Guild of Literature and Art at Stevenage, Herts.
From the *Illustrated Times*, 12 August 1865

Despite its promising beginning, the Guild never succeeded to the extent of Dickens's hopes. Its initial usefulness was much reduced by a stipulation in its Parliamentary Act of incorporation that no pensions were to be paid until it had been in existence for seven years. The Institute – in fact two houses – was eventually completed in 1865, on land donated by Lytton at Stevenage. It was designed 'with due regard to the ordinary habits and necessary comforts of gentlemen' (the figures in the engraving, however, are less than life-size, when measured against the building), but artists and writers were reluctant to reside there, for it was remote from London, and smacked of charity. The building was rented out, and recently demolished, the Guild having been dissolved in 1897.

G 55 [76]
Tavistock House, Tavistock Square
Photograph, copied from an original by J.W. Marchant, 1900, in the British Museum

This shows the back elevation of the house which Dickens bought from Frank Stone (see P 20) in 1851, and which he sold in 1860.

G 56
Playbill for Henry Fielding's *Tom Thumb* at Tavistock House, 6 January 1854
F.MS.180

In this play, Dickens, appearing as 'The Modern Garrick' took the part of the Ghost of Gaffer Thumb, and Glumdalca, the Beautiful Queen of the Giants, was played by 'The Infant Phenomenon' – 'an exquisitely conceived surprise for the audience, who', wrote Canon Ainger, 'by no means expected from the description to recognize in the character the portly form of the editor of *Punch*', Mark Lemon.

G 57
Playbill for J.R. Planché's *Fortunio* at Tavistock House, 8 January 1855
F.MS.180

The phrasing of the playbill bears the stamp of 'our manager, who took upon him the charge of everything, from the writing of the playbills to the composition of the punch, brewed for our refreshment between the acts, but "craftily qualified" . . . to suit the capacities of the childish brain' (Alfred Ainger).

G58
Playbill for Wilkie Collins's *The Lighthouse* at Tavistock House, 18 June 1855
F.MS.180

G59
William Wilkie Collins
Manuscript of *The Storm at the Lighthouse: a play in two acts* [1855]
F.MS.115

The manuscript of *The Lighthouse*, in Collins's handwriting.

1855 was 'a year of much unsettled discontent' with Dickens. In the early summer Collins sent him his play *The Lighthouse*, and Dickens, attracted by the part of Aaron Gurnock the ancient light-keeper, plunged once again into theatricals. Having excelled hitherto as a comic actor, he now turned to a melodramatic part. Gurnock is 'an old man with half-dazed wits and a bewildered sense of some wrong committed in bygone years', Mrs Cowden Clarke observed, and of Dickens's acting she said, 'A wonderful impersonation was this; very imaginative, very original, very wild, very striking'.

G60
Clarkson Stanfield, RA (1793/4–1867)
Backcloth to *The Lighthouse*
Tempera. 103 × 105
Lent by The Dickens House

'For the scene of the Eddystone Lighthouse at this little play, afterwards placed in a frame in the hall at Gadshill, a thousand guineas was given at the Dickens sale. It occupied the great painter only one or two mornings, and Dickens will tell how it originated. Walking on Hampstead Heath to think over his Theatrical Fund speech, he met Mr. Lemon, and they went together to Stanfield. "He has been very ill, and he told us that large pictures are too much for him, and he must confine himself to small ones. But I would not have this, I declared he must paint bigger ones than ever, and what would he think of beginning upon an act-drop for a proposed vast theatre at Tavistock House? He laughed and caught at this, we cheered him up very much, and he said he was quite a man again." April 1855.' (Forster's *Life*.)

G61
Playbill for Wilkie Collins's *The Frozen Deep* at the Gallery of Illustration, 8 August 1857
Enthoven Collection

Dickens and his family were living in Paris at Christmas-time 1855–56, and there were no amateur theatricals. The following year Collins's play *The Frozen Deep* was performed on five nights between 5 and 14 January 1857. Dickens played Richard Wardour, once again running the gamut of melodramatic passion. Of his acting Francesco Berger (who composed the overture) wrote: 'It is fearfully fine throughout – from the sullen despair in the second act, alternating with gusts of passion or with gleams of tenderness, down to the appalling misery and supreme emotion of the dying scene'.

Dickens's friend Douglas Jerrold died suddenly on 8 June 1857. Immediately Dickens set about organizing a fund for his widow and children, and once again adopted amateur theatricals as a means of raising money. *The Frozen Deep* was therefore performed for this purpose in London at the Gallery of Illustration, and in Manchester (M1–3).

MACREADY

The amateur theatricals were observed rather superciliously ('it is quite ludicrous the fuss which the actors make about this play') by the professional actor William Charles Macready (1793–1873). Dickens was introduced to him by Forster on 16 June 1837, and they became firm friends. During Dickens's American tour of 1842 Macready kept an eye on his children.

Macready was the son of an actor and an actress. After an education at Rugby, however, it was with reluctance that he took up his parents' profession, compelled by their financial failure. Throughout his life he was oppressed by 'painful convictions of the uncertainty of my position', and strove always to raise and assert the dignity of his profession. This superior attitude, and his ungovernable temper, made him a difficult colleague, but his friends, mostly chosen from outside the theatrical profession, knew the deeply sensitive and emotional sides of his nature. He succeeded Edmund Kean as the pre-eminent tragedian of the English stage, showing less fire and passion than the older actor, but always interpreting his parts with scrupulous care. During his periods as manager of Drury Lane and Covent Garden he restored to use the original, unimproved texts of Shakespeare's plays, as well as experimenting with elaborate scenic effects, often designed by Clarkson Stanfield. He made three American tours in 1826, 1843, and 1848. He retired from the stage in 1851 to lead the life of a quiet country gentleman at Sherborne, Dorset.

G62
Playbill for *King Lear* at the Theatre Royal, Covent Garden, 25 January 1838
Enthoven Collection

G63
Anonymous
Mr Macready as King Lear
Engraving published by John Tallis & Co. Cut to $10\frac{3}{4} \times 7$
Enthoven Collection

G64
William Shakespeare
King Lear
London, W. and J. Richardson, 1770
Acting copy, marked by Macready
F.PB.7920

Lear was one of Macready's greatest parts. In the Covent Garden production of 1838, he restored to the play the part of the Fool, then usually omitted. The part was given to a woman, Miss Priscilla Horton, who was much complimented. Cordelia was played by Miss Helen Faucit, who was later to become infatuated with Macready and a cause of embarrassing rumours. Many of Macready's acting copies, including that displayed here, are in the Forster Collection.

G65
Charles Dickens
Manuscript of a critique of Macready's production of *King Lear* at the Haymarket Theatre, 1849
F.MS.169

G66
***The Examiner*, 27 October 1849**
F.PB.2914

It is almost certain that Dickens contributed a brief notice of the 1838 *Lear* to the *Examiner*, 28 January 1838: Forster, dramatic critic of the *Examiner*, was kept from the performance by illness, and therefore printed the remarks of 'a friend, on whose judgement we have thorough reliance', very probably Dickens. Dickens certainly reviewed Macready's production of 1849 (in which Miss Horton again played the Fool) for the *Examiner:* the manuscript of the critique, in his hand, survives.

G67
Playbill for J.S. Knowles's *Virginius* at the Theatre Royal, Covent Garden, 13 May 1839
Enthoven Collection

G68
After John Jackson, RA (1778–1831)
Mr Macready as Virginius. 'Does no one speak?'
Dated *20 June 1820*
Stipple engraving by Charles Picart. $13\frac{1}{2} \times 10\frac{3}{8}$
Enthoven Collection

Macready was equally interested in contemporary drama, launching such plays as Talfourd's *Ion*, Bulwer's *Richelieu* and Knowles's *Virginius*.

G69 [38]
Daniel Maclise, RA (1806–70)
William Charles Macready (1793–1873) as Werner in Byron's *Werner*, Act I, scene i
Oil. $68\frac{1}{2} \times 39\frac{1}{2}$
F.P.21

This portrait was exhibited at the Royal Academy in 1851 (no. 644). Macready first played the part at Drury Lane in 1830, and it was considered one of his finest achievements.

G70
Playbill for *Macbeth* at the Theatre Royal, Drury Lane, 26 February 1851
Enthoven Collection

Of this farewell performance, Macready wrote in his Diary: 'Acted Macbeth as I never, never before acted it; with a reality, a vigour, a truth, a dignity that I never before threw into my delineation of this favourite character'. After the performance came a farewell speech, and a tribute of applause from the audience which 'was, in my experience, unprecedented'.

G71
Cutting, with engraving of Macready speaking at a public dinner in his honour
From the *Illustrated London News*, 8 March 1851
Enthoven Collection

Macready's last public appearance was at the dinner given in his honour at the Hall of Commerce on 1 March 1851. Bulwer-Lytton took the chair and paid tribute to Macready. Dickens also spoke and at the conclusion of the speeches Forster read Tennyson's sonnet to Macready:
'Thine is it that our drama did not die,
Nor flicker down to brainless pantomime,
And those gilt gauds men-children swarm to see.
Farewell! Macready: moral, grave, sublime...'

H: Dickens and Christmas

Dickens is firmly associated in most people's minds with the idea of Christmas, primarily through the series of *Christmas Books* which he began in 1843 with *A Christmas Carol* and continued at yearly intervals with *The Chimes*, *The Cricket on the Hearth* and *The Battle of Life*. *The Haunted Man* followed in 1848. All were quickly adapted for the stage. Subsequently he produced a Christmas number of *Household Words* from 1850 till 1858, and of *All the Year Round* from 1859 till 1868; his own contributions to these were generally made in collaboration with other writers.

Although the Christmas tree was becoming fashionable after its introduction by Queen Victoria and the Prince Consort at Windsor in 1841, Dickens disapproved of 'the new German toy'. The aspects of Christmas which delighted him were its feasting, especially if it could be indulged in by the poor, and the feelings of benevolence engendered by the season.

H1
John Callcott Horsley, RA (1817–1903)
The first Christmas card. 1843
Lithograph. $3\frac{1}{4} \times 5\frac{1}{8}$
20717

H2
William Maw Egley (1826–1916)
The second Christmas card. 1848
Two sketches and the finished design
Pencil: etching. Each $3\frac{1}{4} \times 4\frac{3}{4}$
E.11/2–1940; E.13–1940

The increasing concern with Christmas felt in early Victorian times is seen in the advent of the first Christmas cards in the 1840s. H1, designed in 1843 by J.C. Horsley for his friend Henry Cole (see I 30, 31), was put on public sale in 1846. The scenes chosen to decorate both this, the first Christmas card, and W.M. Egley's successor of 1848 emphasize the conviviality and the charity of Christmas.

H3
Illustrations depicting the Poulterer's shop, Holborn Hill, Newgate Market, the Norfolk Coach and Leadenhall Market on Christmas Eve
Illustrated London News, 27 December 1845

H4
After Frederick Eltze (fl. 1867)
The Christmas Dinner
Wood-engraving by Joseph Swain; coloured by hand. $5\frac{1}{2} \times 8$
E.2467–1966

One of a series of Christmas scenes from *The New Table Book*, 1867.

H5
A Christmas Carol. In Prose. Being a Ghost Story of Christmas
London, Chapman and Hall, 1843
F.PB.2416

Written when Dickens was half-way through *Martin Chuzzlewit* and thought out during many long night walks through the London streets, this story of the moral regeneration of Scrooge had an immediate success. Thackeray, who himself later wrote Christmas books (*Mrs. Perkins's Ball*, 1847; *The Rose and the Ring*, 1855) said that *A Christmas Carol* was 'a national benefit'.

H6
John Leech (1817–64)
Three illustrations to *A Christmas Carol*
Etchings, coloured by hand. $3\frac{3}{4} \times 3\frac{3}{8}$; $3\frac{7}{8} \times 3\frac{1}{4}$; $4\frac{3}{4} \times 3\frac{1}{4}$
'Mr. Fezziwig's Ball'
'Marley's Ghost'
'Scrooge's Third Visitor'

H7
The Chimes: a Goblin Story of some Bells that rang an Old Year out and a New Year in
London, Chapman and Hall, 1845 [i.e. December 1844]
Open at the illustration 'Richard and Margaret' by John Leech
F.PB.2414

The Chimes, Dickens's second Christmas book, was written in Italy. Its title gave him difficulty, till at last he sent Forster the message 'We have heard THE CHIMES at midnight, Master Shallow!' After completing the story he paid a brief visit to England during which he gave a memorable reading of it to his friends (see H10).

H8 [48]
Daniel Maclise, RA (1806–70)
Two drawings for illustrations to *The Chimes*
Pencil. $6\frac{1}{4} \times 4$; $6\frac{1}{4} \times 3\frac{3}{4}$
Frontispiece: 'The Tower of the Chimes'
Title page: 'The Spirit of the Chimes'
F.P.75.2 and 1

H9
John Leech (1817–64)
Four drawings for illustrations to *The Chimes*
Pencil. Average size $4\frac{5}{8} \times 2\frac{7}{8}$
'Trotty Veck'
'Alderman Cute and his Friends'
'Sir Joseph Bowley's'
'Richard and Margaret'
Lent by the City Art Gallery and Museum, Nottingham

John Leech shared in the illustration of *The Chimes* with Maclise (see H8), Stanfield and Richard Doyle. Dickens was not satisfied with this drawing for the illustration 'Richard and Margaret'. Although it had already been engraved when he saw it for the first time, Dickens suppressed the cut, and asked Leech to redraw the lower figure, making him younger and less dissipated in appearance.

H10 [12]
Daniel Maclise, RA (1806–70)
Charles Dickens Reading 'The Chimes' to His Friends
Pencil. $4\frac{3}{4} \times 6\frac{7}{8}$
F.P.74

Dickens wrote *The Chimes* in Genoa, and then came to London to read it on 3 December 1844 to an assembly of his close friends in Forster's rooms at Lincoln's Inn. At his special request, Carlyle, who had influenced the social message of this work was invited, as well as Laman Blanchard, Douglas Jerrold, Clarkson Stanfield, Frederick Dickens, Daniel Maclise, the Rev. Alexander Dyce, W.J. Fox, and the Rev. William Harness; many of the group were radicals, many were journalists. Maclise enclosed this sketch in a letter to Mrs Dickens now in the Pierpont Morgan Library. In this he remarked 'I do not think that there ever was such a triumphant hour for Charles – I must make a great historical picture of the subject the first opportunity'.

H11
Letter from Charles Dickens to Catherine Dickens, 2 December 1844
Lent by the Trustees of the British Museum

In this exuberant and affectionate letter Dickens tells his wife that he has arrived in London, has busied himself over the publication of *The Chimes* (persuading, with forceful charm, two of his illustrators to alter their designs) and is about to give a private reading of the novel to a circle of friends. He describes how everyone who has heard the novel has been extraordinarily moved, and in the postscript reflects: 'what a thing it is to have power'.

H12
Playbill for *The Chimes*
Dramatised by Mark Lemon and Gilbert A'Beckett and first performed at the Theatre Royal, Adelphi, 19 December 1844
Enthoven Collection

H13
The Cricket on the Hearth. A Fairy Tale of Home
London, Bradbury and Evans, 1846 [i.e. December 1845]
F.PB.2418

Dickens's third Christmas book; this was illustrated by Maclise, Doyle, Stanfield, Leech and Edwin Landseer.

H14
After Thomas Harrison Wilson (worked 1842–86)
Samuel Anderson Emery (1817–86) as John Peerybingle in *The Cricket on the Hearth*
Dramatised by Albert Smith, in the first performance held at the Lyceum Theatre, 20 December 1845
Lithographed by G.E. Madeley; coloured by hand.
$14\frac{1}{2} \times 9\frac{1}{2}$
Enthoven Collection

H15
The Battle of Life. A Love Story
London, Bradbury and Evans, 1846
Open at the frontispiece by Daniel Maclise
F.PB.2410

Dickens's fourth Christmas book which was illustrated by Maclise, Doyle, Stanfield and Leech

H16
Undated letter from Daniel Maclise to John Forster referring to his illustration for the frontispiece of *The Battle of Life*
F.MS.385

'It is clear to me that Dickens does not care one damn whether I make a little sketch for the book or not.—however if *you* think that the appearance of the volume should be as like the former ones as possible – I will with even pleasure gulp down my jealousy and draw on the wood that apple tree &c for a frontispiece – In which case you must *shut up that* same subject to Doyle – as I saw in his sketch last night. But I do this at your bidding – and not at all for D. and on the whole would much prefer not engaging in the matter at all –'

H17
John Leech (1817–64)
Drawings for illustrations to *The Battle of Life*
Pencil. Each $4\frac{1}{2} \times 2\frac{7}{8}$
'The Parting Breakfast'
'The Night of the Return'
8582, 8583

H18
Letter from John Leech to John Forster, 16 November 1846
F.MS.345

Leech protests about the limited time available for the preparation of his designs, and about Maclise's request that he should portray Clemency Newcome in the same guise as himself. '*Conscientiously* I could not make Clemency Newcome particularly beautiful. If you will read a little *beyond* the words "plump and cheerful" – you will find the following. "But the extraordinary homeliness of her gait and manner would have superseded any face in the world" – "To say that she had two left legs and somebody else's arms . . ."

'The impression made upon me by such a description as I have quoted certainly is that the character so described is both awkward and comic – Of course I may be wrong in my conception of what Dickens intended, but *I* imagined the lady in question to be a sort of clean "Slowboy" – The blessed public (if they consider the matter at all) will hold me responsible for what appears with my name, they will know nothing about my being obliged to conform to Mr. Maclise's idea . . .'

His reluctance to undertake the design may account for Leech's misconception that Michael Warden took part in the elopement with the result that he is portrayed with Marion in the illustration 'The Night of the Return'. Dickens wrote to Forster concerning this illustration: 'When I first saw it, it was with a horror and agony not to be expressed. Of course I need not tell *you*, my dear fellow, Warden has no business in the elopement scene. *He* was never there! In the first hot sweat of this surprise and novelty, I was going to implore the printing of that sheet to be stopped, and the figure taken out of the block. But when I thought of the pain this might give to our kind-hearted Leech, and that what is such a monstrous enormity to me, as never having entered my brain, may not so present itself to others, I became more composed . . .'

H19
The Haunted Man and the Ghost's Bargain. A Fancy for Christmas Time
London, Bradbury and Evans, 1848
F.PB.2429

This story, Dickens's fifth Christmas book, was begun in the autumn of 1847, but not published till the following Christmas. It was the last to appear as a separate volume, and was succeeded by the Christmas stories in *Household Words* and *All the Year Round*. The opening shows the double-page illustration by Sir John Tenniel (1820–1914) for chapter 2. The other illustrators were Stanfield, Leech and Frank Stone.

61

H20
John Leech (1817–64)
Three drawings for illustrations to *The Haunted Man*
Pencil. Average size $3\frac{7}{8} \times 2\frac{7}{8}$
'The Tetterbys'
'The Boy before the Fire'
'Johnny and Moloch'
Lent by the City Art Gallery and Museum Nottingham

H21
'Buz'
The Haunted Druggist, or Bogy's Speculation
London, W. Strange, 1849
F.PAMPH.317

A parody of *The Haunted Man*

H22
Sir John Everett Millais, PRA (1829–96)
John Leech
Signed and dated *JEM* (monogram) *1854*
Water-colour. $6\frac{7}{8} \times 5\frac{7}{8}$
Lent by the National Portrait Gallery

H23
Christmas Stories from the Household Words. Conducted by Charles Dickens
London, Chapman and Hall [1860]
F.PB.4287

Showing 'A Round of Stories by the Christmas Fire. Being the Extra Christmas Number of *Household Words*. Christmas, 1852'.

I: Social novels

DOMBEY AND SON

I 1
Manuscript of *Dombey and Son* [1846–48]. Vol.IB
F.MS.160

The last instalment of *Martin Chuzzlewit* appeared in July 1844. Dickens then allowed two years to elapse before beginning *Dombey* in June 1846. The first six numbers he wrote abroad, in Switzerland and Paris; the inception and progress of the story are therefore well documented in letters to Forster. It deals with a Victorian merchant, Mr Dombey, and his emotional and commercial failure. In portraying Mr Dombey's relations with his family, Dickens also suggests 'a pervasive dissatisfaction with society as a whole.' The eruptive energy of Victorian capitalism seems to be represented by the railway. In chapter 20 Mr Dombey takes a train journey, and Dickens seizes the opportunity for a passage of rhythmic declamation: 'Away, with a shriek, and a roar, and a rattle . . .'. The manuscript shows how carefully he composed this passage.

I 2
Dombey and Son
London, Bradbury and Evans, 1848
F.PB.2422

In the centre of Phiz's frontispiece sit Florence and Paul Dombey on the seashore. Above left are depicted incidents in Paul's life, and above right incidents in Florence's history. Below, in the waves, may be seen the figures of Sol Gills and Walter engaged in their nautical adventures.

I 3
Dealings with the Firm of Dombey and Son, Wholesale, Retail, and for Exportation
In parts. London, Bradbury and Evans, 1846–48
D.PB.3052

The part cover by Phiz is designed to suggest something of the tenor of the story. At the bottom left stands Mr Dombey lightly supporting his prosperity, represented by the precariously balanced ledgers and cash boxes. At the top centre he sits secure upon a cash box; to the left of him are scenes from his business and family life, and to the right he is seen speaking in the House of Commons (Dickens did not in fact give him a political career in the novel) and remarrying at a society wedding. But on the right of the design his edifice of prosperity is revealed as a house of cards, and at its foot he is shown as crippled and crushed by money bags. Dickens wrote concerning it: 'I think the cover very good; perhaps with a little too much in it, but that is an ungrateful objection'.

I 4
Thomas Roscoe
The London and Birmingham Railway
London, Charles Tilt [1838]
Showing a map of the line
14.vii.1874

I 5
***London and Birmingham Railway. Coaching Department. Hours of Departure & Time Table.* On and after Thursday 20th June 1839**
29.vi.1870

In chapter 20, Dombey, with his friend Major Bagstock, takes a journey to Leamington. He travels on the London and Birmingham Railway: the chronology of the book is well worked out, and the journey can be dated to 1839–40, not long after the line was fully opened in September 1838. Occupying his own carriage, which was attached (as was common at the time) to a flat truck, Dombey travelled the length of the line, and then drove from Birmingham to Leamington.

I 6
Enlarged photograph of an advertisement for the Crown Commercial Hotel, Leamington [c.1840]

Dombey and Bagstock stayed at the Royal Hotel, Leamington. This advertisement for another hotel makes clear how much the railway had increased the prosperity of the spa town.

I 7
John Cooke Bourne (1814–96)
Building the Stationary Engine House, Camden Town
Sepia wash heightened with white. $7\frac{7}{8} \times 13\frac{1}{4}$
Lent by Sir Arthur Elton Bt

I 8
John Cooke Bourne (1814–96)
(a) **Excavating at Camden Town with Saint Saviours, Eversholt Street in the distance. 1836–37**
Pencil and wash heightened with blue and ochre. $6\frac{3}{4} \times 10$
Lent by Sir Arthur Elton Bt

(b) **Excavating at Park Street, Camden Town. 1836–37**
Pencil and wash. $5\frac{3}{8} \times 8\frac{1}{2}$
Lent by Sir Arthur Elton Bt

The building to the extreme left was formerly Wellington House where Dickens was educated from 1824–26.

Variations on these sketches of the building of the London and Birmingham Railway were published under the title *A series of Lithographed Drawings on the London and Birmingham Railway by John C. Bourne* with descriptions by John Britton, FSA, 1838–39.

The effects of the railway were by no means all beneficial. The London and Birmingham Railway laid waste large tracts of the London suburbs. Dickens was distressed by the chaos and confusion caused by the digging of the Camden Town cutting, which he described as tearing down 'Staggs's Gardens' – the 'little row of houses, with little squalid patches of ground before them' where Polly Toodle's family lived: 'The first shock of a great earthquake had, just at that period, rent the whole neighbourhood to its centre. Traces of its course were visible on every side. Houses were knocked down; streets broken through and stopped; deep pits and trenches dug in the ground; enormous heaps of earth and clay thrown up . . . in short, the yet unfinished and unopened Railroad was in progress; and, from the very core of all this dire disorder, trailed smoothly away, upon its mighty course of civilisation and improvement'.

I 9
Anonymous
Effects of the Rail Road on the Brute Creation, 1831
Lettered with title and *Published July 12th 1831 by Ino Townsend No. 2 King St., Manchester: Plate 2 & 3 Just Published*
Lithograph. $10\frac{3}{8} \times 14\frac{1}{8}$
Lent by Sir Arthur Elton Bt

I 10
Anonymous
Effects of the Rail Road on the Brute Creation, 1831
Lettered with title and *Published July 6th 1831 by Ino Townsend No 2 King Strt Manchester.*, and with a note on spurious copies
Lithograph. 13×18
Lent by Sir Arthur Elton Bt

I 11
George Cruikshank's Table-Book.
Edited by Gilbert Abbott A'Beckett
London, At the Punch Office, 1845
Showing the etching by Cruikshank: 'The Railway Dragon'
F.PB.2159

The villain of *Dombey and Son*, Carker, haunted by discomfiture and rage, flees to a remote country railway station, and is there run down by a locomotive: '. . . looked round – saw the red eyes, bleared and dim in the daylight, close upon him – was beaten down, caught up, and whirled away upon a jagged mill, that spun him round and round, and struck him limb from limb, and licked his stream of life up with its fiery heat, and cast his mutilated fragments in the air'. Dickens's monstrous locomotive was suggested, perhaps, by some of the caricatures produced at the height of the railway mania in the mid forties.

I 12 [46]
William Maw Egley (1826–1916)
Florence Dombey in Captain Cuttle's Parlour
Signed and dated *W. Maw Egley 1888*
Oil. 24×18
1824–1900

Standing in opposition to the hard capitalist world of Dombey, is the shop of Sol Gills, at the sign of the Wooden Midshipman. Though Sol is commercially inept – 'the world's gone past me. I hardly know where I am myself; much less where my customers are' – his heart is in the right place, and with his nephew Walter he cherishes a secret love of the marvellous and adventurous. When Florence Dombey is driven from her home by her father's harshness, she takes refuge in the Wooden Midshipman, now (in Sol's absence) under the supervision of the lovably eccentric, sententious Captain Cuttle. The painting was retouched in 1890.

I 13
Joseph Edward Carpenter
What Are The Wild Waves Saying
C.1850
Music composed by Stephen Glover
Enthoven Collection

While staying with Mrs Pipchin at Brighton, Little Paul would often break off when talking to Florence by the sea 'to try to understand what it was that the waves were always saying; and would rise up in his couch to look towards that invisible region far away'.

Dickens's description of the death of Little Paul Dombey, the subject of this ballad, was as distressing to contemporary readers as the death of Little Nell. Lord Jeffrey reacted to Little Paul's death with characteristic emotion: 'Oh my dear dear Dickens! what a No. 5 you have given us! I have so cried and sobbed over it last night, and again this morning; and felt my heart purified by those tears... Since that divine Nelly... there has been nothing like it. Every trait so true and so touching ... and yet lightened by that fearless innocence ...'.

ILLUSTRATIONS TO
DOMBEY AND SON, 1846–48,
BY HABLÔT K. BROWNE (PHIZ)
(1815–82)

Each of Phiz's forty illustrations to *Dombey and Son* was etched in duplicate. Either because this was insufficient to meet the demand, or because Phiz was late in supplying the duplicate plate, many of the illustrations, even in the early issues, were reproduced by lithography. In his illustrations to this novel, the artist used the oblong format for the first time.

Dickens was disappointed in some of Phiz's illustrations to the first few parts; however, the success of the later plates redeemed the artist in Dickens's mind. Phiz gave him all the original drawings for the illustrations and a painted portrait of Little Paul.

I 14
Phiz (Hablôt K. Browne) (1815–82)
Studies for the figure of Mr Dombey
Inscribed *Dombey-48 rather bald – rather red – handsome well-made – pompous (?)Sirs. Close Shaved. Close cut and stiffly formal*
Pencil. 9 × 7
F.P.181.3

As Dickens was living in Lausanne when he began to write *Dombey and Son*, he was unable to discuss his conception of Mr Dombey with his illustrator. He was nervous lest Phiz should make him too much of a caricature. The artist sent him this selection of types. The Dombey actually etched was not an absolute transcript of any of these suggestions, but a combination of several.

I 15 [26]
Phiz (Hablôt K. Browne) (1815–82)
(a) **Preliminary drawing in pen and ink,**
(b) **etching of the illustration 'The Dombey Family' to *Dombey and Son*, 1846–48**
(a) inscribed *The Dombey Family & Polly Toodles*, *Dombey* and *Whether 'twere better to have him* [Mr Dombey] *standing thus, stiff as a poker, with a kind of side glance at his daughter – or sitting, as in the other?* (b) Signed *Phiz* and inscribed with the title of the plate
$5 \times 3\frac{5}{8}; 4\frac{7}{8} \times 4$
(a) Lent by the Trustees of the British Museum

Dickens must have preferred the alternative drawing Phiz mentions in the inscription, because in the etching Mr Dombey is represented as seated and Florence is transferred to the other side of the illustration.

(c) **Preliminary drawing in pen and ink and wash,** (d) **etching of the illustration 'Paul and Mrs. Pipchin' to *Dombey and Son*, 1846–48**
(c) Inscribed *Paul & Mrs. Pipchin* and *Dombey*
(d) Signed *Phiz* and lettered with the title of the plate
$5\frac{1}{8} \times 4; 4\frac{3}{4} \times 4$
(c) Lent by the Trustees of the British Museum

Dickens, who was so disappointed in the two illustrations in the preceding part that he felt like 'curling his legs up', was particularly anxious that this illustration should be a success: 'The best subject for Browne will be at Mrs. Pipchin's; and if he liked to do a quiet odd thing, Paul, Mrs. Pipchin and the Cat, by the fire, would be very good for the story. I earnestly hope he will think it worth a little extra care'. This may account for his adverse reaction to the etching, which, notwithstanding his criticism, follows the text closely. 'I am really *distressed* by the illustration of Mrs. Pipchin and Paul. It is so frightfully and wildly wide of the mark. Good Heaven! in the commonest and most literal construction of the text, it is all wrong. She is described as an old lady, and Paul's "miniature arm-chair" is mentioned more than once. He ought to be sitting in a little arm-chair down in a corner of the fireplace, staring up at her. I can't say what pain and vexation it is to be so utterly misrepresented. I would cheerfully have given a hundred pounds to have kept this illustration out of the book. He never could have got that idea of Mrs. Pipchin if he had attended to the text. Indeed I think he does better without the text; for then the notion is made easy to him in short description, and he can't help taking it in.' Dickens's reaction was tempered by unhappy memories of his childhood. Mrs Pipchin was based on Mrs Roylance, with whom the young Dickens lodged during his employment at the blacking warehouse.

(e) **Preliminary drawing in pencil, and**
(f) **etching for the illustration 'Major Bagstock is delighted to have that opportunity' to** *Dombey and Son,* **1846–48**
(e) Signed *PZ*. Inscribed in another hand with titles
$4\frac{3}{4} \times 4\frac{1}{2}$; $5\frac{1}{2} \times 4\frac{1}{2}$
(e) Lent by the Trustees of the British Museum

Edith, Dombey's second wife, makes her debut in this illustration. Dickens wanted her to appear 'handsome, though haughty-looking – good figure, well dressed, showy, and desirable. Quite a lady..., with something of a proud indifference about her, suggestive of a spark of the Devil within'. Whereas her 'Mother affects cordiality and heart, and is the essence of sordid calculation'. He was particularly pleased with Phiz's rendering of them: 'the women *quite perfect*. I cannot tell you how much I like the younger one'. The figure of Mr Dombey is omitted in this early sketch.

I 16
Phiz (Hablôt K. Browne) (1815–82)
Four illustrations to *Dombey and Son,* **1846–48**
(b), (c) and (d) Signed *Phiz*
Etchings. $5 \times 4\frac{3}{4}$; $5 \times 4\frac{3}{4}$; $5\frac{1}{4} \times 4\frac{1}{8}$; $5\frac{1}{4} \times 3\frac{3}{4}$

(a) 'Doctor Blimber's Young Gentlemen as they appeared when enjoying themselves'

(b) 'Poor Paul's Friend'

(c) 'Abstraction & Recognition'

The advertisement for *The Bottle*, which Phiz has etched on the wall in this plate, is an apt comment on Alice Marwood's position as she watches her former lover ride by: 'so easy and so trim, a-horseback while we are in the mud –'. Its presence in the illustrations emphasizes the resounding success of Cruikshank's publication. Dickens bought one of the 100,000 copies which were sold in the first few days after their issue.

(d) 'Let him remember it in that room, years to come!'

BLEAK HOUSE

I 17
Manuscript of *Bleak House* **[1852–53]. Vol.IB**
F.MS.162

Dickens had always attacked social abuses in his novels, but up to *David Copperfield* the attacks had been specific and incidental. *Bleak House* was the first novel to be wholly expressive, in plot and atmosphere, of a discontent with contemporary institutions. The plot demonstrates the destructive effects of Chancery litigation. Dickens makes use of the London fog as a symbol of the unintelligible confusion of the country's legal system. And in his descriptions of the rain falling on the silent, shuttered Chesney Wold (see the page of manuscript displayed) he suggests the decay and enfeeblement of the country's aristocracy and political establishment.

I 18
Bleak House. **Number V**
London, Bradbury and Evans, July 1852
Lent by The Dickens House

The covers of the parts of *Bleak House* (and of the next three novels published in parts) are blue; Dickens reverted to green with *Our Mutual Friend*. Phiz's cover design depicts, in the topmost section and in the bottom corners, lawyers playing games with their clients. The vignettes in the side panels suggest incidents in the story, and in the lower part of the centre panel Mr Jarndyce is seen outside Bleak House (the wind being in the east), surrounded by the foolish philanthropists who take advantage of him.

I 19 [52]
Bleak House
London, Bradbury and Evans, 1853
F.PB.2411

See note to I 25

I 20
(a) *Chancery Reform Association*
[Prospectus and list of officers] [1850]
F.PAMPH.259/13

(b) William Carpenter
Chancery Reform. The Equity Jurisdiction of the Court of Chancery; a Lecture
London, Effingham Wilson [1850]
F.PAMPH.259/6

(c) William Carpenter
Chancery Reform Tracts, No.2. Chancery and Ecclesiastical Courts
7 February 1851
Showing the first and last pages
F.PAMPH.310/20

As early as *Pickwick* Dickens had attacked the Court of Chancery, and in 1844 was himself embroiled in its workings when he stopped a piracy of *A Christmas Carol* by Chancery proceedings. In 1850–51 the state of the Court of Chancery came to the forefront of public interest. A Chancery Reform Association was formed; around the turn of the year the issue was thoroughly ventilated in *The Times*: and in March 1851 Sir John Russell's government proposed measures for Chancery reform. The first part of *Bleak House* appeared a year later; by then Russell's Chancery Reform Act had passed into law, but it is clear from Dickens's portrayal of Chancery in the novel that he did not consider the situation to be much improved.

I 21 [57]
Sir Henry Cole, KCB (1808–82)
Drawing of a parcel of records in the Old Record Office showing the state in which historical records were being preserved in about 1827
Water-colour. $7\frac{7}{8} \times 12\frac{1}{4}$
E.5883–1910

At the end of the Jarndyce Chancery suit, the estate is entirely absorbed in legal costs. All that is left is paper. From the court 'great bundles of paper began to be carried out – bundles in bags, bundles too large to be got into any bags, immense masses of papers of all shapes and no shapes'. The Lord Chancellor is balanced in the novel by a parody Lord Chancellor: Krook, the rubbish merchant, whose shop is full of ancient documents which he cannot read. It was evidently Dickens's conviction that the country's legal system was clogged with waste paper. Curiously, the legal and other public records of the country were treated almost as waste paper. Sir Henry Cole conducted a vigorous campaign to improve the condition of the Public Records, pointing out in an article in the *Westminster Review* (1849) that the Chancery records were dumped in the Tower of London along with gunpowder and ordnance stores, while the Common Law records were kept in the stables of Carlton House. These and other equally strange depositories were replaced, as a result of Cole's efforts, by a new fireproof repository in 1851.

I 22
John Simon
Reports relating to the Sanitary Condition of the City of London
London, John W. Parker and Son, 1854
F.PB.8053

In the early '50s thinking men were concerned no less with sanitary reform than with Chancery reform. Among the most influential exposures of the state of London were Dr Simon's reports, of which the first appeared in 1849. 'The following Reports', Simon explains in his Preface, 'officially addressed to the Commissioners of Sewers of the City of London, were originally printed only for the use of the Corporation; and although, to my very great pleasure, they have been extensively circulated through the medium of the daily press, there has continued so frequent an application for separate copies' that a collected edition has been issued. Simon begs the reader to 'devote an hour to visiting some very poor neighbourhood in the metropolis.... Let him fancy what it would be to himself to live there, in that beastly degradation of stink, fed with such bread, drinking such water.... Let him ... gravely reflect whether ... it be not a jarring discord in the civilization we boast – a worse than pagan savageness in the Christianity we profess, that such things continue....'

I 23 [53]
(a) *The Public Health a Public Question. First Report of the Metropolitan Sanitary Association*
London, Published by the Association, 1850
F.PAMPH.245/7

(b) George Godwin
London Shadows; a Glance at the 'Homes' of the Thousands ... Illustrations by John Browne
London, Routledge and Co., 1854
F.PAMPH.369/6

Dickens's interest in sanitary reform had long been active; in 1850 he became a member of the committee of the Metropolitan Sanitary Association, and referred to it in the 1850 Preface to *Oliver Twist*. At the first meeting of the Association on 6 February 1850 Lord Ashley paid tribute to him, as one 'who had done more to advance the interests of the working classes than any other writer of the age'. Dickens spoke at this meeting and at another the following year; and in 'Tom-all-Alone's' in *Bleak House* he gave his picture of the conditions the Association were trying to improve. That Phiz's representation of 'Tom-all-Alone's' is in accord with reality, may be proved by a comparison with the illustrations in George Godwin's *London Shadows*.

I 24
(a) Mrs Caroline Chisholm
Family Colonisation Loan Society ... or, A System of Emigration to the Colonies
[Prospectus] [London, 1849]
F.PAMPH.249/13

(b) **Enlarged photograph of a portrait of Mrs Caroline Chisholm** From *The People's Illustrated Journal*, 29 May 1852
F.PAMPH.495

Even in small details *Bleak House* was topical. Mrs Jellyby, who devotes herself to organizing 'the happy settlement, on the banks of the African rivers, of our superabundant home population' is probably based on Mrs Caroline Chisholm, who established the Family Colonisation Loan Society in 1850. Dickens supported the society (but did not approve of Mrs Chisholm's domestic disorder) and published an article on it in the first number of *Household Words*.

I 25 [51]
Enlarged photograph of a cartoon: 'Alarming Case of Spontaneous Combustion' in *Diogenes*, 8 January 1853
F.PAMPH.494

In the Preface to *Bleak House*, the extraordinary death of Krook, through spontaneous combustion, is defended by Dickens against critics (notably G.H.Lewes) who had claimed it to be an impossibility. Dickens quotes scientific accounts and authenticated cases, but nonetheless common-sense laughed at Krook's demise, effective as it was on a symbolic level. This cartoon is clearly suggested by Phiz's plate 'The Appointed Time' (see I 19).

ILLUSTRATIONS TO *BLEAK HOUSE* 1852–53 BY HABLÔT K. BROWNE (PHIZ) (1815–82)

Only 10 out of the customary 40 illustrations were etched in duplicate. The rest of the plates were reproduced by lithography, and the etched and lithographic illustrations were mixed indiscriminately in the same parts. Those etched in duplicate were the so-called 'dark plates' on which Phiz used a technique combining machine ruling and engraving, which was particularly well suited to giving exciting and dramatic effects of chiaroscuro. Only two dark plates had been issued previously: 'On The Dark Road' in *Dombey and Son* and 'The River' in *David Copperfield*.

I 26
Phiz (Hablôt K. Browne) (1815–82)
(a) and (b) **Impressions from different plates for the illustration 'A new meaning in the Roman' to *Bleak House*, 1852–53**
Engraving and etching. Each $5\frac{3}{8} \times 3\frac{7}{8}$
Lent by Professor Kathleen Tillotson

Marked differences between these two 'dark plates' are visible. In (a) there are three floor boards between the rugs to the right, the left candle stub is dark, there is a decoration between the top of the book-case and the cornice at the extreme right, and there are two cherubs in attendance behind the Roman. In (b) there are only two floor boards between the rugs, the right candle stub is dark, the space between the book-case and cornice is shaded and there is only one cherub behind the Roman.

(c) and (d) **Impressions from different plates for the illustration 'The Night' to *Bleak House*, 1852–53**
Engraving and etching. Each $3\frac{3}{4} \times 6\frac{1}{4}$
Lent by Professor Kathleen Tillotson

Apart from such minor differences as those visible in the tripod-like structures to the left of each plate, or in the lamps, the treatment of the backgrounds is completely different.

I 27
***Diogenes*, 3 September 1853**
Showing an article: 'A Browne Study'
F.PAMPH.494

This is a contemporary comment on Phiz's 'dark plates' (see I 26).

I 28 [54-5]
Phiz (Hablôt K. Browne) (1815–82)
Five illustrations to *Bleak House*
(d) signed *Phiz*
(a), (b), (d) and (e) Etchings. (c) Engraving and etching. Average size $4\frac{1}{2} \times 4\frac{3}{4}$

(a) 'The Lord Chancellor copies from memory'

(b) 'Consecrated ground'

(c) 'Tom-all-Alone's'

(d) 'The visit at the Brickmaker's'

(e) 'Mr. Guppy's entertainment'

I 29
Phiz (Hablôt K. Browne) (1815–82)
(a) **Preliminary drawing in pencil and wash, and** (b) **etching of the illustration 'Attorney and Client, fortitude and impatience' to *Bleak House*, 1852–53**
$4\frac{3}{4} \times 4\frac{3}{4}$; $4\frac{1}{8} \times 5\frac{1}{8}$
(a) Lent by the Trustees of the British Museum

HARD TIMES

I 30
Manuscript of *Hard Times* [1854]
F.MS.163

George Bernard Shaw observed that, while in *Bleak House* Dickens 'was still denouncing evils and ridiculing absurdities that were mere symptoms of the anarchy that followed the industrial revolution of the XVIII and XIX centuries', in *Hard Times* he turned his attack on the industrial revolution itself.

Certainly there is a new emphasis in *Hard Times*: 'the increase in strength and intensity is enormous'. But Shaw perhaps overstates his case when he claims that the novel expresses 'a passionate revolt against the whole industrial order of the modern world'. For in the second chapter of *Hard Times*, Dickens hits out, quite incidentally to the main purpose of the novel, at the Department of Practical Art and caricatures Sir Henry Cole, its General Superintendent, who also directed the museum which became the Victoria and Albert Museum. And in this attack, it has been claimed, he writes from the standpoint of the middle-class Philistine. His intention to caricature Cole is revealed by the fact that he has jotted down that name in his notes for chapter 2 on the Number Plan here displayed.

I 31
Sheet of the corrected proof of *Hard Times* [1854]
F.MS.170

The character based on Sir Henry Cole is the 'government officer' who accompanies Mr Gradgrind into the school classroom, and questions the pupils on artistic matters. In the manuscript the 'government officer' is more like Cole than he appears in the printed text, for Dickens excised from the proofs several phrases which seize on Cole's characteristic attitudes. On his first appearance, the 'government officer' is described as 'a bustling pleasant little gentleman', and the deleted phrases on the displayed proof sheets reveal more of his spry, cheerful personality.

I 32
***Household Words*, 1 April 1854**
Showing the first instalment of *Hard Times*
F.PB.4285

Hard Times was published weekly in *Household Words* between 1 April and 12 August 1854. Dickens found it very difficult to adjust his narrative to short weekly instalments: 'the difficulty of the space is *crushing*'. But it may have helped him to achieve an unusual forcefulness in this work.

I 33
Sir Joseph Edgar Boehm (1834–90)
Sir Henry Cole, KCB (1808–82)
Terracotta bust. $21\frac{1}{2}$ high
525–1883

See notes to I 30, I 31

I 34 [58]
Arthur Fitzwilliam Tait (1819–1905)
Stockport Viaduct
c.1850
Lithograph. 10×15
Lent by The British Railways Board

Hard Times is the first of Dickens's novels to take place in the industrial North of England; in a typical manufacturing town– 'Coketown'. Coketown may have been based on Preston; but it stands for any industrial town.

'It was a town of red brick, or of brick that would have been red if the smoke and ashes had allowed it; but as matters stood it was a town of unnatural red and black like the painted face of a savage. It was a town of machinery and tall chimneys, out of which interminable serpents of smoke trailed themselves forever and ever, and never got uncoiled. It had a black canal in it, and a river that ran purple with ill-smelling dye, and vast piles of buildings full of windows . . . which looked, when illuminated, like Fairy Palaces – or the travellers by express-train said so . . . [as they] whirled in full sight of the Fairy Palaces over the arches near, little felt amid the jarring of the machinery, and scarcely heard above its crash and rattle. . . . The streets were hot and dusty on the summer day, and the sun was so bright that it even shone through the heavy vapour drooping over Coketown. . . . The atmosphere of these Fairy Palaces was like the breath of the simoom, and their inhabitants, wasting with heat, toiled languidly in the desert.'

I 35
George Frederick Watts, OM, RA (1817–1904)
Thomas Carlyle (1795–1881)
1868
Oil. $25\frac{1}{2} \times 20\frac{1}{2}$
F.P.39

Dickens dedicated *Hard Times* to Thomas Carlyle, whom he had known well since 1840, and greatly admired. In a letter asking Carlyle's permission, Dickens assured him: 'I know it contains nothing in which you do not think with me, for no man knows your books better than I'.

I 36
Hard Times and Pictures from Italy
London, Chapman and Hall, 1866
Showing the wood-engraved frontispiece by A. Boyd Houghton
F.PB.2399

Dickens's main attack is directed at the ethics, not the practice, of the Victorian industrialists. He shows how hard-headed political and economic philosophies damage people, not only the 'hands' exploited by their masters, but the masters themselves. The political philosopher Mr Gradgrind is forced to realize that he has ruined his children by cramming them with facts and starving their fancies, by educating their minds and not their hearts. In Arthur Boyd Houghton's illustration Mr Gradgrind acknowledges the worthlessness of his son Tom.

I 37
(a) J.R. McCulloch
A Dictionary, Geographical, Statistical and Historical, of the Various Countries, Places and Principal Natural Objects in the World
2 vols. London, Longman, 1854
F.PB.5642

(b) Anonymous [J.R. McCulloch]
A Catalogue of Books, the Property of the Author of the Commercial Dictionary
London, privately printed, 1856
Showing a portrait of McCulloch engraved by W. Mote
F.PB.5641

Gradgrind wreaks damage not only in his own home but on a wider scale. The book opens in a schoolroom where he announces his educational principle: 'Facts, facts, facts'. Of his many real-life counterparts, J.R. McCulloch is typical. McCulloch was a political economist who wrote a standard theoretical treatise on the subject, but whose chief works were huge compilations of densely accumulated information: 'facts, facts, facts'. His fat *Dictionary* contains the material with which Gradgrind wished to fill the pupils in his school, and which was packed away behind his own 'square wall of a forehead', in his bald head which swelled as if it 'had scarcely warehouse-room for the hard facts stored inside.'

I 38
Enlarged photograph of a wood-engraved illustration of the Preston Strike
From the *Illustrated London News*, 12 November 1853

In 1838 Dickens had expressed a resolve to 'strike the heaviest blow in my power' for the Lancashire cotton operatives. At the very beginning of 1854 he returned to the idea and began *Hard Times*. Almost at once he took a trip to Preston to see at first hand the strike which had prevailed there for some months.

In the *Illustrated London News* for 4 March 1854, the writer of 'Town and Table-Talk on Literature, Art, &c' reported: 'the title of Mr Dickens's new work is *Hard Times*. His recent inquiry into the Preston strike is said to have originated the title, and, in some respects, suggested the turn of the story'. In fact Dickens concluded on his arrival at Preston that 'I shall not be able to get much here', and there is no strike in *Hard Times*.

I 39 [56]
Playbill advertising a performance by Powell's Circus Royal, at Arbour Square, Stepney, 1848
Wood-cut. $29\frac{1}{2} \times 10$
Lent by A.D. Hippisley Coxe Esq.

It has been conjectured that in *Hard Times* the proprietor of the 'Horse-riding' or Circus, Mr Sleary, whose slogan was 'People mutht be amuthed', was based on John Clarke (1786?–1864) listed on this playbill as 'The King of the Clowns'. Later Clarke became Powell's partner and joint owner of the circus.

LITTLE DORRIT

See also Section K

I 40
Manuscript of *Little Dorrit* [1855–57]. Vol.IIB
F.MS.165

The tone of melancholy in the close of *Little Dorrit* makes it unusual among the endings of Dickens's novels.

'They went quietly down into the roaring streets, inseparable and blessed; and as they passed along in sunshine and shade, the noisy and the eager, and the arrogant and the froward and the vain, fretted and chafed, and made their usual uproar.'

I 41
***Little Dorrit*. Number X**
London, Bradbury and Evans, September 1856
Lent by Mrs J. Brain

Dickens at first intended to call this novel *Nobody's Fault*, an ironic comment on the state of the nation in 1855–56. It has been pointed out that Phiz's cover design supports the notion of 'Nobody's Fault'.

'Its two sides seem to typify society in decay, and images of doom are combined with complacence and self-absorption. On the left is part of a crumbling castle, on whose tottering top is seated a sleeping man in an arm-chair with a handkerchief over his eyes and a newspaper on his knee. Against the castle lies a falling tree; the "supporters" of the coat of arms are rats. This is "the world" in its material aspect. Opposite stands part of a church, crowned by a raven, while a child plays leap-frog among the graves, and in a wheel-chair sits the life-in-death figure of Mrs Clennam attended by Flintwinch. So much for "religion". Overlapping these two scenes, and extending across the bottom of the design, is a motley crowd of travellers, each clinging to his belongings, all moving different ways, colliding, harassed, unhappy. Across the top of the design is what is virtually a political cartoon. Two aged figures, crippled and half blind, lead the procession, followed by a line of dotards and a dandy; Britannia in a bath-chair, asleep, is propelled by a line of men in fools' caps, followed by a crowd of toadies, behind whom are women and children; all, save the last, are smiling inanely. The centre-piece is Little Dorrit herself, at the gate of the prison, in a shaft of sunlight.'

I 42
Little Dorrit
London, Bradbury and Evans, 1857
F.PB.2430

The Marshalsea prison looms over Little Dorrit and her family; in the end it receives the ruined Arthur Clennam into its custody, and it is only through 'the daughter of the Marshalsea' that he is saved from despair. The prison is a symbolic presence in the novel.

I 43
Fifth Report from the Select Committee on the Army before Sebastopol; with the Proceedings of the Committee and an Appendix
Ordered, by the House of Commons, to be printed, 18 June 1855
F.PB.6737

I 44
The Queen Visiting the Imbeciles of the Crimea
Wood-engraved cartoon
Punch, 14 April 1855

In the months before Dickens began *Little Dorrit*, the whole of England had been roused to indignation at the incompetence of governmental administration. The Northcote-Trevelyan report of 1853 had given a stimulus to the movement to reform the civil service, but it was the revelations in 1854 and 1855 of the mismanagement of the Crimean War which inflamed public feeling. W.H. Russell's reports in *The Times* were amply confirmed by the investigations of the Roebuck

Committee, which disclosed, in Dickens's words, 'a confused heap of mismanagement, imbecility, and disorder, under which the nation's bravery lies crushed and withered'. In *Little Dorrit* Dickens bitingly satirized governmental administration in the 'Circumlocution Office'.

I 45
(a) ***Civil Service Reform. Observations upon the Report by ... Trevelyan ... and ... Northcote. By a Civil Subaltern***
London, William Edward Painter [1854]
F.PAMPH.381/19

(b) ***Official Paper. – No.3. Unfitness of the Present Home Government for ... New and Important Public Duties***
London, Administrative Reform Association, 1855
F.PAMPH.434/27

(c) ***Red-Tapeism; it's Cause. By One behind the Scenes***
London, James Ridgway, 1855
F.PAMPH.434/15

(d) Bernard Cracroft
The Right Man in the Right Place
Cambridge, E. Johnson, 1855
F.PAMPH.434/20

(e) John P. Gassiot
The Present Crisis in Administrative Reform
London, Smith, Elder and Co., 1856
F.PAMPH.434/12

(f) ***Administrative Reformers, What Have They Done? A Letter to Samuel Morley, Esq.***
London, Effingham Wilson, 1855
F.PAMPH.434/5

(g) ***Dangers of Administrative Reform, clearly pointed out in A Letter to the Editor of 'The Times'***
London, Thomas Harrison, 1855
F.PAMPH.434/14

When the Administrative Reform Association was founded in May 1855, Dickens at once joined it, and on 27 June delivered a speech at the Drury Lane Theatre on Administrative Reform, in which he 'denounced Palmerston for his heartlessness and for his *insouciance* of behaviour, when he knew how disastrously the campaign had gone on in the Crimea, and that the whole nation was bowed down in grief.... Dickens had acquired the habit ... of opening wide his mouth to give full effect to the charm of oral delivery. This gave him rather the appearance of gnashing his teeth...'

I 46
Enlarged photograph of a woodcut portrait of John Sadleir
From the *Illustrated London News*, 9 March 1850

Merdle, the financier in *Little Dorrit*, was based, at least as regards his death, on John Sadleir MP, the swindler, who committed suicide on 17 February 1856 after the failure of the Tipperary Bank, of which he was a director. On 16 February Sadleir 'was busy in the city, still endeavouring to bolster up his credit', but in the evening 'he sent a servant to a chemist's for a large quantity of the essential oil of almonds. The next morning his body was found in a retired spot on Hampstead Heath, not far from Jack Straw's Castle, to which tavern he had been a visitor on former occasions. The bottle which had held the poison, and a silver cream-jug used for drinking its contents, were lying by his side' (*Gentleman's Magazine*).

I 47
Phiz (Hablôt K. Browne) (1815–82)
(a) **Preliminary drawing in pencil with touches of red chalk, and** (b) **etching for the illustration 'Under the Microscope' to** *Little Dorrit,* **1855–57**
(a) signed *Phiz* and initialled in ink by the author C.D. Inscribed *Dickens* and with titles and note in another hand
$5 \times 3\frac{7}{8}; 5\frac{1}{8} \times 3\frac{3}{4}$
(a) Lent by the Trustees of the British Museum

(c) **Drawing in pencil and wash, and**
(d) **etching for the illustration 'Mr. Merdle a borrower' to** *Little Dorrit,* **1855–57**
(c) signed *Phiz*, and inscribed with titles in another hand
$4\frac{3}{4} \times 5\frac{1}{4}; 4 \times 5\frac{1}{2}$
(c) Lent by the Trustees of the British Museum

I 48
Phiz (Hablôt K. Browne) (1815–82)
Four illustrations to *Little Dorrit,* **1855–57**
(a), (c) and (d) etchings. (b) Engraving and etching
Average size $4\frac{1}{8} \times 6$

(a) 'Flora's Tour of Inspection'

(b) 'Little Dorrit's Party'

(c) 'The Marshalsea becomes an Orphan'

(d) 'The Patriotic Conference'

THE UNCOMMERCIAL TRAVELLER

Some of Dickens's best writing on social questions is found in the series of articles which appeared during 1860 in *All the Year Round* under the title 'The Uncommercial Traveller'. This series occupied Dickens in the interval between *A Tale of Two Cities* and *Great Expectations*; further articles appeared in 1863, 1868 and 1869. The series contains several autobiographical pieces, as well as many keenly observed and vividly recorded reports on the life of the lonely, the shabby, the 'houseless' and the broken. Dickens sometimes gathered his material on expeditions deliberately made for the purpose of reporting; but some of his strangest and saddest observations came to him on night walks, taken to combat the insomnia from which he suffered at this troubled period of his life. *The Uncommercial Traveller* was published in book form in 1861, 1866 (in the Cheap Edition of the Works; enlarged), 1868 (in the Charles Dickens Editions of the works) and 1875 (in the Illustrated Library edition of the Works; further enlarged). G.J. Pinwell designed a frontispiece 'Ain't this a lovely spot' for the 1866 edition, and three further illustrations (of which two are exhibited) for the 1868 edition.

I 49
George John Pinwell, RWS (1842–75)
(a) **and** (b) **2 studies in pencil, one heightened with chinese white and** (c) **proof of the wood-engraving for the illustration 'Leaving the Morgue' to** *The Uncommercial Traveller,* **1868**
(b) Signed with initials *GJP*.
(c) Signed with a monogram *GJP* and *Dalziel*
Each $5 \times 3\frac{1}{2}$
E.4165, 4166–1909; E.2493–1904

This illustration is of an incident in 'Travelling Abroad'. 'Whenever I am at Paris, I am dragged by invisible force into the Morgue', Dickens records, and describes a visit 'to see a large dark man whose disfigurement by water was in a frightful manner comic.... It was very hot weather, and he was none the better for that, and I was much the worse. Indeed, a very neat and pleasant little woman with the key of her lodging on her forefinger, who had been showing him to her little girl while she and the child ate sweetmeats, observed monsieur looking poorly as we came out together, and asked monsieur, with her wondering little eyebrows prettily raised, if there were anything the matter?'

I 50
George John Pinwell, RWS (1842–75)
(a) **Study in pen and ink, pencil and chinese white and** (b) **proof of the wood-engraving for the illustration 'Time and his Wife' to** *The Uncommercial Traveller,* **1868**
Each signed with a monogram *GJP*.
(b) Dated '68 and signed *Dalziel*
Each $5 \times 3\frac{1}{2}$
E.4167–1909, E.2491–1904

In the essay 'The City of the Absent', Dickens recalls visits made to London churchyards. In one of them 'with astonishment I beheld an old old man and an old old woman ... making hay.... Gravely among the graves, they made hay, all alone by themselves. They looked like Time and his wife. There was but the one rake between them, and they both had hold of it in a pastorally-loving manner, and there was hay on the old woman's black bonnet, as if the old man had recently been playful'.

DICKENS AS A REFORMER OF SOCIETY

I 51
William Acton
Prostitution in Relation to Public Health
London, John Churchill, Princes Street, Soho, 1851
F.PAMPH.298/7

As a result of the work of men like Dr William Acton, the acknowledged authority of his age on prostitution, this problem was recognised as one which should be understood and fought rather than shunned. In an address to the London Dialectical Society in 1868, Acton welcomed 'the change of tone that had occurred since he first began to write on this subject'. Twenty years earlier it was a subject ignored by almost everyone, whereas, he said, by the late 1860s it was discussed even in the presence of women.

I 52
Henry Mayhew
The Great World of London
London, 1856
Showing a wood-engraved illustration of 'Workroom, on the Silent System, at the House of Correction, Tothill Fields'
Lent by the Trustees of the British Museum

153
'Ah! Fanny! How long have you been *Gay*?'
Wood-engraved cartoon by John Leech. *Punch*
12 September 1857

This cartoon of two prostitutes meeting is an example of the changing attitude to the problem.

154
Dante Gabriel Rossetti (1828–82)
Study for 'Found'
Signed with a monogram *DGR* and inscribed
'*I remember thee; the kindness of thy youth, the love of the betrothal*' *Jerem. II. 2*
Pen and ink. $8 \times 7\frac{1}{4}$
Lent by the City Art Gallery, Birmingham

The theme of the 'fallen' woman was a favourite subject for paintings and poems by the Pre-Raphaelites. In 'Found' a drover recognizes in a woman of the streets his lost sweetheart, who shrinks from him in shame, cowering against the wall of a graveyard. The model for the woman was Fanny Cornforth. This was the only painting of a contemporary subject that Rossetti ever attempted, and it was in fact never finished. Although commissioned in 1853 it was not begun until late the following year when Rossetti, staying with the Madox Browns at Finchley, painted the wall, the calf and the cart; he continued to work on the painting at intervals until his death. The oil painting is in the Bancroft Foundation, Wilmington, Delaware, U.S.A.

155 [61]
(Paul) Gustave Louis Christophe Doré (1832–83)
Glad to death's mystery, Swift to be hurl'd Anywhere, anywhere out of the World!
Drawing for the illustration to 'The Bridge of Sighs' by Thomas Hood
Signed *GD*
Indian ink, heightened with white. $9\frac{3}{4} \times 7\frac{1}{4}$
E.358-1948

'The Bridge of Sighs' and a 'Threatening Letter to Thomas Hood, from an Ancient Gentleman by Favour of Charles Dickens' were published in *Hood's Magazine*, May 1844. Both Hood's poem and Dickens's ironic letter (in which he assumes the character of an old Tory who grumbles about Young England and finds only one thing to be praised, a 'Judge who knows how to do his duty') were provoked by the widely discussed case of Mary Furley. She had been sentenced to death the preceding April for attempting suicide and for drowning one of her illegitimate sons, whom she had clutched to her as she threw herself into the Regent's Canal in a bid to escape returning to the work-house after her savings had been stolen. For artistic reasons Hood did not mention the child and shifted the scene to Waterloo Bridge, a notorious favourite for suicides. Dickens is said to have been overcome with emotion when he heard Hood's poem sung.

156
Sir William Charles Ross, RA (1794–1860)
Baroness Angela Georgina Burdett Coutts (1814–1906)
Exhibited at the Royal Academy, 1847
Miniature on ivory. $16\frac{1}{2} \times 11\frac{1}{2}$
Lent by the National Portrait Gallery

Dickens and Angela Burdett Coutts probably met through Edward Majoribanks in 1838 or '39. Miss Coutts was immediately impressed by the 'restlessness, vivacity, impetuosity, generous impulses, earnestness and frank sincerity' of the young novelist and a relationship of sympathy and understanding sprang up between them. Miss Coutts was a kind and generous friend to his wife Catherine and to his children; she nominated Walter for his cadetship and provided capital to set Charley up in the paper business. More important, however, than these personal ties was the fact that Dickens was the guiding influence in her philanthropic career. When Dickens confided his marital problems to her she tried to bring about a reconciliation between him and his wife; after their separation in 1858 the relationship between Dickens and Miss Coutts was irrevocably strained.

157
***Once a Week,* 25 October 1862**
Showing a wood-engraved illustration by George Du Maurier to verses entitled 'Only'

By May 1846 Dickens was planning, and from November 1847 helping to organize, Miss Coutts's home for the rehabilitation of prostitutes, which he referred to as the 'Home for Homeless Women' in an anonymous article published in *Household Words* in 1853. Dickens rented for the purpose a house at Shepherd's Bush, which had room for thirteen girls and two superintendents; he renamed it Urania Cottage. The girls spent two hours of every week-day morning in 'book education of a very plain kind'; the rest of the working day was spent in domestic training. The girls were made to understand that 'they were not going through a monotonous round of occupation and self-denial which began and ended there; but which began, or was resumed, under that roof, and would end, by God's blessing in happy homes of their own'. Dickens believed that they needed to be '*tempted to virtue. They cannot be dragged, driven or frightened*' and that the best incentive was the hope of marriage. When they left the home the girls were sent abroad to start their reformed lives.

The only statistics of its success are given by Dickens in his article in *Household Words*. Of the 57 girls who had been through the school by 1853, 7 married, 23 did well in Australia or elsewhere, 'seven went away by their own desire during their probation; ten were sent away for misconduct in the Home; seven ran away; three emigrated and relapsed on the passage out'.

Although Dickens's part in the Home was not publicly known during his life, this was the only charitable organization to which he gave his constant attention over a prolonged period. From about 1854 he spent less time at Urania Cottage, and his association with it ceased completely after his separation from his wife in 1858.

I 58
Alexander Maconochie
The Mark System of Prison Discipline
London, Thomas Harrison, 1855
F.PAMPH.449/19

Although Dickens had certain reservations about this method of discipline, which Maconochie had been advocating from the mid-1840s, he used a modified version of it at Urania Cottage; he felt sure that under its influence a girl 'must . . . rise somewhat in her own self-respect'. Every girl received marks daily for her various achievements; she could also lose a mark for bad behaviour, but 'A bad mark is very infrequent, and occasions great distress in the recipient and great excitement in the community'. The marks were valued not only as a recognition of achievement but also because they were convertible into money when the girl left the home.

I 59
Letter from Dickens to Miss Burdett Coutts, 28 October 1847, and the printed text of Dickens's 'Appeal to Fallen Women' originally enclosed in the letter
Lent by the Pierpont Morgan Library, New York

Dickens wrote the 'Appeal to Fallen Women' for distribution amongst such women before or after they were taken by the police. Captain George Chesterton, the governor of Coldbath Fields Prison, which was the source of many recruits for Urania Cottage, handed it to suitable girls and assured Dickens that 'it affects them very heartily indeed'.

I 60
Letter from Dickens to Miss Burdett Coutts, 15 November 1856
Lent by the Pierpont Morgan Library, New York

Dickens aimed at reducing the institutional atmosphere at Urania Cottage. He rejected the idea of clothing the girls in a uniform and chose dresses for them 'as cheerful in appearance as they reasonably could be – at the same time very neat and modest'. In this letter he returned to Miss Coutts the sample of dull cotton called Derry, which she had suggested for the girls' overalls and other garments: 'I return Derry. I have no doubt it's a capital article, but it's a mortal dull color. Color these people always want, and color (as allied to fancy), I would always give them. In these cast-iron and mechanical days, I think even such a garnish to the dish of their monotonous and hard lives, of unspeakable importance. One color, and that of the earth earthy, is too much with them early and late. Derry might just as well break out into a stripe, or put forth a bud, or even burst into a full blown flower. Who is Derry that he is to make quakers of us all, whether we will or no!'

I 61
George Cruikshank (1792–1878)
The Ragged School, In West Street (late Chick Lane) Smithfield
Plate illustrating 'London Penetralia, No. II the Ragged Schools' from *Our Own Times*, 1846
Signed *George Cruikshank*
Etching. $4\frac{1}{2} \times 7\frac{1}{2}$
F.PAMPH.121/18

Ragged Schools were volunteer institutions set up to provide free teaching, with an emphasis on religious instruction, for poor children. In 1843 Dickens visited one such school situated in 'wretched rooms . . . of a rotten house' in Field Lane, Holborn at Miss Coutts's request. He was appalled by the state of the children: 'I have seldom seen . . . anything so shocking as the dire neglect of soul and body exhibited among these children', and, although he doubted the practicality of impressing them with the existence of God 'when their own condition is so desolate', he warmly recommended that Miss Coutts should give the schools her support. Dickens contributed an article to the *Daily News* in 1846 describing the work of these schools and praised it also in an article entitled 'The Devil's Acre' in *Household Words* in 1858.

162 [59]
(a) **Overcrowding**
Photographs of wood-engraved illustrations in *Sanatory Progress: being the Fifth Report of the National Philanthropic Association*, 1850

When in *Nicholas Nickleby* Dickens describes the overcrowded rooming-house in which the Kenwigs family lives, he makes of it something picturesque and even attractive. In the 1840s and '50s numerous reports emphasized the horror of slum overcrowding, 'the obscenity and crime engendered by this brutal herding of a promiscuous and fluctuating multitude, comprising males and females, children and adults, the innocent and the depraved, pressed together, by night, in a way which renders privacy impossible, and breaks down every barrier to lust' (*Quarterly Review*, Sept. 1850). Dickens became seriously concerned over the problem, and assisted Miss Coutts in her housing projects.

(b) **Nova-Scotia Gardens**
Photograph of a wood-engraved illustration in *The Builder*, 25 April 1857

This slum with its 'huge mountain of refuse' (see L 16) was cleared to make way for a cheap housing project which was planned by Miss Coutts, with Dickens as her adviser, in the 1850s, and which materialized as the Columbia Developments in the 1860s. Dickens pointed out that blocks of flats with spacious public gardens, good foundations and efficient drainage were more satisfactory than rows and rows of small separate houses. In the course of elaborating his ideas, he outlined a complete plan of schools, savings banks and public libraries to be established with each group of buildings.

163

***The Illustrated London News*, 8 May 1869**
Showing a wood-engraved illustration of the official opening of Columbia Market

Columbia Market was built, at a cost of £170,000 to Miss Coutts, near the set of model homes for working class families erected on the site of the Nova Scotia Gardens, Bethnal Green. The Archbishop of Canterbury was present at the official opening of the market in 1869. It has now been demolished.

164
Joel T. Hart (1810–77)
Thomas Southwood Smith, MD (1788–1861)
Incised on the base *Southwood Smith* and *J.T. Hart. Sculpt. 1856*
Marble bust. 26 high
Lent by the National Portrait Gallery

Southwood Smith wrote reports for the Poor Law Commissioners on the causes of sickness and mortality among the poor. He was one of the principal founders of both the Health of Towns Association, 1839, and the Metropolitan Association for the Improvement of the Dwellings of the Industrial Classes, 1842. He was the medical member on the General Board of Health from 1848 to 1854. Dickens was well acquainted with him, not only through their association as officers of the Sanatorium, which was founded by Southwood Smith in 1840 and opened in 1842 at Devonshire House, York Gate, close to Dickens's home at 1 Devonshire Terrace, but from their common interests. They were both concerned about the employment of children and the bad housing and sanitary conditions which prevailed. In the fifties, Southwood Smith helped Dickens in deciding on a site and drawing up plans for the Columbia Estate (see 162 and 63).

165
George Cruikshank (1792–1878)
'The maniac father and the convict brother are gone.—The poor girl, homeless, friendless, deserted, destitute, and gin mad, commits self murder'
Drawing for the last plate of *The Drunkard's Children*, published 1 July 1848
Signed in ink *George Cruikshank*
Pencil and pink wash. $9\frac{3}{4} \times 13\frac{7}{8}$
9429.H

On acquiring a copy of *The Drunkard's Children*, a publication which recorded the downfall of the Drunkard's family in eight plates, attributing all their troubles to alcohol, Dickens felt compelled to write 'a few words by way of gentle protest' in the *Examiner*. He praised the plates lavishly and limited his criticism to Cruikshank's philosophy. Dickens believed that the artist's teaching should begin with the causes of alcoholism rather than with its effect. Dickens retained the attitude expressed in 'Gin Shops' in 1835 all his life. Drinking 'is a vice in England, but wretchedness and dirt are greater'. If 'temperance societies would suggest an antidote against hunger, filth and foul air, or could establish dispensaries for the gratuitous distribution of bottles of Lethe-water, gin palaces would be numbered among the things that were'. Later he tried to cure the roots of the trouble with his work on the Committee of the Metropolitan Sanitary Association and with Miss Burdett Coutts.

I 66 [60]
Sanatory Progress: being the Fifth Report of the National Philanthropic Association
London, J. Hatchard, 1850
Showing a wood-engraved illustration: 'Enon-Chapel Cemetery, and Dancing Saloon'
F.PAMPH.260/2

London was everywhere polluted by sewage and decomposing corpses. 'The 17 million cubic feet of decaying residuum, now lying a subterranean chaos under London, debilitate us all, without exception,' wrote the *Quarterly Review* (Sept. 1850).

I 67 [73]
Sir Samuel Luke Fildes, KCVO, RA (1843–1927)
Applicants for Admission to a Casual Ward
Oil. 56 × 97½
Signed and dated *Luke Fildes* 1874
Lent by the Royal Holloway College (University of London)

This composition is based on a drawing by Fildes which appeared with the title 'Houseless and Hungry' in the first issue of *The Graphic*, 4 December 1869. Its success led to Millais' recommending Fildes as the illustrator for *Edwin Drood*. When elaborating it into the painting he exhibited at the Royal Academy in 1874, he added after the title a quotation from Forster's *Life* [VII, 2] extracted from Dickens's description of a scene he had witnessed on 8 November 1855 outside the door of Whitechapel Workhouse: 'Dumb, wet, silent horrors! Sphinxes set up against that dead wall, and none likely to be at the pains of solving them until the *general overthrow*'.

I 68
Alexander Farmer (d. 1869)
An Anxious Hour
Signed and dated *Alexr Farmer 1865*
Oil on panel. 12 × 16
541–1905

The theme of the sick child is frequent in Victorian art and literature; the large families and high mortality rate made the event one which was all too familiar in real life. Dickens not only treated it in such fictional passages as the deaths of Little Nell and Paul Dombey; he made one of his finest speeches in support of the Hospital for Sick Children, Great Ormond Street, in 1858.

J: Dickens as editor

For an uninterrupted period of twenty years, from 1850 until his death, Dickens edited his own weekly magazine, in addition to all his other work. In its earlier form the magazine was named *Household Words*; in 1859, when Dickens changed publishers, *Household Words* was succeeded by a new magazine *All the Year Round*, almost identical save in name. Dickens's editorial control over these periodicals was absolute, signalized by the appearance at the beginning of each issue of the legend 'Conducted by Charles Dickens', and by the almost total absence of other contributors' names.

Throughout his earlier life, Dickens had hankered after such a means of communicating with his public. In 1837, at the age of 24, he was given the editorship of a new monthly magazine, *Bentley's Miscellany*, but abandoned it after disputes with Bentley over his editorial independence. In 1840 he persuaded Chapman and Hall to publish *Master Humphrey's Clock*, a weekly in which he could display his varied talents with the help of occasional contributors. Although this magazine did not develop according to his intentions, Dickens's enthusiasm was not dashed, and in 1845 he was proposing to Forster to launch another new periodical: 'The Cricket'. The name was in fact turned to account in a Christmas book, while Dickens turned to newspaper journalism, helping to found and editing the *Daily News*.

Dickens wished his magazines to express consistent attitudes, and for 'The Cricket' he succinctly prescribed a Christmas philosophy: '*Carol* philosophy, cheerful views, sharp anatomisation of humbug, jolly good temper . . . and a vein of glowing, hearty, generous, mirthful, beaming reference in everything to Home and Fireside'. The philosophy of the later magazines was less exuberantly expressed, but as clearly manifests his desire to communicate his personal qualities of generosity and good humour to his readers (see J18, 25).

BENTLEY'S MISCELLANY

On 4 November 1836 Dickens signed an agreement to become editor of a monthly magazine projected by the publisher Richard Bentley, and to be entitled 'The Wits' Miscellany'. The title was soon changed to *Bentley's Miscellany*, causing William Jerdan to inquire: 'What need was there to have gone to the other extreme?' Dickens's editorial prerogatives were clearly set down in his contract, but he had no experience, and Bentley doubtless felt justified in his occasional interpositions. But after the very first number (January 1837) Dickens wrote to him: 'I must beg you once again, not to allow anybody but myself to interfere with the Miscellany'. Fiercer quarrels over this issue developed in the summer. Dickens's relations with Bentley became strained on other counts (see c58–9) and at the end of January 1839 Dickens relinquished the editorship to Harrison Ainsworth.

J1
***Bentley's Miscellany*. Number XXII**
London, Richard Bentley, October 1838
Lent by The Dickens House

J2 [15]
***Extraordinary Gazette. Speech of His Mightiness on opening the second number of Bentley's Miscellany*
[February 1837]**
F.PAMPH.72

This advertising circular was composed by Dickens. When drawing up a prospectus in November 1836 he had written to Bentley: 'I think that until we are actually afloat, we had better not be *too facetious*'. By February 1837 he evidently felt confident enough to cast his circular in the form of a facetious speech to his readers.

The wood-engraving, after a design by Phiz, shows Dickens leading a stout porter, who carries a huge quantity of copies of the magazine.

J3
Photograph of a portrait of Richard Harris Barham
Engraved by Joseph Brown after R.J. Lane

The Rev R.H. Barham (1788–1845), minor canon of St Paul's, had been a friend of Bentley's since their schooldays at St Paul's, and contributed frequently to the *Miscellany* from its first issue. Many of his *Ingoldsby Legends* appeared there (see J4). Dickens did not meet him until June 1837, but was soon numbered among his friends. Barham endeavoured to mediate in the disputes between Dickens and Bentley.

J4
***Bentley's Miscellany,* January 1838**
London, Richard Bentley, 1838
Lent by Bedford College, University of London

Here is shown one of Barham's *Ingoldsby Legends*, 'The Temptations of St Anthony', as it appeared in the *Miscellany* in February 1838. The accompanying etching is by Cruikshank, who, as chief illustrator of the *Miscellany* until 1843, provided illustrations for many small articles as well as for *Oliver Twist* and several novels by Ainsworth.

J5
Daniel Maclise, RA (1806–70)
The Rev. Francis Mahony ('Father Prout')
Pencil. 6½ × 6¼
F.P.80

Another frequent contributor to the *Miscellany* under Dickens's editorship was 'Father Prout'. Francis Sylvester Mahony (1804–66), after a Jesuit training, was dismissed from the order in 1830 and ordained a secular priest in 1832. He soon came to prefer literary life in London to his religious vocation, and established himself as a periodical writer. In 1846 he worked as a correspondent for the *Daily News*.

One of Father Prout's contributions to *Bentley's Miscellany* was an absurd 'Poetical Epistle . . . to Boz' dated 'Genoa, 14th December 1837' which included the lines:
'Write on, young sage! still o'er the page pour forth
  the flood of fancy;
Wax still more droll, wave o'er the soul Wit's wand
  of necromancy.
Behold! e'en now around your brow the immortal
  laurel thickens;
Yea, SWIFT or STERNE might gladly learn a thing
  or two from DICKENS.'

J6
***Bentley's Miscellany,* March 1839**
London, Richard Bentley, 1839
Lent by Bedford College, University of London

Dickens's resignation from the editorship of the *Miscellany* took effect from 31 January 1839. He was succeeded by Ainsworth, and, to help smooth over the disturbance, he contributed to the March 1839 number a 'Familiar Epistle from a Parent to a Child', in which he committed the magazine to the care of 'one of my most intimate and valued friends, Mr. Ainsworth'.

MASTER HUMPHREY'S CLOCK

As the end of *Nicholas Nickleby* approached, Dickens began to consider what form his next published work should take. Inclined to give himself a rest from full-length novels and 'to shorten the intervals of communication between himself and his readers', he proposed to Chapman and Hall, through Forster, that they should publish a weekly miscellany to be written chiefly by himself. 'The best general idea of the plan of the work,' he wrote, 'might be given perhaps by reference to *The Tatler*, *The Spectator*, and Goldsmith's *Bee*; but it would be far more popular both in the subjects of which it treats and its mode of treating them.' He went on to throw out many interesting suggestions. Few were adopted in the end, because his readers did not react favourably to a miscellany, and after the first few numbers Dickens gradually abandoned the miscellany form, and used the periodical as a vehicle for serializing two novels, *The Old Curiosity Shop* and *Barnaby Rudge*.

J7
Dickens's diary (*The Law and Commercial Daily Remembrancer*) for 1840
F.MS.182

The periodical was first mooted to the publishers in July 1839, but it was early 1840 before Dickens had decided on a name for it. On 9 January he noted two possible titles in his diary:
'Old Humphrey's Clock
Master Humphrey's Clock'.
He then wrote to Forster to explain their significance: 'I have a notion of this old file in the queer house, opening the book by an account of himself, and, among other peculiarities, of his affection for an old quaint queer-cased clock. . . . Then I mean to tell how that he has kept odd

manuscripts in the old, deep, dark, silent closet where the weights are; and taken them from thence to read . . .'

J8
Advertising leaflet for *Master Humphrey's Clock* [? April 1840]
Lent by The Dickens House

The engraving by Phiz shows Dickens opening the door of Master Humphrey's clock, and freeing the creatures of his imagination who have lurked within.

J9
Manuscript of the Preface to Vol. I of *Master Humphrey's Clock*, with Dickens's additions
F.MS.168

J10
Corrected proof, with a further addition, of the Preface to Vol. I of *Master Humphrey's Clock*
F.MS.70

In the Preface (dated September 1840) which Dickens wrote to introduce the first volume of *Master Humphrey's Clock*, he explained what his intentions had been, adjusting his account a little to conceal the degree to which they had not been fulfilled. To the Preface as first drafted he added a paragraph to combat a rumour, apparently widely circulated, that he had gone mad and was receiving treatment in an asylum.

J11
***Master Humphrey's Clock*. Part I**
London, Chapman and Hall, 4–25 April 1840
Lent by The Dickens House

The periodical appeared in both weekly and monthly parts, the former having white covers and the latter green. The same cover design by Cattermole was used for both series.

J12
***Master Humphrey's Clock*. Vol. I**
London, Chapman and Hall, 1840
Showing the illustration by Phiz: 'Master Humphrey meets Mr. Pickwick'
F.PB.2433

One of Dickens's original intentions was the reintroduction of Mr Pickwick, who took his place as one of Master Humphrey's guests; the Wellers also appear and found a below-stairs club, 'Mr. Weller's Watch'.

J13
Three illustrations to *Master Humphrey's Clock*
Wood-engravings

(a) George Cattermole (1800–68)
'Master Humphrey's room'
$3\frac{1}{8} \times 4\frac{3}{8}$

(b) Phiz (Hablôt K. Browne) (1815–82)
'*Barnaby Rudge* in Master Humphrey's imagination'
Lettered *Gray* and · *HKB* ·
$3\frac{1}{2} \times 4\frac{1}{2}$

(c) George Cattermole (1800–68)
'Master Humphrey's room deserted'
Lettered *Landells*
$3\frac{3}{4} \times 4\frac{5}{8}$

The first number of the periodical began with an illustration of Master Humphrey's chamber and his clock. After the eighth chapter of *The Old Curiosity Shop* Master Humphrey disappears, but comes back to bridge the gap between this novel and *Barnaby Rudge*: Phiz's illustration shows him dreaming of the characters who are to appear in the new novel. Master Humphrey is absent during *Barnaby Rudge* but appears for a last bow at the very end. The illustration by Cattermole (for which Dickens gave precise instructions) shows the clock stopped and the room empty, 'Master Humphrey being supposed to be no more'.

J14
Phiz (Hablôt K. Browne) (1815–82)
Preliminary drawing for 'Master Humphrey and his companion'
Inscribed by Dickens *Master Humphrey admirable. Could his stick (with a crooked top) be near his chair? I misdoubt the deaf gentleman's pipe and wish he could have a better one* and "*Master Humphrey's Clock*" and with a note in another hand.
Pencil. $7\frac{1}{4} \times 6\frac{1}{4}$
Lent by the Trustees of the British Museum

THE DAILY NEWS

From 1842 Dickens had occasionally entertained the idea of founding and editing a new liberal daily newspaper: it would provide him with a commanding platform from which to address the public. In 1845 Bradbury and Evans approached him with a scheme; financial backers were found, including Joseph Paxton; and Dickens, accepting the editorship after some hesitation, gathered his staff, placing his father John Dickens, an efficient newspaperman, in charge of the reporters.

The paper first appeared in January 1846 – a good moment, it seemed, to raise a new radical voice in political affairs, since the Corn Law crisis was at its height and repeal imminent. The running of a newspaper was perhaps the most taxing organizational task Dickens had undertaken, and he found himself so wearied by it, and so much at odds with Bradbury his publisher, that he resigned after only seventeen issues had appeared. Forster took over the editorship until October 1846.

J15
Trial specimen issue of the *Daily News*, dated 19 Jan 1846
Lent by the Comtesse de Suzannet

In preparation for the first issue of the *Daily News*, which appeared on 21 January 1846, the printers ran off a trial issue. It contains the first of Dickens's 'Travelling Letters' (the text differing somewhat from the published version), an editorial describing vividly the execution of Tapping the murderer, and a humorous leading article on the (imaginary) trial of one Jones for the murder (the verdict was 'Justifiable Homicide') of 'five bricklayers, seven carpenters, two furniture-warehouse porters, three painters, and a plasterer'. This was a private joke at the expense of Mr Jones, the newspaper's master-printer, who had been obliged to settle into new premises in a hectic rush.

J16
***Mephystopheles*, 14 February 1846**
Showing a cartoon 'Titania Dickens to Bottom, the Daily News'
Lent by the Trustees of the British Museum

J17
Photograph of a cartoon 'The Jackdaw disguised, and the Peacocks' from *Mephystopheles*, 31 January 1846

The *Daily News* was greeted with hostility by the established daily papers, for it sold more cheaply and paid better salaries. The magazine *Mephystopheles* poked fun at the state of rivalry in these two cartoons, the one being a parody of Landseer's 'A Midsummer Night's Dream', and the other alluding to the fable of the jackdaw and the peacocks.

HOUSEHOLD WORDS AND ALL THE YEAR ROUND

Dickens had long cherished the 'dim design' of *Household Words* and began to plan it during a holiday at Bonchurch in the summer of 1849. His plan, as it developed, was once again for a miscellany, but, he told Forster, 'to bind all this together, and to get a character established . . . I want to suppose a certain SHADOW . . . a kind of semi-omniscient, omnipresent, intangible creature . . . I want him to loom as a fanciful thing all over London.' This did not seem 'feasible' to Forster, and indeed it is not so much a plan as a vision on Dickens's part of his own influence pervading the magazine. One of the titles he suggested for the magazine was 'Charles Dickens: A weekly journal . . . conducted by Himself', and when the magazine was finally launched (with the name *Household Words*) Dickens, as 'Conductor' lavished immense care and labour upon it, to ensure that every word, no matter who had originally written it, represented his own attitudes and sense of style. He issued to his indispensable sub-editor, W.H. Wills, a 'solemn and continual Conductorial injunction': '*Keep Household Words Imaginative*'. He insistently urged his team of writers to 'brighten it', and Percy Fitzgerald later recalled how they had all had to acquire the rather desperate habit of 'colouring up for effect', for they could not naturally sparkle as brightly as the Conductor.

In 1858 Dickens quarrelled with Bradbury and Evans. Although they acquiesced in his extraordinary decision to publish in *Household Words* a statement about his separation from Mrs Dickens, they declined to allow such an announcement in *Punch*, and Dickens, incensed, terminated *Household Words*. Returning to Chapman and Hall, he began *All the Year Round* (Forster having rejected his suggested title *Household Harmony*), running it on the same lines but with rather more fiction.

J18
***Household Words*, 30 March 1850**
Showing Dickens's article 'A Preliminary Word'
F.PB.4285

In the first number Dickens expounded the magazine's policy. 'No mere utilitarian spirit, no iron binding of the mind to grim realities, will give a harsh tone to our Household Words. In the bosoms of the young and old, of the well-to-do and of the poor, we would tenderly cherish that light of Fancy which is inherent in the human breast.' Whatever the attractions of the matter in *Household Words*, there was nothing fanciful about the typography and layout.

J19
Portion of the corrected galley-proof of an article 'Foreigners' Portraits of Englishmen' published in *Household Words*, 21 September 1850
F.MS.171

The *Household Words* Contributors' Book records that the article 'Foreigners' Portraits of Englishmen' was by E.C. Grenville Murray (who probably wrote it in the first place), Wills (who probably revised it before it was set up in type) and Dickens (who transformed it at proof stage). Dickens frequently rewrote his contributors' work in this way, and after his attentions a proof was likely, as he said, to 'look like an inky fishing-net'.

J20
George Richmond, RA (1809–96)
Elizabeth Cleghorn (Stevenson) Gaskell (1810–65)
Signed and dated in pencil *George Richmond delt 1851*
Coloured chalks on tinted paper. 17 × 13
Lent by the National Portrait Gallery

J21
***Household Words*, 13 December 1851**
Showing 'Our Society at Cranford'
F.PB.4285

Elizabeth Stevenson married the Rev. William Gaskell, minister of Cross Street Unitarian Chapel, Manchester, and after the death of their only son in 1844 turned for occupation to writing a story of life in the industrial North of England. Published as *Mary Barton* in 1848, it was a great success, giving her an entrée to literary circles in London, where she became acquainted with Dickens. When he began *Household Words* he enlisted her among his contributors. 'I should set a value on your help which your modesty can hardly imagine,' he assured her, and she wrote *Lizzie Leigh* for the magazine, following it some time later with the sketches of village life published as *Cranford*.

J22
Mrs Gaskell
North and South
2 vols. London, Chapman and Hall, 1855
F.PB.3332

When *North and South* was serialized in *Household Words*, Mrs Gaskell was obliged, as she records in an introductory note to the two volume edition, 'to conform to the conditions imposed by the requirements of a weekly publication'. Besides the problem of breaking it into instalments, she disliked having her work subjected to Dickens's revisions, and protested; in the end he gave way, and watched the magazine's circulation drop as her story proceeded without the benefit of his revisions.

J23
Photographs of William Henry Wills and Henry Morley

W.H. Wills (1810–80) had been Dickens's secretary and assistant on the *Daily News*, and was his sub-editor on *Household Words* and *All the Year Round*. Though not distinguished as a man or as a writer, he was quick and thoroughly dependable, and Dickens, who described him as 'a very intelligent person (though I could wish him not quite so thin and sharp-nosed)', relied on his aid in private as well as business matters. Henry Morley (1822–94) came to journalism after medicine and schoolteaching, and wrote in the *Examiner* for Forster as well as in Dickens's magazines. He exercised his talents as a teacher of literature so successfully that in 1865 he was appointed Professor of English at University College, London.

J24

Tallis's Dramatic Magazine, **November 1850**
Showing an engraved portrait of R.H. Horne
after a daguerrotype by Paine of Islington
F.PAMPH.492

Richard Henry or Hengist Horne (1803–84) met Dickens probably in the late 1830s and wrote perceptively about the early novels in his rather idiosyncratic *A New Spirit of the Age*, 1844; he was Irish correspondent on the *Daily News*. Appointed assistant editor of *Household Words* in 1849 Horne contributed effective pieces of picturesque reporting until, commissioned to write a 'Digger's Diary' from Australia, he let Dickens down by his extreme tardiness in leaving England. 'We had in type at one time eighty-four columns' of the diary, Dickens complained, 'and the man not aboard ship at the London docks until within the three last.'

J25

Household Words, **28 May 1859**
Showing Dickens's announcement of the merging of *Household Words* with *All the Year Round*.
F.PB.4285

In announcing his new magazine, Dickens emphasizes that its policy will not differ from that of *Household Words*. 'That fusion of the graces of the imagination with the realities of life, which is vital to the welfare of any community, and for which I have striven from week to week as honestly as I could during the last nine years, will continue to be striven for "all the year round".'

J26

All the Year Round, **30 April 1859**
Showing the first instalment of *A Tale of Two Cities*
F.PB.122

J27

All the Year Round, **26 November 1859**
Showing the first instalment of Wilkie Collins's *The Woman in White*
F.PB.122

Collins's serialized novel followed at once on *A Tale of Two Cities*. Introducing it, Dickens wrote: 'We purpose always reserving the first place in these pages for a continuous original work of fiction. . . . And it is our hope and aim, while we work hard at every other department of our journal, to produce, in this one, some sustained works of imagination that may become a part of English Literature'. Collins's *No Name* and *The Moonstone* were also serialized in *All the Year Round*.

J28

Photographs of Charles Lever, Charles Reade, Charles Collins, Edward Bulwer-Lytton and Edmund Yates

Dickens tried to persuade George Eliot to write for *All the Year Round*, but without success, and he had to be content to serialize the work of less distinguished novelists in the 'first place' in *All the Year Round*. Lever's *A Day's Ride, a Life's Romance* appeared in 1860–61, and *A Strange Story* by Dickens's old friend Lytton was serialized in 1861–62. Charles Reade contributed *Hard Cash* in 1863, and Charles Collins, the brother of Wilkie, *At the Bar* in 1865. Yates's *Black Sheep* occupied the opening pages of the magazine in 1866–67.

J29

Enlarged photograph of a cartoon 'The Committee of Concoction' from *The Queen*, 21 December 1861

One of the special features of *Household Words* and of the first series of *All the Year Round* was the yearly extra Christmas Number, made up predominantly of stories suitable for the festive season. This cartoon shows an editorial conference for the 'concoction' of the 1861 Christmas Number, 'Tom Tiddler's Ground'. The figures are (*l to r*) Sala, Wilkie Collins, Dickens and John Hollingshead.

J30

Portion of a corrected proof of Percy Fitzgerald's 'Autobiography of a Small Boy' which appeared in *All the Year Round*, 15 and 22 August 1868
Lent by The Dickens House

Until the end Dickens continued relentlessly to revise the work of his contributors. Of Percy Fitzgerald, whose proofs he here corrects, he once said that he 'writes so loosely, that he really seems sometimes to write in his sleep'. Fitzgerald remembered Dickens at work on proofs: 'When one of the long slips had been corrected it looked like a blue network covering the print – so profuse and lavish were his alterations. He inserted, cut out, wrote between the lines and in the margins. . . . The expense might be called terrific. . . . He seems to have dealt with every article in the same way'.

J31
All the Year Round, 5 December 1868
F.PB.122

A new series of the magazine began on this date. Announcing it Dickens pointed out that it would permit 'some desirable improvements in respect of type, paper, and size of page'. He reassured his readers that 'my fellow-labourers and I will be at our old posts'.

J32
All the Year Round, 25 June 1870
Showing a statement by Charles Dickens Jun.: 'Personal'
F.PB.122

In April 1870 Dickens installed his son Charley as sub-editor, and a month and a half later, by a codicil to his will, bequeathed the magazine to him. When his father died, Charley took over the editorship, which he held until 1894.

ART CRITICISM IN *HOUSEHOLD WORDS*

J33
Copy by Rebecca Solomon after Sir John Everett Millais, PRA (1829–96)
Christ in the House of His Parents
Oil. 15 × 24
Lent by Sir David Scott, KCMG

This version by Rebecca Solomon of the painting which Millais exhibited at the Royal Academy in 1850 (now in the Tate Gallery, No. 3584) was considerably worked on by Millais in 1863; he painted in all the heads and the greater part of the background.

Following the lead given by Frank Stone in the *Athenaeum* and other adverse criticism Dickens made a vehement attack on the original work in *Household Words*.

J34
Portion of the corrected galley-proof of Dickens's article 'Old Lamps for New Ones' published in *Household Words*, 15 June 1850
F.MS.171

In this article Dickens attacks Millais' picture 'Christ in the House of His Parents', which he characterizes as 'the lowest depths of what is mean, repulsive and revolting'. He seems particularly to have disliked the medievalism of the Pre-Raphaelites ('a great retrogressive principle').

Although Dickens later became a friend of Millais, meeting him through Wilkie and Charles Collins, he did not recant. In a letter sending him a copy of *Household Words* after their first meeting in January 1855 he wrote: 'Objecting very strongly to what I believe to be an unworthy use of your great powers, I once expressed the objection in this same journal. My opinion on that point is not in the least changed, but it has never dashed my admiration of your progress in what I suppose are higher and better things'.

K: Dickens at work

Dickens preserved most of the manuscripts of his novels and bequeathed them to John Forster, who in turn left them to this Museum as part of his collection. The surviving portions of *Pickwick Papers* and *Nicholas Nickleby*, four of the five Christmas Books, *Great Expectations* and *Our Mutual Friend* are elsewhere; but the Forster Collection includes all that survives of *Oliver Twist* (except for a few pages) and the complete MSS. of the other ten novels and one Christmas Book: *The Old Curiosity Shop*, *Barnaby Rudge*, *Martin Chuzzlewit*, *The Chimes*, *Dombey and Son*, *David Copperfield*, *Bleak House*, *Hard Times*, *Little Dorrit*, *A Tale of Two Cities* and *Edwin Drood*. Many of these MSS. contain Dickens's preliminary plans; and the Forster Collection also includes many of the corrected proofs for most of the novels. We can therefore see Dickens at work at every stage in the composition of a novel.

DEVELOPING CRAFTSMANSHIP

K1 [62]
Manuscript of *Oliver Twist* [1837–38]. Vol.IA
F.MS.151

K2 [63]
Manuscript of *Barnaby Rudge* [1841]. Vol.IA
F.MS.155

K3 [64]
Manuscript of *The Chimes* [1844]
F.MS.158

K4 [65]
Manuscript of *A Tale of Two Cities* [1859] Vol.A
F.MS.166

An instinctive confidence and fluency mark Dickens's early literary productions: the MS. of *Oliver Twist* is boldly written with less deletion and hesitation than in later work.

Later MSS. show how Dickens grew gradually more laborious and deliberate over composition: his handwriting becomes more cramped, and his pages become dense with correction.

OLIVER TWIST: THE HISTORY OF THE TEXT

K5
Manuscript of *Oliver Twist* [1837–38]. Vol.IIA
F.MS.151

Oliver Twist, like all Dickens's novels, was published in instalments. When the first instalment appeared in February 1837, Dickens had not written beyond it, and he was never far ahead of publication; up to late 1837 he was concurrently writing *Pickwick*, and after February 1838, *Nickleby*. He had little time for revision until the novel was republished in later editions.

The novel was written fast and the MS. shows relatively few corrections. But Dickens took the opportunity to make some changes before the first printed version. The lower half of the page of MS. shown – an altercation between Mr and Mrs Bumble – was omitted from the printed text. It reads:

'"Is that" – said Mr. Bumble with sentimental sternness "is that the woice as called me a irresistible duck in the small one-pair ? Is that the creetur that was all meekness, mildness, and sensibility ?"
"It is indeed, worse luck" – replied his helpmate; "not much of sensibility though, or I should have had more sense than to make the sacrifice I did."
"The sacrifice Mrs. Bumble ?" – said the gentleman with great asperity . . .'

K6
***Bentley's Miscellany*, July 1838**
London, Richard Bentley, 1838
Lent by Bedford College, University of London

The 24 instalments of the novel appeared month by month (with 3 gaps) in the magazine *Bentley's*

Miscellany. They were illustrated with etchings by George Cruikshank, illustrator of the magazine.

The printed version of Book II, ch. xiv omits the passage shown in K 5, which must have been excised at proof stage. The proofs do not survive.

K 7
Oliver Twist
3 vols. London, Richard Bentley, 1838
F.PB.2439

The novel first appeared in book form in three volumes, published by Richard Bentley, some months before its conclusion in the magazine.

Here is shown the set which Dickens presented to Forster, specially bound by Hayday. It has the second title-page with the author's name instead of 'Boz', which appeared in the earliest copies.

K 8
The Adventures of Oliver Twist; or the Parish Boy's Progress . . . A New Edition, revised and corrected
In parts. London, Bradbury and Evans, 1846
D.PB.3051

In 1840 *Oliver Twist* was transferred from Bentley to Dickens's other publishers, Chapman and Hall. They issued in 1846 a completely new edition of the novel, for which Dickens thoroughly revised the text. This edition appeared in monthly parts with green paper covers, which since 1836 had been Dickens's normal method of publication for full-length novels.

Cruikshank, whose illustrations were again used (though touched up), designed the woodcut cover for the parts. His preliminary sketch is displayed at K8A.

K 8A
George Cruikshank (1792–1878)
Two drawings for the wrappers of the 1846 edition of *Oliver Twist*
$8\frac{3}{4} \times 7\frac{1}{4}$; $8\frac{3}{4} \times 6\frac{1}{2}$
9995.A,B.

K 9
The Adventures of Oliver Twist
London, Chapman and Hall, 1850
F.PB.2399

The 'Cheap Edition' of Dickens's novels began to appear in 1847: *Oliver Twist* was included in the series in 1850. Dickens made many further small revisions for this edition.

Cruikshank provided the new frontispiece: his preliminary sketch is shown at K9A.

K 9A
George Cruikshank (1792–1878)
Drawing, tracing and wood-engraving for the frontispiece of the 1850 edition of *Oliver Twist*
$5\frac{1}{2} \times 4\frac{1}{2}$; $5\frac{1}{8} \times 3\frac{1}{4}$
9995.E, 9797.G, 9996.12

K 10
The Adventures of Oliver Twist
London, Chapman and Hall, and Bradbury and Evans, 1858
F.PB.2400

The next collected edition was the Library Edition which began to appear in 1858. *Oliver Twist* came out in December 1858, and was not revised, except for the Preface.

K 11
The Adventures of Oliver Twist
London, Chapman and Hall, 1867
F.PB.2401

The last collected edition which Dickens supervised was the 'Charles Dickens Edition', so named to indicate 'his present watchfulness over his own Edition'. He added descriptive headlines on each right-hand page.

Oliver Twist received minor revisions. The most significant were designed to modify what had been construed as anti-Semitism. 'The Jew' is therefore altered fairly consistently in later chapters to 'Fagin'. Compare the heading of chapter lii in the Library edition (K 10) and this edition.

K 12
Oliver Twist
Edited by Kathleen Tillotson
Oxford, at the Clarendon Press, 1966
L.4105–1966

This edition of *Oliver Twist* is the first volume to appear in 'The Clarendon Dickens'. Here a critical text is for the first time established. It takes account of all the changes made in the various editions shown in this display.

LITTLE DORRIT: FROM PLAN TO PRINT

K13
Photograph of the first page of Dickens's Memorandum Book
From the original in the Berg Collection, New York Public Library

Dickens recorded his first ideas for *Little Dorrit* in a Memorandum book which, according to Forster, he began to keep in January 1855. The first page includes two motifs used in the novel, as he has later noted. They are the first and third notes.

'The unwieldy ship taken in tow by the snorting little steam Tug. [*Done in Casby and Pancks*]'

'Our house. Whatever it is, it is in a firstrate situation and a fashionable neighbourhood. (auctioneer called it "a gentlemanly residence".) A series of little closets squeezed up into the corner of a dark street – but a Duke's mansion round the corner. The whole house just large enough to hold a vile smell. The air breathed in it at the best of times, a kind of Distillation of Mews. [*Done in The Barnacles*]'

K14
First Number Plan of *Little Dorrit* [1855]
F.MS.168

For each instalment of *Little Dorrit* Dickens made a plan. The plan for the first instalment, begun in May 1855, shows that he intended to call the book *Nobody's Fault*. He changed his mind after writing the third instalment in September; the novel was advertised in October as *Little Dorrit* and the first instalment appeared in December.

The plans are written on sheets of paper folded to make two pages. On the left-hand page Dickens jotted down, often well ahead, ideas of what to include in the whole Number; and on the right-hand page he wrote the chapter headings with notes on their contents.

K15
Manuscript of *Little Dorrit* [1855–57]. Vol.IA
Showing the Plan for Number VIII
F.MS.165

The different inks reveal the order in which Dickens made these notes. He first wrote in black ink the suggestions on the left and the chapter headings on the right. When he began to write the instalment (see K16) he changed to blue ink. He evidently checked off the left-hand suggestions as he used them, and probably inserted the notes beneath the chapter headings while he was writing or afterwards. (See Transcript p.90.)

K16
Manuscript of *Little Dorrit* [1855–57]. Vol.IB
Showing chapter xxvii, part of Number VIII
F.MS.165

On this page, Dickens is gathering up threads before proceeding to 'work out Tattycoram's spiriting away', which is the first topic noted on his plan for this chapter (see K15).

K17
Corrected proofs of *Little Dorrit* [1855–57]. Vol.I
Showing page proofs of chapter xxvii
F.PB.2431

Although the MS. of chapter xxvii is quite heavily revised, Dickens made further large changes on the proofs.

K18
The part issues of *Little Dorrit*
London, Bradbury and Evans, 1855–57
Lent by Mrs J. Brain

The novel appeared in 19 monthly parts (the last a double number) between December 1855 and June 1857. The part-covers for this novel are blue. The woodcut design is by Phiz.

K19
Little Dorrit
London, Bradbury and Evans, 1857
F.PB.2430

The one-volume edition of *Little Dorrit* appeared in June 1857.

PLANS

K20
Manuscript of *Martin Chuzzlewit* [1843–44]. Vol.IA
Showing notes for Number IV
F.MS.157

The notes for the contents of two Numbers, IV and VI, of *Martin Chuzzlewit* (1843–44) mark a change in Dickens's practice. The slightness of his notes for earlier novels is indicated by the survival of a very sketchy plan for Numbers XLI–XLIV of *The Old Curiosity Shop* (1840–41). But from *Dombey and Son* (1846–48) onward, Dickens made for every novel except *Great Expectations* and *A Tale of Two Cities* a series of Number Plans, i.e. plans of each instalment.

K21 [66]
Manuscript of *David Copperfield* [1849–50]. Vol.IIB
Showing the plan for Number XVII
F.MS.161

On the left Dickens has noted the topics to be dealt with in the number. Uppermost in his mind is the death of Dora. But this must be kept as the closing scene of the number, in chapter liii. In the preceding chapter, therefore, Dickens places Micawber's exposure of Uriah Heep, which he has also noted on the left. Chapter li follows naturally from the previous number. The basic structure of the number is thus established.

On the right Dickens has noted the important motifs of each chapter, including significant phrases in the characters' speeches. He has also written instructions to himself, which interestingly reveal his intentions. 'Present little Dora's death, through Jip's death.'

The printed text shows this strong curtain scene at the end of the number. Its effect is reinforced by Phiz's illustration.

K21A
The Personal History of David Copperfield
London, Bradbury and Evans, 1850
F.PB.2420

K22, K23
Manuscript of *Bleak House* [1852–53]. Vols IA and IIB
Showing the plans for Numbers V and XVIII
F.MS.162

These plans show Dickens working on a larger scale.

In the notes on the left of Plan V he has proposed to himself more ideas than he can use in a single number, and beside one of these he writes 'Next time', thus beginning to shape the following number.

But his mind has already moved much farther ahead in the story. The closing scene of Number V is a deliberate anticipation of the curtain scene in Number XVIII. At the end of Number V, Jo points out to Lady Dedlock an obscure and decayed churchyard. Dickens describes this incident on his plan as a 'shadowing forth of Lady Dedlock at the churchyard'. What is shadowed forth is the death of Lady Dedlock. On the left of Plan XVIII, Dickens notes his intention: 'Ending with the churchyard gate, and Lady Dedlock'. On the right the Number Plan records Esther Summerson's dramatic discovery of Lady Dedlock's body: 'And it was my mother cold and dead'.

K22A, K23A
Bleak House
London, Bradbury and Evans, 1853
F.PB.2411
Another copy
L.1199–1948

K24
Manuscript of *Little Dorrit* [1855–57]. Vol.IIA
Showing extra Memoranda for Numbers XIX–XX
F.MS.165

Dickens rarely supplemented his Number Plans with any other kind of plan. Occasionally, however, he found that he had let his plots grow so complicated, that he could not round them off until he had reviewed and analysed the narrative already written. Here, he compiles some 'Mems: for working the Story round', classifying them as 'Retrospective' and 'Prospective'. (See Transcript p.91.)

PROOFS

Dickens treated proofs as the modern author treats typescript, making large changes for artistic reasons. He made changes also in order to adjust the length of an instalment. The instalments were of a fixed number of printed pages, and Dickens had to try to write exactly the right amount. Sometimes, when the instalment had been set up in type, he discovered that he had written too much or (more rarely) too little. Sometimes he wrote too much: and then he cut passages in proof.

K25
Part of the corrected proofs of *The Old Curiosity Shop* [1840–41]
F.MS.170

Dickens wrote to Forster on 4 October 1840: 'In number thirty there will be some cutting needed, I think. I have, however, something in my eye near the beginning which I can easily take out'.

The passages he cut can be seen in the proofs.

K26
Corrected proofs of *David Copperfield* [1849–50]. Vol.I
F.PB.2421

Number VII should end on page 224, but Dickens's text runs on to the next page, which the printer has labelled 'Overmatter'. In order to reduce the text, Dickens has excised an amusing conversation between Steerforth and Mrs Gummidge.

K27
Part of the corrected proofs of *The Old Curiosity Shop* [1840–41]
F.MS.170

Occasionally Dickens did not write enough. He did not like to give short measure and usually tried to fill up any empty space left on the last page of an instalment.

Someone has indicated on the page how much space ought to be filled up, and has noted '10 lines may be br[ough]t forw[ar]d'. Dickens has, however, filled the space by adding to the text.

K28 [67]
Corrected proofs of *Bleak House* [1852–53]. Vol.II
F.PB.2412

Dickens here appeals to the printer to rearrange the last page.

'(Printer – Manage to bring this down. as I would rather not write more in. It can be easily done by bringing the previous chapter over, a little. CD)'.

K29
Part of the corrected proofs of *The Old Curiosity Shop* [1840–41]
F.MS.170

Forster helped Dickens regularly by reading proofs, and occasionally by acting as his agent with the printer. Here, in a marginal note on the proof of *The Old Curiosity Shop*, he reproaches the printer's reader.

Dickens's text contains a characteristically bold metaphor ('. . . so screwed himself up that he seemed to be squinting all over . . .') which the printer's reader has queried, thinking it nonsense. Forster angrily comments: 'Why q[uer]y? Its capital, you donkey reader'.

TRANSCRIPT OF THE PLAN OF *LITTLE DORRIT*, NUMBER VIII

LEFT:

Clennam and Pet?   Yes
       Gowan?   Yes
Sprightly Young Barnacle?   No
    Tattycoram?   Yes
    Miss Wade?   Yes
       Merdle?

RIGHT:

(Little Dorrit. ——————————————— No.VIII.)

          Chapter XXVI
          Nobody's state of mind

Dissection of Clennam's feelings in respect of Gowan. He ashamed of them in his own eyes – thinking it ungenerous to entertain them – always contending with them. Resolves never to disparage him.
Hampton Court Palace and Mrs Gowan
    A Noble Refrigerator in company – British Embassy
Nothing but Barnacles, Stiltstalkings, and Mob.

                            Mrs Gowan and Clennam
                            The Ride home.

          Chapter XXVII
          Five and Twenty

Work out Tattycoram's spiriting away.
     Dark Lane Picture. Evening

        Empty house – Interview with Miss Wade & Tattycoram
        A common cause between them.

          Chapter XXVIII
          Nobody's disappearance

Mr. Meagles's advertisement
       Clennam on the Summer Evening – Scene with Pet, delicately shewing that the father and mother have been for him, and that they all know of his affection.   Very delicate.   The dead twin daughter   And the roses, floating
                                                          away.

          Chapter XXIX
          Mrs Flintwinch goes on dreaming

The old house in the City – Carry through.
     Glimpse of Little Dorrit and Pancks, to carry through.
        Arrival of Rigaud to close the chapter. Mysterious sounds
                      again, as he enters.

TRANSCRIPT OF THE FIRST PAGE OF MEMS FOR *LITTLE DORRIT* NUMBERS XIX AND XX

LEFT:
Mr Flintwinch has a brother just like him – or a twin brother – who appeared in the beginning of the book, and took away with him a box (31 and 32) *Affery saw him.*

Arthur Clennam in his interview with his mother, and on his first opportunity after coming home, asked her if it had ever occurred to her to suspect that his father had unhappily wronged any one and made no reparation? Also reminded her with what earnestness his father, dying, had given him his watch for her, containing the watchpaper "Do not forget," and had tried to write some word. Also, how that "I knew that your ascendancy over him was the cause of his going to China to take care of the business there, while you took care of it here"; and that "it was your will that I should remain with you until I was twenty, and then go to him as I did". (35) He said all this at forty.

When he connected his suspicions with Little Dorrit, and asked her (in the Marshalsea, on his first visit there) whether she had known his mother long? – she replied, "I think, two years" – "She does not even know that I live here. We have a friend, father and I – a poor laboring man, but the best of friends – and I wrote out that I wished to do needlework, and gave his address. And he got what I wrote out, displayed at a few places where it cost nothing, and Mrs Clennam found me that way, and sent for me (62).

Mr Flintwinch once being alone with Mrs Clennam, reproached her for "not having cleared Arthur's father to him and for "leaning against the dead." (131.) *Affery overheard.*

RIGHT:
How connected with the Dorrits?

Arthur's father's Uncle who had no other relation, left a will; by which he made him his sole heir, except a legacy of two thousand guineas (?) to the girl, under the charge of Frederick Dorrit, or in default of her being alive – to his youngest [*deletions*] female relative, daughter or Niece. Mrs Clennam with-held this will – "I will make restitution when I see fit – I will find it one day. He was not in his right mind when he made it. It was weakness – imbecility."

L: Last novels

The four novels of 1859–70, years when Dickens was also occupied with his public readings and with editing his weekly periodical, are more widely spaced, and three of the four are short. All appeared in serial form, in 'monthly numbers' or in *All The Year Round*, and one in both forms. These novels are strikingly different from each other; Dickens was experimenting to the end. When he died he left *The Mystery of Edwin Drood* only half written, and only a quarter of it published.

A TALE OF TWO CITIES

L1
Manuscript of *A Tale of Two Cities* [1859]. Vol.B
F.MS.166

On 30 April 1859 Dickens inaugurated his new weekly magazine *All the Year Round*, and, to get it off to a good start, serialized his novel *A Tale of Two Cities* in its opening numbers. In order to keep up his more comfortable method of monthly publication as far as possible, he 'struck out a rather original and bold idea'. Although the story appeared week by week in *All the Year Round*, he resolved 'at the end of each month to publish the monthly part in the green cover, with the two illustrations, at the old shilling. This will . . . give me my old standing with my old public'. He found, as he had found with *Hard Times*, that writing in weekly instalments was a tiresome constraint: 'the small portions . . . drive me frantic'. The manuscript of *A Tale of Two Cities* contains no number plans, and it may perhaps be assumed that Dickens made none.

L2
A Tale of Two Cities
London, Chapman and Hall, 1859
Another copy
F.PB.2452

After breaking with Bradbury and Evans as a result of disagreements over *Household Words*, Dickens returned to Chapman and Hall, his former publishers. It was they who published *A Tale of Two Cities*. Here are shown a presentation copy of the first edition given to Forster, and a copy in the red publisher's cloth binding.

L3
Véney and Girardet
Fusillade Au Faubourg St. Antoine [Paris] Le 28 Avril 1789
Lettered with title, 2 lines of descriptive text and *Dessiné par Véney et Girardet. Gravé à l'Eau-forte par Pélicier et terminé par Cl. Niquet*
Etching. $10\frac{5}{8} \times 13\frac{3}{8}$
E.1785-1952

This etching, contemporary with the scene it depicts, portrays an incident similar to that described by Dickens in Book II, chapter 21, of *A Tale of Two Cities*, which Phiz illustrated with a plate entitled 'The Sea Rises' (see L5d).

L4
Jan Bulthuis (1750–1801)
Prisoners released from the Bastille walking down the rue St. Antoine towards the Hotel de Ville, 14 July 1789
Copy of a stipple engraving by L. Charpentier
Lettered *Verloste Gevangenen der Bastille. J. Bulthuis, delin. R. Vinkeles & D.Vrydag, sculp.*
1795
Etching. $8\frac{7}{8} \times 10\frac{3}{8}$
E.269-1953

Among the prisoners represented are Claude Auguste Tavernier (born 1745), Count Jacques François Xavier Whyte de Malleville (born 1730) and the Count of Solanges (1746–1825). Their confused, bewildered expressions resemble that of the formerly distinguished Dr Manette, when he is found by his daughter Lucie, working at shoe-making, the trade he learnt during his 18 years confinement in the Bastille (see L5c).

L5 [69]
Phiz (Hablôt K. Browne) (1815–82)
Illustrations to *A Tale of Two Cities*, 1859

(a) Preliminary drawing in pencil heightened with white and (b) etching of the illustration 'The Stoppage at the Fountain'
(a) signed *Phiz*
$4\frac{7}{8} \times 3\frac{3}{8}; 4 \times 6$
(a) Lent by the Trustees of the British Museum

(c) 'The Shoemaker'
Etching. $3\frac{1}{2} \times 5$

(d) 'The Sea Rises'
Etching. 4×7

A Tale of Two Cities was the last of Dickens's novels to be illustrated by Phiz (see C 50).

The artist naturally felt perplexed and aggrieved at 'Dickens's strangely silent manner of breaking the connection' and could only surmise the reason in an undated letter to his friend Robert Young: 'Marcus [Stone] is no doubt to do Dickens. *I* have been a "good boy", I believe. The plates in hand are all in good time, so that I do not know what's "up", any more than you. Dickens probably thinks a new hand will give his old puppets a fresh look, or perhaps he does not like my illustrating Trollope neck-and-neck with him – though, by Jingo, he need fear no rivalry *there*! Confound all authors and publishers, say I. There is no pleasing one or t'other. I wish I had never had anything to do with the lot'. It is possible that Dickens was annoyed that Phiz contributed illustrations to *Once a Week*, the magazine which was published by Bradbury and Evans after Dickens abruptly terminated *Household Words* (see Section J).

GREAT EXPECTATIONS

L6
Manuscript of *Great Expectations* [1860–61]
Lent by the Wisbech and Fenland Museum

Dickens began to form his ideas of *Great Expectations* during 1860, and at first contemplated publishing it in the usual twenty monthly parts. However, the current serial in *All the Year Round*, a novel by Charles Lever entitled *A Day's Ride, a Life's Romance*, was proving unsuccessful, and Dickens felt obliged to 'strike in' with his own novel, in order to restore the magazine's falling circulation.

The manuscript of *Great Expectations* (which, like that of *A Tale of Two Cities*, has no Number Plans but has other memoranda) was given by Dickens to his friend the Rev. Chauncy Hare Townsend (see P22, 23), who bequeathed it, along with the rest of his library, to the Wisbech Literary Institution.

L7
Sheet of the corrected galley-proofs of *Great Expectations*
F.MS.170

L8
***All the Year Round*, 1 December 1860**
Showing the first instalment of *Great Expectations*
F.PB.122

The novel appeared weekly in *All the Year Round* between 1 December 1860 and 3 August 1861.

L9
Great Expectations
3 vols. London, Chapman and Hall, 1861
F.PB.2425

Here is shown a copy of the three-volume first edition of *Great Expectations* in the original purple publisher's cloth. Because the first edition was largely bought up by circulating libraries, where copies were worn out or rebound, fine specimens of the first edition in their original binding are rare and valuable. This novel was not illustrated.

OUR MUTUAL FRIEND

L10
***Our Mutual Friend*. Number X**
London, Chapman and Hall, February 1865
Lent by The Dickens House

Dickens gave the manuscript of *Our Mutual Friend* to Eneas Sweetland Dallas and it is now in the Pierpont Morgan Library. He did not begin publication until he had completed five numbers. Even so, he found it tiring to keep to his programme. 'Work and worry, without exercise, would soon make an end of me,' he wrote in 1865, as he snatched a holiday in France. 'If I were not going away now, I should break down.'

L11
Our Mutual Friend
2 vols. London, Chapman and Hall, 1865
Another copy
F.PB.2441

Our Mutual Friend, after appearing in twenty monthly parts, from May 1864 to November 1865, was published in two volumes, an unusual format for Dickens's novels. Here are shown a specially bound presentation copy given to Forster, and a copy in publisher's cloth.

L12 [71]
Richard Doyle
Bird's Eye Views of Society
London, Smith, Elder and Co., 1864
Open at 'A State Party'. Wood-engraving
9.i.1865

Doyle's 'A State Party', drawn in the same year in which Dickens began *Our Mutual Friend*, makes an apt illustration of the banquet given by the 'bran-new' Veneerings in 'a bran-new house in a bran-new quarter of London', with their new friends, servants, plate, carriage, pictures and baby.

L13
Tombleson's Panoramic Map of the Thames and Medway
London, J. Reynolds [?c.1848]

L14
Mogg's Panorama of the Thames from London Bridge, to its Junction with the Medway and continuation of the Coast of Kent to Ramsgate
London, E.J. Mogg, 1842
22.ix.1875

L15 [70]
Henry Mayhew
London Labour and the London Poor
Vol.II. London, George Woodfall, 1851
Showing a wood-engraved illustration: 'View of a Dust Yard'
F.PB.5985

L16 [68]
'A Court for King Cholera'
Wood-engraved cartoon by John Leech.
Punch, 25 September 1852

Two features of Victorian London are employed by Dickens as recurring motifs with symbolic overtones in *Our Mutual Friend*. One is the river Thames. From its slimy waters Gaffer Hexam salvages the bodies of the drowned, and earns a miserable living by despoiling them. Many of the early scenes in the novel are set on the Limehouse waterside near Hexam's home and the tavern of the Six Jolly Fellowship Porters. Later in the book the scene changes to the neighbourhood of Henley, further upstream, where Lizzie Hexam has taken refuge and where Bradley Headstone makes his murderous assault on Eugene Wrayburn. The other motif is the 'dust heaps'. The rubbish and sewage of the city were removed by contractors and dumped in huge insanitary mounds in the suburban outskirts. Some of the 'dust' could be made use of in industrial processes (ashes in brickmaking, for example), and among the rubbish might be found many objects which could be turned to profit. Contractors made fortunes out of 'dust', and in *Our Mutual Friend*, Dickens tells the story of one such fortune, amassed by old Mr Harmon.

L17
Marcus Stone, RA (1840–1921)
Photograph by Lock and Whitfield, c.1882
X.551.VI.p.33

Dickens and Frank Stone, the father of Marcus, were warm friends (see P20). Marcus wrote of the novelist: 'I saw him constantly in his own home, often for weeks together. He used to treat me as though I were his son'. After the death of Frank Stone, Dickens tried to find commissions amongst his literary friends for the young illustrator and arranged for Stone to provide the frontispieces for some volumes in the Cheap Edition of his *Works*, and the illustrations for several volumes in the Library Edition. In 1864 Dickens invited Stone to illustrate his new novel *Our Mutual Friend*. The blocks were engraved on wood by W.T. Green and Dalziel Brothers in almost equal proportions. By 1870, when Dickens was searching for an illustrator for *Edwin Drood*, Stone was enjoying considerable success with his paintings and no longer worked as an illustrator.

L18

Marcus Stone, RA (1840–1921)

(a) Proof of the illustration 'The Bird of Prey'. Frontispiece to Vol. I of *Our Mutual Friend*, 1864–65

Lettered *Dalziel*

Wood-engraving. $3\frac{5}{8} \times 6\frac{1}{8}$

E.2590–1904

(b–e) Four illustrations to *Our Mutual Friend*, 1864–65

(b) Lettered *Dalziel*; (c) and (d) lettered *W.T. Green. Sc:* and (e) *Green Sc.*

Wood-engravings. $3\frac{5}{8} \times 6$; $3\frac{3}{4} \times 6$; $5 \times 3\frac{5}{8}$; $4\frac{7}{8} \times 3\frac{1}{2}$

(b) 'Mr. Venus surrounded by the trophies of his art.'

Stone suggested taxidermy to Dickens when the author was looking for a 'striking and unusual' vocation to feature in this novel. He took Dickens to the premises of a Mr Willis, who had provided a stuffed dog for him to paint in his picture 'Working and Shirking'. Although Dickens never actually met the taxidermist Willis, Mr Venus was based on him and Stone made several sketches at his shop to give verisimilitude to this illustration.

(c) 'The Happy Pair'

(d) 'More Dead than Alive'

(e) 'The Dutch Bottle'. Frontispiece to Vol. II

Dickens gave his illustrator these suggestions for this plate: 'the dustyard with the three mounds, and Mr. Boffin digging up the Dutch Bottle, and Venus restraining Wegg's ardour to get at him. Or Boffin might be coming down with the bottle, and Venus might be dragging Wegg out of the way as described'.

L19

Manuscript agreement between Charles Dickens and Chapman and Hall

Lent by Harry Dickens Esq.

In this agreement, which relates to *Our Mutual Friend*, Dickens contracts with Messrs Chapman and Hall to produce a new serial tale in 20 monthly parts, to be commenced before the end of 1864, for the sum of £6000.

EDWIN DROOD

L20

Manuscript of *Edwin Drood* [1870]

F.MS.167

When Dickens died on 9 June 1870, he had almost completed six of the proposed twelve parts of *Edwin Drood*, and only three had been published. The manuscript contains plans for the completed numbers, but the sheets on which Dickens intended to note his plans for remaining numbers are blank, and the ending of the novel remains a mystery.

The page on view is part of chapter 2; it contains a description of a sudden seizure from the effects of opium which overcomes John Jasper, and for which Jasper faintly utters an excuse. After writing Jasper's words Dickens covered them over with a slip of paper, firmly attached with sealing wax, on which he rewrote the speech. He commonly made corrections to his manuscripts in this way. It was thought by some *Drood* solutionists that the words covered by the slip of paper might contain a clue to the mystery, but when the slip was removed in 1963 nothing very significant was discovered; Jasper's murderous tendencies under opium are perhaps more clearly hinted than Dickens wished.

For the last page of the manuscript see M45.

L21

Sheets of the corrected page-proofs of *Edwin Drood*

F.MS.170

The only surviving corrected proofs of *Edwin Drood* in the Forster Collection are a set of page proofs for Number V. These were the last proofs to be corrected by Dickens, and it will be seen that he cancelled a number of passages for reasons of space. He died two months before Number V was published, and Forster, seeing it through the press, restored the cancelled passages in order to make up for the lack of the final chapter in Number VI. On page 143 Dickens intended to cancel a paragraph in which Mr Datchery, a mysterious disguised investigator who appears in Cloisterham after Edwin Drood's disappearance, cunningly interrogates Mrs Tope.

L22
The Mystery of Edwin Drood
In parts. London, Chapman and Hall, 1870
L.725/725e–1933

The cover was designed by Charles Collins and touched up and altered by Luke Fildes (see L25).

L23
The Mystery of Edwin Drood
London, Chapman and Hall, 1870
F.PB.2435

L24 [74]
Gustave Doré and Blanchard Jerrold
London. A Pilgrimage
London, Grant and Co., 1872
Showing the wood-engraved illustration: 'Opium Smoking – The Lascar's Room in *Edwin Drood*'

In chapter 18, 'Whitechapel and Thereabouts', Jerrold describes and Doré illustrates a visit made to 'the room in which *Edwin Drood* opens'.

L25
Sir Samuel Luke Fildes, KCVO, RA (1843–1927)
Photograph by Frederick Hollyer, 1884
7749–1938

When illness prevented Dickens's son-in-law, Charles Collins, who was to have illustrated *Edwin Drood*, from completing his designs for more than the cover for the parts, Dickens was left with little time to find a replacement. Millais, after seeing an illustration 'Houseless and Hungry' in the *Graphic* by the then little-known Fildes, suggested him to the author as a suitable illustrator for his new novel. Although Fildes was gratified by the invitation, he hesitated until Dickens reassured him that he was not expected to imitate the humorous style of Phiz, of which the author confessed himself a little tired. Fildes drew his subjects from life; for the scene of the opium smokers' den he ventured into an actual den in the East End. Later Fildes made his name as a painter and gave up book illustration.

L26
Letter from Dickens to Frederic Chapman, 18 January 1870
Lent by Sir Paul Fildes, FRS

In the letter Dickens asks his publisher to arrange a meeting for him with Fildes. Fildes later remembered the initial effect the author had on him: 'I felt a little oppressed – I don't know why – he loomed so large, and was so great in my imagination'.

L27
Sir Samuel Luke Fildes, KCVO, RA (1843–1927)
'Under the Trees.' Illustration to *Edwin Drood*, 1870

(a) Proof of the illustration
Signed *Dalziel* and *S.L.F.*
Wood-engraving. $4 \times 6\frac{1}{4}$

The background of this illustration was taken from a sketch of the cloisters at Chester Cathedral, drawn by the artist some time previously.

(b) Photocopy of the original drawing for the illustration on an uncut block.
Signed *S.L.F.* and on the back *J.Contenem*
$4\frac{1}{4} \times 6\frac{1}{2}$

Fildes's illustrations, drawn on paper, were photographed on to box-wood blocks. The engraving was first entrusted to Dalziel Brothers; after the first two engravings the process of reproduction was transferred to a former colleague of the artist, Charles Roberts, at Fildes's request.

(c) Study for the figure of Edwin Drood
Pen and ink and black chalk. $5\frac{1}{4} \times 4$

(d) Study for the hands of Rosa Bud
Pencil and black chalk. 3×2
Lent by Sir Paul Fildes, FRS

L28
Sir Samuel Luke Fildes, KCVO, RA (1843–1927)
'At the Piano'. Illustration to *Edwin Drood*, 1870

(a) Studies for the figures of Helena Landless and Rosa Bud
Black chalk heightened with chinese white. $6\frac{1}{2} \times 9$

(b) Study for the figure of Mr Crisparkle
Black chalk heightened with chinese white, squared for reduction in pencil. $5 \times 3\frac{3}{4}$
Lent by Sir Paul Fildes, FRS

L29 [72]
Sir Samuel Luke Fildes, KCVO, RA (1843–1927)
'Up the River'. Illustration to *Edwin Drood*, 1870

(a) Study for the background of the illustration
Inscribed with note on its engraved size *2¼ high*
Black chalk. $3\frac{1}{2} \times 8\frac{1}{2}$

A view of Putney Church and the wooden bridge which used to span the Thames at that point.

(b) Study for the figure of Rosa Bud seated
Black chalk heightened with chinese white
$5\frac{1}{8} \times 5\frac{1}{8}$
Lent by Sir Paul Fildes, FRS

M: Final years

THE BREAKDOWN OF DICKENS'S MARRIAGE

Dickens and his wife separated in 1858. Happy as the earlier years of the marriage had been, at the time of the final break he wrote a number of self-justificatory letters declaring that it had never been a success. Restless by nature, his restlessness in his middle forties, after 21 years of marriage during which his wife had borne him ten children, is scarcely surprising; nor is his falling in love with a girl young enough to be his daughter, Ellen Ternan, whom he met through his production of *The Frozen Deep*. There has been much speculation about his later relations with Ellen, but most of the details are still obscure. In the '60s he visited her frequently in a cottage at Slough, which she possibly shared with her mother, and later at a house in Peckham; and from time to time she came to Gad's Hill. But only a few of Dickens's friends knew her and of her importance to him.

M1 [41]
The Frozen Deep
Wood-engraving from the *Illustrated London News*, 17 January 1857
Enthoven Collection

Dickens suggested the theme of *The Frozen Deep* to Wilkie Collins in 1856 and made many suggestions for the dialogue and action. The first performances were given in the 'Smallest Theatre in the World' at Tavistock House in January 1857. After some performances in July at the Gallery of Illustration in aid of Jerrold's widow, the first of which was attended by Queen Victoria and the Prince Consort, it was decided to play it at the Free Trade Hall, Manchester. The female parts, which had been played by Dickens's daughters and a friend, were taken over by professional actresses for these performances; for this purpose Mrs Ternan and her daughters, Maria and Ellen, were employed. After the performance at Manchester Dickens wrote to Collins 'The domestic un-happiness remains so strong upon me that I can't write, and (waking) can't rest, one minute. I have never known a moment's peace or content since the last night of *The Frozen Deep*. I do suppose that there never was a man so seized and rended by one spirit'.

M2
Playbill for the performance of *The Frozen Deep*, Free Trade Hall, Manchester, 24 August 1857
Lent by the Manchester Public Libraries

This is the bill for the third and last performance in Manchester, an extra one arranged to meet the demand for seats.

M3
R. Dudley
The Frozen Deep. Performance in the Free Trade Hall, Manchester
Signed and dated *R. Dudley, 1857*
Water-colour. $7\frac{1}{2} \times 5\frac{1}{4}$
Lent by the Manchester Public Libraries

Dickens played the part of Wardour at Manchester with a power of which Wilkie Collins wrote: 'he literally electrified the audience'. Of Maria Ternan, the sister of Ellen, Dickens reported to Miss Coutts: 'when she had to kneel over Wardour dying, and be taken leave of, the tears streamed out of her eyes into his mouth, down his beard, all over his rags'.

M4, M5 [79]
Ellen Ternan
Photographs
Enthoven Collection

M6
Ellen Ternan with her sisters, Maria and Frances
Photograph
Enthoven Collection

M7

Household Words, 12 June 1858

F.PB.4285

Dickens decided to print this personal statement about his separation from Mrs Dickens on the advice of John T. Delane, Editor of *The Times.* In it he denies the rumours circulating about the causes for the breakdown of his marriage. These concerned Georgina Hogarth as well as Ellen Ternan.

M8

Letter from Dickens to Arthur Smith, 29 May 1858

From a facsimile printed in the *Dickensian*

Dickens drafted this letter so that Arthur Smith, then manager of his readings, could amplify his public statement (M7) with an informed private account of the innocence of Georgina Hogarth and a 'young lady' (Ellen Ternan), of whom he says 'there is not on this earth a more virtuous and spotless creature . . . I know her to be as innocent and pure, and as good as my own dear daughters'.

Although it was intended to be private, this letter found its way into print in the *New York Tribune,* and was copied in English newspapers. This increased Dickens's sense of being wronged, and he always referred to this document as the 'violated letter'.

M9

Letter from John Forster to Sir Edwin Landseer, 20 June 1858

L.1316–1962

This letter shows Forster trying to justify Dickens's separation to one of their friends.

'I think, with you, that both are in the wrong – in some respects it *must* in such cases, after so large a part of life has been lived together, almost invariably be so. But yet I wish you could know *everything* – because, upon the whole, Dickens bears this test better than you would be prepared to think – and, after all the critical experience I have had of him lately, I am more than ever prepared to say, that a man more truthful and honourable, a man more genuinely worthy of the feeling he has generally inspired, does not exist.'

M10 [80]

The Staplehurst Railway Accident, 9 June 1865

Photograph from the original in the possession of the British Railways Board

M11

The Staplehurst Railway Accident, 9 June 1865, showing Charles Dickens working among the dying and dead

Photograph from the *Penny Illustrated Paper,* 24 June 1865

The accident occurred when Dickens, Ellen Ternan and (almost certainly) her mother were returning from a brief holiday in France. Dickens climbed out of the compartment to assist with the injured. A staggering man covered with blood had 'such a frightful cut across the skull', Dickens said, 'that I couldn't bear to look at him. I poured some water over his face, gave him some drink, then gave him some brandy and laid him down in the grass . . .'. Only on his return to Gad's Hill did he realise how shaken he was. Nevertheless, although his hand was unsteady and he dictated the replies to most of the enquiries after his health, he wrote himself to the Stationmaster at Charing Cross: 'A lady who was in the carriage with me in the terrible accident on Friday, lost, in the struggle of being got out of the carriage, a gold watch-chain with a smaller gold watch-chain attached, a bundle of chains, a gold watch-key, and a gold seal engraved "Ellen".

I promised the lady to make her loss known at headquarters . . . I would have spoken to you instead of writing, but that I am shaken; – not by the beating of the carriage, but by the work afterwards of getting out the dying and dead.'

Dickens was unable to throw off the effects of the accident. He wrote to Forster 'I am curiously weak – weak as if I were recovering from a long illness'. And sometime later 'I begin to feel it more in my head. I sleep well and eat well; but I write half a dozen notes, and turn faint and sick'.

M12

The Gad's Hill Gazette, **30 December 1865**

Lent by Dr Margaret Whinney

This number of the *Gazette* contains a reference to the Staplehurst Railway accident. Mr Dickenson, who was visiting the Dickens family, had 'not yet entirely recovered from the effects of a most disastrous railway accident in which he was a sufferer, and had it not been for the courage and intrepidity of Mr Dickens, he would not now be spending his Christmas at Gad's Hill'. The *Gazette* continues with a description of Dickens's part in the accident; he 'managed to crawl out of the window and then, caring little for his own safety, busied himself in helping the wounded . . .'.

GAD'S HILL

In 'Travelling Abroad' (*The Uncommercial Traveller*) Dickens relates what a treat it was to him as a 'very queer small boy' to be brought to see the big house at Gad's Hill, and how his father had said to him, 'If you were to be very persevering and were to work hard, you might some day come to live in it'. In 1855 the house, Gad's Hill Place, came on to the market and Dickens was able to buy it. It became his permanent residence after he sold his London home in 1860.

M13 [77]
The Dining Room at Gad's Hill Place
Photograph
Lent by Dr Margaret Whinney

Amongst the pictures are to be seen the 'Nickleby' portrait of Charles Dickens by Maclise (O 4), 'Dolly Varden looking back at her lover' by Frith, and the portrait of Kate Dickens by Marcus Stone (B 27).

M14
The Drawing Room at Gad's Hill Place
Photograph
Lent by Dr Margaret Whinney

M15 [78]
Artist Unknown, c.1868
Cricket at Gad's Hill, with Dickens bowling
Inscribed with title and date
Oil. $11\frac{1}{2} \times 15\frac{1}{2}$
Lent by the Marylebone Cricket Club

It was Charles Dickens's custom to act as scorer at the cricket matches which were played in aid of charities in the field in front of Gad's Hill Place. Here he is seen opening the bowling.

M16–M18
***The Gad's Hill Gazette,* 19 August 1862 and 6 January 1866. Circular letter, January 1867**
Lent by Dr Margaret Whinney

This paper, with personal, social and sporting news of the Dickens household and the local community at Gad's Hill was mainly edited by H.F. (Harry) Dickens, and printed by hand. The issue of 19 August 1862 appears to be the earliest recorded, though evidently not the first of the series. The issue of 6 January 1866 is unusual because produced by an outside printer, and the circular letter of January 1867 records the termination of the *Gazette*. For the issue of 30 December 1865 see M12.

M19
Sale Catalogue of the Modern Pictures, Water-colours, Drawings and Objects of Art
Christies, 9 July 1870
Another copy, with prices
F.PB.2458

The sale of the works of art belonging to Charles Dickens was held by Christies a month after his death. Amongst the items in the sale to be seen in this exhibition are 'The S.S. Britannia at Liverpool embarking Charles Dickens' (E 10), 'The Eddystone Lighthouse' (G 60) and 'The Logan Rock' (D 10) by Clarkson Stanfield, 'Sintram and his Companions' (F 46) and 'The Grave of Little Nell' (F 8) by G. Cattermole, 'Charles Dickens as Sir Charles Coldstream in Used Up' (G 43) by A. Egg, and 'Girl at the Waterfall at St. Nighton's Kieve, Cornwall' (P 4) by D. Maclise, R A. The prices reached were regarded as extremely high in the context of the time. Frith's 'Dolly Varden looking back at her lover' fetched 1,000 guineas; the 'Nickleby' portrait by Maclise, 660 guineas.

M20
Sale catalogue of the house and grounds, Gad's Hill Place
Norton, Trist, Watney & Co., 5 August 1870

The illustrations show the chalet given to Dickens by Fechter, in which he wrote the last pages of *Edwin Drood*; and include views of the exterior and plan of the house and establishment.

SECOND VISIT TO AMERICA

Dickens paid a second visit to America twenty-five years after his first (see Section E), giving a series of readings. He sailed from Liverpool on 9 November 1867, and arrived back there on 1 May 1868. The tour was a financial and personal success, but on his return his friends noticed that his health had been impaired. At a farewell banquet given in his honour in New York on 18 April 1868 Dickens gave a pledge that he would add to future editions of *Martin Chuzzlewit* and *American Notes* his testimony to the gigantic changes he had found in the country since his last visit and the kindliness with which he had been received.

M21
Farewell Banquet in honour of Charles Dickens before his visit to America: Invitation and ticket issued to Sir Edwin Landseer, RA

M22
Invitation to the Rev. Alexander Dyce for the Banquet

M23
List of the Stewards for the Banquet

On the announcement of Dickens's imminent departure for the United States a number of his friends resolved to hold a farewell banquet in his honour. It was held at the Freemasons' Hall, with Lord Lytton in the Chair, and nearly four hundred and fifty guests. Dickens was almost overcome by the warmth of the reception given him.

M24
Au Revoir. Charles Dickens leaving England for his second American visit
Caricature, showing Dickens being seen off by his characters and John Bull
Judy, 30 October 1867
Lent by the Trustees of the British Museum

M25
Map of Charles Dickens's second tour in America

M26
'A Man and A Brother'. Uncle Sam – 'Wal, Charley, I Guess you're welcome, let me introduce to you our new brother from down South'. The most remarkable man in the country
Photograph of cartoon showing Dickens being introduced to a negro published in *Banter*, 2 December 1867

M27
Caricature of Dickens and George Dolby gloating over the money earned on the Reading tour
Photograph

M28 [83]
Letter from Longfellow to John Forster, 23 November 1867
F.MS.366

In the letter Longfellow writes: 'It is a great pleasure to see Dickens again after so many years, with the same sweetness and flavor as of old, and only greater ripeness. The enthusiasm for him and for his Readings is immense. One can hardly take in the whole truth about it, and feel the universality of his fame. The Readings will be as triumphant a success here as in England. Every ticket is sold for the whole course, and the public clamorous for more'.

READINGS

By far the most interesting love-affair of Dickens's life, it has been said, was his lifelong love-affair with his public; and when his marriage broke down in 1858, it was to his public that he turned for reassurance. Since 1853 he had given occasional public readings for charity; now, seeking to intensify 'that particular relation (personally affectionate and like no other man's) which subsists between me and the public', he embarked on a series of paid readings. So successful was he that he embraced public reading virtually as a second and highly profitable profession, alternating it with authorship.

The first work which he adapted for reading was *A Christmas Carol*, and this remained a favourite. When he expanded his repertoire, he drew heavily on other Christmas Books and on the Christmas stories which he wrote for *All The Year Round* and

Household Words. He also extracted readings from his earlier novels, usually choosing cheerful incidents such as the Bardell v. Pickwick trial, or pathetic ones such as the death of Paul Dombey.

The excitement and satisfaction of the readings must have done much to invigorate his troubled middle age. Yet the hectic activity that was involved must surely also have hastened his death. In all he gave over four hundred readings. The first series of London readings in 1858 was followed by an autumn tour of the provinces, ending in London again with a series of Christmas readings. During most of 1859 and '60 Dickens was at work on *A Tale of Two Cities* and *Great Expectations*, but from October 1861 until June 1862 he again toured the country reading. In the next year, 1863, he undertook a London season of readings in the spring and summer; and after an interval devoted to the writing of *Our Mutual Friend*, there followed two more series of readings, April–June 1866 and January–May 1867. At the height of his success as a reader, Dickens toured America from November 1867 to April 1868.

Forster, seeing him on his return, considered that 'America had told heavily on him'. Yet Dickens now drew from *Oliver Twist* a new reading 'Sikes and Nancy', which, unlike the other readings, was designed to excite the audience to terror, and which, in performance, made great demands on Dickens's stamina and histrionic power. This tale of horror had a compulsive fascination for him, and, despite failing health, he gave repeated readings of it.

His farewell series of a hundred readings (for £8,000) in London and the provinces began in October 1868, and broke off when the strain brought him to the verge of collapse in April 1869. After a period of rest, he insisted on resuming the series, partly to compensate his backers for the loss caused by his breakdown. His doctor forbade travel by rail, and so, early in 1870, twelve final performances were given in London. By now Dickens was prostrated with exhaustion after every reading, the rate of his pulse rising as high as 124. But he reached the last reading on 15 March 1870.

M29
A Christmas Carol. In prose. Being a Ghost Story of Christmas
London, Chapman and Hall, n.d.
F.PB.2417

Several of the texts of Dickens's works as he had adapted them for public reading were published in England and America.

M30
Ticket for Dickens's reading of *A Christmas Carol* in the Music Hall, Worcester, on Tuesday evening, 10 August 1858
with F.PB.2417

M31
***Household Words*, 31 July 1858**
Showing an advertisement for Dickens's reading tour of 1858
F.PB.4285

M32
Mrs. Gamp. A Facsimile of the Author's Prompt Copy
Introduction and notes by John D. Gordan.
The New York Public Library, 1956
L.199–1957

On a copy of a reading version printed for him in 1858 by Bradbury and Evans, Dickens has marked further revisions. This prompt copy is in the Berg Collection, New York Public Library.

M33
Letter from Dickens to W.P. Frith, 16 November 1868
L.186–1922

'Come (early in January) and see a certain friend of yours do the murder from Oliver Twist. It is horribly like, I am afraid! I have a vague sensation of being "wanted" as I walk about the streets.'

M34
Sikes and Nancy: a reading from Oliver Twist
Privately printed [?1870]
Lent by The Dickens House

Dickens's own copy of this reading, with marginal stage-directions and revisions, is in the Berg Collection, New York Public Library. From this copy a few other copies seem to have been printed, probably in 1870. One, into which the actress Mrs Adeline Billington transcribed Dickens's notes, is in the Suzannet Collection. The copy displayed here was given to John Billington by Mary Dickens.

M35
Harry Furniss (1854–1925)
Charles Dickens exhausted after his 'Death of Nancy' Reading
Signed *Hy.F.* Inscribed in pencil with title and *Chap.XVII*
Pen and ink on card. $10\frac{5}{8} \times 9\frac{3}{4}$
Lent by the National Portrait Gallery

Harry Furniss saw Dickens only once, when he was a young boy. This drawing is reproduced with the title 'Charles Dickens Exhausted' on p. 174 of *Some Victorian Men* written by the artist in 1924. It illustrates the chapter on 'Charles Dickens as an Actor', in which Furniss insists that the public readings showed Dickens to be almost as great an actor as he was an author; and that 'his "reading" undoubtedly resulted in Dickens's breakdown and death; he sacrificed his life for his dramatic art'.

M36
***Penny Illustrated Paper*, 19 March 1870**
Open at the page showing the cut of Dickens's farewell reading in St. James's Hall, 15 March 1870
Lent by the Trustees of the British Museum

M37 [82]
***Illustrated London News*, 19 March 1870**
Open at the pages showing the cut of Dickens's farewell reading in St James's Hall, 15 March 1870, and the speech made by him at its conclusion.

DEATH

Dickens never fully recovered from the effects of the Staplehurst railway accident in 1865 and, as has been noted, his friends found a serious decline in his health on his return from America in 1868. The end came suddenly two years later when he had half finished *Edwin Drood*; he died at Gad's Hill Place on 9 June 1870.

M38
Letter from Charles Dickens to William Charles Kent, 8 June 1870
Lent by the Trustees of the British Museum

After completing his work for the day on *Edwin Drood* Dickens wrote some letters, including this note making an appointment to meet Charles Kent in London on the following day. Shortly after quoting 'These violent delights have violent ends' from *Romeo and Juliet* he suffered the stroke from which he died on the following day.

M39 [88]
Sir John Everett Millais, PRA (1829–96)
Charles Dickens on his deathbed
Signed with monogram and inscribed *Gads Hill 10th June 1870*
Pencil. $5\frac{1}{4} \times 9\frac{1}{4}$
Lent by Mrs Alec Waley

In spite of his onslaught on Millais' painting 'Christ in the House of his Parents' (cf. J33) Dickens became a friend of the painter. On hearing of Dickens's death, Millais travelled down to Gad's Hill with the sculptor Thomas Woolner the following day. After Millais drew this portrait, Woolner took a death mask from which he later modelled a portrait bust. Millais gave his portrait to Dickens's second daughter, Kate, who wrote to thank him with these words: 'It is quite impossible to describe the effect it has had upon us. No one but yourself, I think, could have so perfectly understood the beauty and pathos of his dear face as it lay on that little bed in the dining-room, and no one but a man with genius bright as his own could have so reproduced that face as to make us feel how, when we look at it, that he is still with us in the house. Thank you, dear Mr. Millais, for giving it to me. There is nothing in the world I have, or can ever have, that I shall value half as much. I think you know this, although I can find so few words to tell you how grateful I am'.

M40
Leading article from *The Times*, 13 June 1870
Photograph

In this leader *The Times* suggested that Dickens should be buried in Westminster Abbey. This was done on 14 June, and in accordance with the instructions in his will: 'I emphatically direct that I be buried in an inexpensive, unostentatious, and strictly private manner; that no public announcement be made of the time or place of my burial; that at the utmost not more than three plain mourning coaches be employed; and that those who attend my funeral wear no scarf, cloak, black bow, long hat-band, or other such revolting absurdity. I DIRECT that my name be inscribed in plain English letters on my tomb, without the addition of "Mr." or "Esquire". I conjure my friends on no account to make me the subject of any monument, memorial, or testimonial whatever. I rest my claims to the remembrance of my country upon my published works, and to the remembrance of my friends upon their experience of me in addition thereto'.

M41
The Grave of Charles Dickens in Poets' Corner
Photograph of a wood-engraving from the *Illustrated London News*, 25 June 1870

The engraving was accompanied by a plan of Poets' Corner and an explanation of the surrounding graves. Dickens was buried between Handel and Sheridan.

M42 [89]
After Sir Samuel Luke Fildes, KCVO, RA (1843–1927)
The Empty Chair, Gad's Hill – Ninth of June 1870
Signed and dated *S.L. Fildes 1870*
Wood-engraving from the *Graphic*, 25 December 1870. $12\frac{1}{2} \times 19\frac{1}{2}$

This engraving after a water-colour by Fildes of Dickens's study at Gad's Hill was published in the 1870 Christmas Number of the *Graphic* emphasizing the point that there would be no further Christmas stories from his hand. Amongst the admirers of this illustration was Van Gogh, who wrote of Dickens: 'There is no writer, in my opinion, who is *so* much a painter and black-and-white artist'.

M43 [87]
Sir Samuel Luke Fildes, KCVO, RA (1843–1927)
The Grave of Charles Dickens, Poets' Corner, Westminster Abbey
Signed, and dated [*18*]*73*
Water-colour. $13\frac{7}{8} \times 8\frac{7}{8}$
F.62

This water-colour was commissioned by John Forster, and was engraved by J. Saddler for the first edition of the *Life of Charles Dickens*.

M44
The Will of Charles Dickens
Lent by the Principal Probate Registry

Written in Dickens's own hand, the passage quoted at M40 can be seen on the side shown.

M44A
Death certificate of Charles Dickens
Photographic copy of the entry in the original death register now deposited at the Register Office, Chatham

M45
The last page of *Edwin Drood*
F.MS.167

This page was written in the Swiss Chalet in the grounds of Gad's Hill during the afternoon of 8 June 1870. Later, in the evening of the same day, Dickens suffered his fatal collapse. 'The reader will observe with a painful interest', says Forster, 'the direction his thoughts had taken'; and he refers to the words at the head of the page.

'A brilliant morning shines on the old city . . . Changes of glorious light from moving boughs, songs of birds, scents from gardens, woods and fields – or, rather, from the one great garden of the whole cultivated island in its yielding time – penetrate into the Cathedral, subdue its earthy odour, and preach the Resurrection and the Life'.

N: Personalia

N1
Chair used by Charles Dickens from Gad's Hill Place
Lent by the Athenaeum

N2
Gladstone bag, used by Charles Dickens on his later travels
Lent by Cedric C. Dickens Esq.

N3
Flower vase
Lent by Mrs Terence McHugh

This vase descended with N4 and N5 to the present owner from her grandfather, the eldest son of Charles Dickens. It may have been bought during one of Dickens's Continental journeys, and used to stand on or near his desk filled with simple flowers and sweet herbs.

N4
Nutmeg grater used by Charles Dickens
Maker's mark TB (Thomas Brough); hall-marked 1799
Lent by Mrs Terence McHugh

This nutmeg grater was constantly used by Charles Dickens for flavouring the milk punch which was his favourite beginning to a meal. It was the family tradition that he used the sharp scent of freshly grated nutmeg as an antidote to bad smells when he explored the more unsavoury parts of London.

N5
Bracelet given by Charles Dickens to Catherine Dickens
Lent by Mrs Terence McHugh

N6
Cuff-links worn by Charles Dickens
Lent by H.C.D. Whinney Esq.

Mary Angela Dickens, Charles Dickens's eldest grand-daughter, wrote to her nephew, the present owner: 'My father, your grandfather, Charles Dickens, was the eldest son of your great-grandfather Charles Dickens. My father had the links after his father's death and he wore them *always*. They were inseparable from him in my memory. I happen to have an orderly mind – the only thing, I fear, which I inherit from both my father and grandfather! When I was quite a girl I thought the dent looked dilapidated and I suggested to my father that it should be taken out. He then told me how it came there. In the readings which your great-grandfather used to give from Oliver Twist the great moment was the murder of Nancy by Bill Sykes. In this there occurs the phrase 'beat twice upon her upturned face' – I quote from memory as to the exact words – and as he spoke them your great-grandfather, half-acting the scene, used to beat his clenched fist upon the reading desk at which he stood. One night, when he was wearing those links, he caught the edge of the desk and the force which possessed him was such that the gold links dented'.

N7
Three plates and a fruit-dish from a dessert service
Made during the partnership of William Taylor Copeland and Thomas Garrett (1833–47)
Lent by H.C.D. Whinney Esq.

The original works was established by Josiah Spode in 1770 at Stoke-on-Trent, Staffordshire. This fruit service belonged to Charles Dickens.

N8
Desk slope used by Charles Dickens
W.54-1935

This desk slope (on which Dickens wrote much of his later work, including the last page of *Edwin Drood*) was given by Georgina Hogarth to Edmund Yates. It was acquired at Yates's sale by Sir Squire Bancroft, who gave it to the Museum.

N9
Pencase used by Charles Dickens
W.67-1938

The pencase was given to E.V. Lucas by Sir Seymour Hicks, who stated that when he bought it, it was accompanied by a letter from Miss Georgina Hogarth guaranteeing its authenticity. From E.V. Lucas the pencase passed to the Museum.

N10
Punch ladle used by Charles Dickens
Lent by Dr Margaret Whinney

O: Portraits of Dickens

Leigh Hunt said of Dickens 'what a face to meet in a drawing room! It has the life and soul in it of fifty human beings'. Portraits have been included at appropriate points in the exhibition. They show the transformation in his appearance from that of a keen, clean-shaven young man to the more familiar image of him in later years, bearded, moustached, and sometimes latterly showing signs of illness and fatigue.

O1
George Cruikshank (1792–1878)
Charles Dickens, with various sketches in the margin
C.1837
Inscribed with notes and *sketch of Charles Dickens*
Pencil. $9\frac{1}{2} \times 7\frac{1}{2}$
9995.C

In April or May 1837 Dickens wrote excusing himself for not seeing a friend who called at Doughty Street because 'I was sitting for my portrait to George Cruikshank . . . and George being a ticklish subject could not leave him'. The sketch shows him when he was beginning to be known as an elegant man-about-town.

O2 [3]
Samuel Laurence (1812–84)
Charles Dickens
Signed, and dated *1837*. Signed by the sitter *Charles Dickens*
Exhibited at the Royal Academy in 1838
Chalks. $18 \times 12\frac{1}{2}$
Lent by Major Sir Charles E. Pym, CBE, DL

Laurence drew two other portraits of Charles Dickens at about this date. The present whereabouts of one, worked up from a sketch drawn when the artist was engaged on this version, are unknown: it is reproduced as the frontispiece to *Dickens by Pen and Pencil* by Frederic G. Kitton, 1890. The other, signed *Boz*, was given by the artist to Dickens, who gave it to his sister, Fanny Burnett: it is now owned by Lord Glenconner. It is almost a replica of the exhibited portrait, and there is some confusion as to which was the model for the lithographs by the artist and by Weld Taylor. The portrait on exhibition remained, during the artist's lifetime, in a place of honour in his sitting-room.

O3
Richard James Lane (1808–72)
Charles Dickens
Exhibited at the Royal Academy in 1843
Pencil. 6×8
Lent by Her Majesty the Queen

Lane may have begun this portrait of Dickens during one of their meetings at the house of their common friend, George Cattermole, who bought it. Earlier, Lane lithographed a portrait of the novelist by Count D'Orsay.

O4 [84]
Daniel Maclise, RA (1806–70)
Charles Dickens
Signed and dated *D. Maclise pinxit 1839*
Oil. $35\frac{1}{4} \times 27$
Lent by the National Portrait Gallery

When this portrait was exhibited at the Royal Academy in 1840 Thackeray wrote in *Fraser's Magazine:* 'As a likeness perfectly amazing; a looking glass could not render a better facsimile. Here we have the real identical man Dickens: the artist must have understood the inward Boz as well as the outward before he made this admirable representation of him'. Later, George Sala said that 'for grace, and refinement, and intellectual force we must go to Maclise's canvas, and ponder over the excellent delineation of the young man with the long silky hair, the fascinating smile, the marvellously clear and enquiring eyes which seem to follow the beholder everywhere. This was the Charles Dickens who was, in the early days of Queen Victoria's reign, one of the best looking and best dressed young fellows about town; or who, a few years later, in a blue frock, white vest and white trousers, looked even nattier and comelier'.

The portrait was commissioned by Chapman and Hall, who had the central portion engraved by Finden, as the frontispiece to *Nicholas Nickleby*. During June 1839, Maclise paid Dickens many visits at Elm Cottage, Petersham, studying the novelist in countless sketches which he destroyed in dissatisfaction. 'Maclise has made another face of me', Dickens reported at the end of the month, 'which all people say is astonishing'. Out of this grew the 'Nickleby' portrait. It was presented to Dickens by the publishers at the Nickleby dinner, 5 October 1839.

Dickens did not like the proof of the engraving. On sending an early one to J.P. Collier he wrote 'I send you the best "proof" I have – bad *is* the best, I fear, but I have the consolation of believing that bad as it is, you could not buy so good a one from a most excellent and most mangled picture'.

05
Angus Fletcher (1799–1862)
Charles Dickens
Exhibited at the Royal Academy in 1839
Marble bust. $25\frac{1}{2}$ high
Lent by The Dickens House

Dickens met Angus Fletcher at the offices of his publisher, John Macrone, who owned, among his collection of literary busts, several by this sculptor. The Dickens bust, Fletcher's last exhibit at the Royal Academy, did not receive favourable reviews. 'We cannot think it like. The features are not sufficiently bold or characteristic of his mind'; and Dickens's comment, when it came into his possession in 1841, 'The Bust ... is considered by everybody (by Maclise at the head of them) *much more like* in Marble than in cast' indicates that it must have received some adverse criticism within Dickens's circle. After the novelist's move to Gad's Hill, the bust stood on a pedestal in the greenhouse, until his death.

According to Forster, Fletcher, the son of Mrs Fletcher of Lancrigg, one of the Wordsworth circle, abandoned the profession of sculptor, as a result of his character –'too fitful and wayward to concentrate on a settled pursuit'. This was part of his appeal for Dickens, who delighted in writing humorous accounts of Fletcher's eccentricities, when the sculptor, himself a Scot, acted as the novelist's guide in the Highlands, or stayed with the Dickenses at Broadstairs. At Broadstairs, Dickens told Maclise, Fletcher sketched the beggars and idiots, dressing them up in his own clothes. To the passers-by, he recited Wordsworth and Mrs Hemans with the vehemence of a preacher.

Fletcher was the original of Dickens's Mr Kindheart in 'The Medicine-Men of Civilization', first published in *All The Year Round*, 26 September 1863.

06
Schloss's English Bijou Almanac for 1842. Poetically Illustrated by the Hon. Mrs. Norton
London, A. Schloss, 1842
L.1320–1954

Albert Schloss, a German by birth, had been in business in London for about four years as a book and print seller, when in 1839 he brought out the first of his English Bijou Almanacs, which appeared annually until 1843. Each of these tiny books, which achieved great success ('A more beautiful or fairy-like production was never seen' was one reviewer's comment), contained a calendar and six portraits of eminent persons accompanied by tributes in verse. In the 1842 *Almanac* appears a portrait of Dickens, based no doubt on Maclise's 'Nickleby' portrait (see 04) accompanied by verses by Mrs Norton.

07 [11]
Daniel Maclise, RA (1806–70)
Charles Dickens, his wife, Catherine and sister-in-law, Georgina Hogarth
1843
Pencil. $6 \times 5\frac{1}{2}$
F.P.76

Dickens referred to his wife and sister-in-law as his 'pair of petticoats'. After he and Catherine returned from America Georgina Hogarth, Catherine's sister, came to live with them permanently; she remained a devoted member of Dickens's household until his death.

John Forster considered this profile drawing one of the best portraits of Dickens, 'nothing ever done of Dickens has conveyed more vividly his look and bearing at this yet youthful time. He is in his most pleasing aspect; flattered if you will; but nothing that is known to me gives a general impression so life-like and true of the then frank, eager, handsome face'.

08
Ary Scheffer (1795–1858)
Charles Dickens
Signed and dated *Ary Scheffer 1855*
Oil. $37\frac{1}{8} \times 24\frac{3}{4}$
Lent by the National Portrait Gallery

Soon after Dickens arrived in Paris for an extended visit in October 1855, he met the artist Ary Scheffer, who insisted on painting his portrait. That the sittings, which began almost immediately, caused the novelist pleasure mingled with agitation and acute frustration, is evident from his correspondence. In November he wrote to John Forster 'You may faintly imagine what I have suffered from sitting to Scheffer every day since I came back. He is a most noble fellow, and I have the greatest pleasure in his society, and have made all sorts of acquaintances at his house; but I can scarcely express how uneasy and unsettled it makes me to have to sit, sit, sit with *Little Dorrit* on my mind.... On Monday afternoon, *and all day on Wednesday*, I am going to sit again. And the crowning feature is, that I do not discern the slightest resemblance, either in his portrait or his brother's! They both peg away at me at the same time'. Early the following year he wrote to Wilkie Collins, 'I have been sitting to Scheffer to-day – conceive this, if you please, with No. 5 upon my soul – four hours!! I am so addleheaded and bored, that if you were here, I should propose an instantaneous rush to the Trois Frères'. The portrait became known privately as 'The Nightmare portrait'. At one of the sittings, Scheffer tried to relieve the boredom by inviting an audience of sixty to hear Dickens read *The Cricket On The Hearth*. Not until March was Dickens able to write to Forster 'Scheffer finished yesterday... As a work of art I see in it spirit combined with perfect ease, and yet I don't see myself'. However, even then the interminable sittings were not over because Scheffer, himself, was not satisfied with the likeness. Dickens was proud of the painting's success at the Royal Academy, although gratified to feel he was not alone in his dissatisfaction with it. He wrote to his wife in Paris: 'It is in the best place in the largest room, but I find the *general* impression of the artists exactly mine. They almost all say that it wants something; that nobody could mistake whom it was meant for, but that it has something disappointing in it, etc., etc.... When you see Scheffer, tell him from me that Eastlake, in his speech at the dinner, referred to the portrait as "a contribution from a distinguished man of genius in France, worthy of himself and of his subject"'.

09
Wilhelm Auguste Rudolf Lehmann (1819–1905)
Charles Dickens
Dated 1861. Signed and dated *R. Lehmann del. London. May 20th 1861* and by the sitter *Charles Dickens*
Pencil. $6 \times 4\frac{1}{2}$
Lent by the Trustees of the British Museum

010 [85]
William Powell Frith, RA (1819–1909)
Charles Dickens in his study at Tavistock House
Signed and dated *W P Frith fecit 1859*
Oil. $27\frac{1}{2} \times 22$
F.P.7

This portrait was commissioned by John Forster in 1854, at about the same time as Dickens began to grow a moustache. It was not painted until five years later because Forster, who believed the moustache to be a 'fancy' which would pass, asked the artist to wait until 'the hideous disfigurement' (an opinion of the moustache shared by many of Dickens's friends) should be removed. When the moustache grew into a beard, Forster, alarmed lest whiskers might follow, gave the order for Frith to begin work, while there was still some of the face visible.

As a result of the growing use of photography along with the novelist's reluctance to sit, the number of painted portraits of Charles Dickens declined towards the end of his life. Frith availed himself of photography for this portrait; Dickens was photographed by Mr Watkins in the black velvet coat he wears in the painting; however, the artist found the photograph of no assistance. Dickens is shown seated in his study at Tavistock House, with the first pages of *A Tale of Two Cities* on the desk.

Forster was full of praise for the portrait. 'I never doubted your perfect success from the first moment I saw the canvas. The picture is, indeed, all I wished – more than I dared to hope – because I know what a ticklish thing a likeness is, and how portraits, otherwise admirable, fail often in that without which all other merits must fall short.' But the sitter was less enthusiastic. 'It has received every conceivable pains at Frith's hands, and ought on his account to be good. It is a little too much (to my thinking) as if my next door neighbour were my deadly foe, uninsured, and I had just received tidings of his house being afire; otherwise very good.'

011
Charles Dickens. C. 1852
Photograph by Henri Claudet
Lent by Dr Margaret Whinney

This is one of the last known representations of Dickens before he started growing a moustache in 1854.

012
Charles Dickens, writing. 1858 or '59
Photograph by John and Charles Watkins
Lent by The Dickens House

Despite his frequent protestations that it was torture for him to sit to photographers, Dickens was their subject many times.

013
Charles Dickens. C.1859
Photograph attributed to Herbert Watkins
Lent by The Dickens House

014
Charles Dickens, standing. 1859
Photograph by Herbert Watkins
Lent by The Dickens House

015 [81]
Charles Dickens seated. 1859
Photograph by Herbert Watkins
Lent by The Dickens House

016
Charles Dickens, seated. Three slightly varying poses. C.1860
Photographs by John and Charles Watkins
Lent by The Dickens House

Dickens was not always satisfied with his photographs. He wrote to John Watkins on 28 September 1861: 'A general howl of horror greeted the appearance of No. 18, and a riotous attempt was made to throw it out of window. I calmed the popular fury by promising that it should never again be beheld within these walls. I think I mentioned to you when you showed it to me, that I felt persuaded it would not be liked. It has a grim and wasted aspect, and perhaps might be made useful as a portrait of the Ancient Mariner'.

017
Caricature of Charles Dickens, 'From Whom We Have Great Expectations', 1861
Photograph

018
Letter from Charles Dickens to Mrs Richard Watson, 8 July 1861
Photograph of the original in the Henry E. Huntington Library, San Marino

Dickens refers in this letter to the recently published caricature 017: 'I hope you may have seen a large-headed photograph with little legs, representing the undersigned, pen in hand, tapping his forehead to knock an idea out. . . . It seems to me extraordinarily ludicrous, and much more like than the grave portraits done in earnest. It made me laugh when I first came upon it, until I shook again, in open sun-lighted Piccadilly'.

019
Charles Dickens. 1867
Photograph by J. Gurney & Son
Lent by The Dickens House

020 [86]
Charles Dickens, standing. Two similar poses. 1867
Photographs by J. Gurney & Son
Lent by The Dickens House

Several photographic houses vied with one another to obtain the exclusive rights to photograph Dickens during his second visit to America in 1867–68 (see Section M). J. Gurney and Son were chosen. After spending a tiring day posing for the photographs, which were probably taken by the son, Benjamin, Dickens swore he would never again sit for a photographer. Nevertheless, when the photographs were submitted to him, he declared that they were the best that had ever been taken of him.

021
Anonymous
Charles Dickens
After 1860
Miniature on card. Oval 4×3
Lent by H.C.D. Whinney Esq.

022
Dickens Souvenir Playing Cards (3)
Manufactured by Chas. Goodall and Son Ltd, London
Each inscribed with the facsimile signature of the sitter *Charles Dickens*
Colour lithographs. Each $3\frac{1}{2} \times 2\frac{1}{2}$
Lent by H.C.D. Whinney Esq.

These cards were issued to commemorate the centenary of the novelist's birth in 1912. They were lithographed after the miniature in Mr H.C.D. Whinney's possession (see 021)

023
William Ward Gallimore (worked 1858–81)
Bust of Charles Dickens
Probably made at the factory of William Henry Goss of Falcon Pottery, Stoke, Staffordshire
Signed *W. W. Gallimore*. Inscribed *published as the Act Directs (sec. 54, Geo III C.56) by Turner & Co. June 1870*
Biscuit porcelain (parian ware). $27\frac{1}{2}$ high
Lent by the Lady Lever Art Gallery, Port Sunlight, Liverpool

Gallimore worked with Goss from 1858 to 1863 when he went to Belleek in Ireland to help establish a new factory with a man named William Bromley. He returned to Goss in 1866, when he was made general manager until his retirement to the U.S.A. in 1881.

P: Dickens's friends

P1
Daniel Maclise, RA (1806–70)
William Harrison Ainsworth (1805–82)
Oil. $30\frac{1}{4} \times 25\frac{1}{8}$
Lent by the Walker Art Gallery, Liverpool

Harrison Ainsworth first saw Dickens in 1834 or '5, shortly after the publication of his successful novel, *Rookwood*, possibly at the *Chronicle* offices. At his home, Kensal Lodge, Ainsworth introduced him to his circle of friends, which included John Macrone, the original publisher of *Sketches by Boz*, and the illustrator, George Cruikshank. In the winter of 1836, through Ainsworth, Dickens met his lifelong friend John Forster; for about a year they formed the Cerberus Club, which consisted only of themselves. In 1839 Ainsworth succeeded Dickens as editor of *Bentley's Miscellany*. Later in life they drifted apart, Ainsworth declining into comparative obscurity.

P2
Letter from Ainsworth to the Rev. Alexander Dyce, 21 Dec [no year]
Dyce Collection

'... I have got together a little party in a great hurry to meet Dickens, and I am delighted to be able to include you among the number...'

P3
Edward Mathew Ward, RA (1816–79)
Daniel Maclise, RA (1806–70)
Signed and dated *E M Ward 1846*
Oil on panel. $18 \times 13\frac{7}{8}$
Lent by the National Portrait Gallery

Daniel Maclise was one of the earliest and closest friends of both Dickens and Forster, and took Ainsworth's place in the Cerberus Club. He was born in Cork, and came to London in 1827 to further his studies in art. Recognized as the outstanding young British painter of the 1830s and 1840s, he was handsome and had a most attractive personality.

P4 [8]
Daniel Maclise, RA (1806–70)
Girl at the waterfall at St. Nighton's Kieve, Cornwall
Signed and dated *D. Maclise, R.A., 1842*
Oil. $35\frac{1}{2} \times 24\frac{3}{4}$
F.P.22

This picture, which was exhibited in the Royal Academy in 1843, was a studio production painted from sketches made during the artist's holiday in Cornwall with Dickens, Forster and Clarkson Stanfield (see D 10). Miss Georgina Hogarth, Dickens's sister-in-law, posed for the figure. A note in the Department records that Mr B.S. Long, formerly Keeper of Paintings, saw her looking at the picture in the Museum, seventy years after it was painted. Dickens wished to buy the painting, but knew that the artist would either insist he should accept it as a gift or ask a ridiculous price for it. Dickens enlisted the help of Thomas Beard, who bought it for him, on the pretext that it was for an imaginary friend in Sussex. Maclise was absent through illness from the dénouement, when Dickens unveiled the picture at a party for his friends, but was rather indignant when he discovered the deception.

P5
Frank Stone, ARA (1800–59)
William Makepeace Thackeray (1811–63)
Painted c.1839
Oil. Oval, 24×20
Lent by the National Portrait Gallery

The paths of Thackeray and Dickens first crossed when the former applied to replace Seymour as illustrator to *Pickwick Papers*. Although Dickens considered his drawings quite unsuitable they became better acquainted at the Garrick Club, and in September 1837 Dickens published a story, *The Professor*, by Thackeray in *Bentley's Miscellany*. Their relations, friendly in the early 1840s, were later uneasy (see P6 for one example). They were reconciled only weeks before Thackeray's death.

P6
Artist unknown
Edmund Yates (1831–94)
Signed illegibly. Inscribed in pencil in capitals *Edm. Yates*
Water-colour. $10\frac{7}{8} \times 7\frac{3}{4}$
Lent by the National Portrait Gallery

Edmund Yates, journalist and contributor to *All The Year Round*, was one of the younger friends the novelist made in later life. Yates followed a sympathetic article on Dickens, at the time of his separation from his wife, in *Town Talk*, with a disparaging one on Thackeray. Thackeray claimed the material was taken from conversations at the Garrick Club and appealed to the Club's committee for protection of his privacy. Dickens, while agreeing that Yates's article was unfortunate, felt Thackeray's reply made an apology impossible; he resigned from the committee on hearing that Yates was to be brought before it. After a painful altercation, Yates's name was struck off the list of Club members.

P7
Edmund Yates
Mr. Thackeray, Mr. Yates, and the Garrick Club. The Correspondence and Facts
London, printed for private circulation, 1859
F.PAMPH.499

In this pamphlet, Yates states his version of the affair.

P8
Edward Hodges Baily, RA (1788–1867)
Douglas William Jerrold (1803–57)
Inscribed on the back of the base *E.H. Baily. R.A. Sculp. 1853*
Marble bust. $23\frac{7}{8}$ high
Lent by the National Portrait Gallery

Douglas Jerrold, playwright, contributor to *Punch*, where *Mrs. Caudle's Curtain Lectures* first appeared, and editor of several publications, probably met Dickens in the summer of 1838. They shared radical sympathies, and Dickens employed Jerrold as leader-writer on the *Daily News* in 1846. Jerrold took a lively part in Dickens's amateur theatricals, playing Master Stephen in *Every Man in His Humour*.

P9
Daniel Maclise, RA (1806–70)
Sir Thomas Noon Talfourd (1795–1854)
Pencil. $7\frac{1}{8} \times 6\frac{7}{8}$
F.P.87

Dickens reported the speeches of Talfourd, barrister (later Judge) and Whig Member of Parliament (1835–41, 1847–49) in the House and in the Law Courts. They met, perhaps through Forster, soon after Talfourd's introduction of the Copyright Bill into Parliament in 1837, and in recognition of this service to authors, Dickens dedicated *Pickwick Papers* to him. They saw each other constantly in the 1840s. Talfourd helped Dickens in negotiations with Bentley in 1838–39 and acted as his counsel in the case of the piracy of *A Christmas Carol* in 1844.
Talfourd was Lamb's literary executor, and was well known as an essayist and as a dramatist. His plays were produced by Macready.

P10
Thomas Noon Talfourd
Manuscript: 'Sonnet to Charles Dickens Esq. on reading the completed "Oliver Twist" … 16 February 1839'
Bound, with two other MS sonnets in a copy of Talfourd's *Ion*, London, Edward Moxon, 1837, with *The Athenian Captive*, London, Edward Moxon, 1838
F.PB.8627

P11
Daniel Maclise, RA (1806–70)
James Henry Leigh Hunt (1784–1859)
Pencil. $7\frac{5}{8} \times 5\frac{1}{4}$
F.P.88

Although Dickens was well acquainted with Leigh Hunt's work, they may not have met until the summer of 1838, the introduction being made by Forster, a close friend of Hunt's. In 1847 Dickens's amateur theatrical company gave benefit performances of *Every Man in His Humour* in Manchester and Liverpool in order to alleviate Hunt's financial difficulties. He contributed to *Household Words*. Harold Skimpole in *Bleak House* is certainly based on him; however, after his death, Dickens in *All The Year Round* categorically denied that Hunt's character had suggested the most unpleasant features in the portrait. 'In the midst of the sorest temptations he maintained his honesty unblemished by a single stain. He was in all public and private transactions the very soul of truth and honour.'

P 12
Phiz (Hablôt K. Browne) (1815–82)
'Coavinses'. Illustration to *Bleak House*
Etching. 4¾ × 4½

The central figure is Harold Skimpole. Dickens wrote to Forster: 'Browne has done Skimpole, and helped to make him singularly unlike the great original'.

P 13
Daniel Maclise, RA (1806–70)
Samuel Laman Blanchard (1804–45)
Pencil. 5¼ × 4¾
F.P.87

Blanchard, essayist, verse-writer and journalist, was a staunch Liberal who edited a succession of newspapers and contributed to the *Examiner* and other periodicals. He was a friend of Dickens by 1838, and present at the reading of *The Chimes* (H 10).

P 14
Clarkson Stanfield, RA (1793/4–1867)
Carte-de-visite photograph, 1864, by John and Charles Watkins
553–1885

Clarkson Stanfield, marine and landscape painter, met Dickens in December 1837, through their mutual interest in the theatre. They were always close friends. Stanfield painted the scenery for four of Dickens's amateur theatrical productions: *Every Man in his Humour, Not So Bad As We Seem, The Lighthouse*, and *The Frozen Deep*. He also contributed illustrations to four of the Christmas Books: *The Chimes, The Cricket on the Hearth, The Battle of Life* and *The Haunted Man*. *Little Dorrit* is dedicated to him, and Dickens wrote his obituary in *All The Year Round*.

P 15
After Alfred-Edward Chalon
(1780–1860)
Marguerite, Countess of Blessington (1789–1849)
Water-colour. 6 × 6½
Painted c.1836
Lent by the National Portrait Gallery

Dickens was probably first introduced to Gore House by Forster about 1839, and was a frequent visitor in the 1840s. A wide variety of well-known men in London, including Disraeli, Captain Marryat, Albany Fonblanque, Barry Cornwall, Sir Martin Archer Shee, Louis Napoleon, and the Lords Durham, Abinger, Strangford and Lyndhurst, were to be met in the relaxed atmosphere of the Countess's salon, but few women entered her house on account of her close friendship with Alfred, Count D'Orsay, whose wife was still alive. Dickens admired his hostess, writing of her in 1842: 'Lady Blessington wears brilliantly, and has the gloss upon her yet'. He contributed to one of her annuals, and at his request, and on her own terms, she wrote social gossip for the *Daily News* for a few months in 1846.

P 16
Alfred Guillaume Gabriel Count D'Orsay
(1801–52)
Self-portrait
Marble bust. 32½ high
Lent by Lady Galway

Dickens met Count D'Orsay, who became godfather to his sixth child, at Gore House (see P 15). He had moved to London in 1831 with Lady Blessington and his wife, Harriet, her daughter. Later that year his wife left him, causing scandalous rumours that he was Lady Blessington's lover and had only married Harriet as a cover. A formal separation followed in 1838. The strikingly handsome Count D'Orsay, whom Carlyle humorously alluded to as the 'Phoebus Apollo of Dandyism' lived a brilliant social life from 1832 to 1841. He also had friends outside the fashionable world, such as Dickens, Forster and Macready. In 1840 to '41, when his creditors, finding he had overspent his marriage settlement, closed in on him, he began to use his artistic talent seriously, making portrait-drawings and busts. Late in 1841 he drew two portraits of Dickens. He was not satisfied with the first but had the second reproduced by lithography. A year later he drew a third portrait. The two later drawings are now in the Suzannet Collection. On the Count's death Dickens wrote his obituary in *Household Words*.

P 17
Sir William Boxall, RA (1800–79)
Walter Savage Landor (1775–1864)
Exhibited at the Royal Academy in 1853
Oil on panel. 23½ × 17½
F.P.3

Dickens described Landor as 'like forty lions concentrated in one poet'. They met at Gore House in 1840, and with a friendship based on respect for one another's work remained close until the older man's death. Landor was godfather to Dickens's fourth child. The poet reacted with great emotion to Dickens's novels, writing as early as April 1839 that he 'has drawn from me more tears and more smiles than are remaining to me for all the rest of the world, real or ideal'. The story of Little Nell was conceived one evening in 1840 while Dickens and Forster were staying with him at 35, St James Square, Bath. Later Landor claimed he regretted nothing so much as his having failed to buy 'that house . . . and then and there to have burnt it to the ground . . . that no meaner association should ever desecrate the birthplace of Nell'.

Lawrence Boythorn in *Bleak House* was based on Landor and was in the novelist's words 'a most exact portrait'.

P18
Enlarged photograph of a facsimile of a letter from Landor to Forster [31 January 1849]

'My dear Forster, My thanks were not spoken to you and Dickens for your journey of two hundred miles upon my birthday. Here they are – not visible on the surface of the paper nor on any surface whatever, but in the heart that is dictating this letter.

On the night you left me I wrote the following, which you may insert or not in the Examiner.
    Ever affectionately yrs

Dying speech of an old philosopher.
    I strove wth none, for none was worth my strife:
    Nature I loved, and, next to Nature, Art:
    I warm'd both hands before the fire of Life;
    It sinks; and I am ready to depart.

    Walter Savage Landor'

The facsimile is used in Forster's biography of Landor (1869).

P19
Frank Stone, ARA (1800–59)
Samuel Rogers (1763–1855), the Hon. Caroline Norton (1808–77) and the niece of the poet, Mrs Phipps
Painted c.1845
Oil. $24\frac{1}{2} \times 29\frac{3}{8}$
Lent by the National Portrait Gallery

Dickens had met Samuel Rogers by August 1838 and was invited to the select literary breakfasts at his home, crammed full with art treasures and beautifully bound books. His guests included the Carlyles, Thomas Macaulay, Lady Blessington and Mrs Norton. Rogers was particularly fond of Dickens's wife, Catherine. Dickens dedicated *Master Humphrey's Clock* to him. In 1836 Dickens reported for the *Morning Chronicle* the case of Norton v. Melbourne, in which scandalous evidence, resting on nothing but the spiteful tattle of discharged servants, was advanced to show that Caroline Norton had been his mistress; some features of Bardell v. Pickwick recall the case. After the failure of the action against Melbourne the Nortons separated and Mrs Norton supported herself by the earnings from her poems, novels and editorship of annuals; one of her controversial pamphlets, *English Laws for Women in the Nineteenth Century*, 1854, took as its text Dickens's 'It won't do to have truth and justice on our side: we must have law and lawyers'. Her beauty and wit made her a welcome guest in many circles, including Holland House. Dickens first met her in 1837. She contributed two poems to *Household Words*.

P20
Frank Stone, ARA (1800–59)
Self-portrait
Oil. 30×24
Lent by the City Art Gallery, Manchester

Dickens met Frank Stone at the Shakespeare Club in 1839; the artist took part in productions of *Every Man in His Humour*, *Not So Bad As We Seem* and *Mr. Nightingale's Diary*. He also contributed three illustrations to *The Haunted Man*.

P21
After Joseph Kenny Meadows (1790–1874)
Dr John Elliotson (1791–1868)
Lithograph by R. Martin, coloured by hand.
$7\frac{1}{4} \times 4\frac{1}{8}$
Lent by the National Portrait Gallery

Dr John Elliotson was Professor of the Practice of Medicine at London University from 1831 to 1838, when he resigned after attacks on his practice of mesmerism in the *Lancet*. He was the first President of the Phrenological Society. Dickens became interested in mesmerism on meeting Elliotson in about 1838 and practised it on his wife and friends with some success. In 1849 he magnetized John Leech into mesmeric slumber at Bonchurch, when the artist was feverish after being knocked down by a wave. 'I talked to the astounded little Mrs. Leech across him, when he was asleep, as if he had been a truss of hay . . . What do you think of my setting up in the magnetic line, with a large brass plate ? "Terms twenty-five guineas per nap"!'

P 22
The Rev. Chauncy Hare Townshend
The Three Gates. In verse
London, Chapman and Hall, 1859

2nd edition. London, Chapman and Hall, 1861

Another copy. With an engraved portrait as frontispiece.
F.PB.8934–5

P 23
Religious Opinions of the late Rev. C.H. Townshend. Published as directed in his Will, by his Literary Executor (i.e. **Charles Dickens**)
Chapman and Hall, 1869
F.PB.8936

Dickens met Townshend (1798–1868) the author of a small book *Facts of Mesmerism*, 1840, while dining with Dr John Elliotson. Egg, Wilkie Collins and Dickens were his guests at Lausanne during their European tour of 1853. In his will Townshend appointed Dickens his literary executor with directions to publish his *Religious Opinions*. Although privately Dickens regarded his notes as 'Religious Hiccoughs' he faithfully edited them, and they were published a year after their author's death.

He bequeathed his important collection of modern paintings and gem stones to the Victoria and Albert Museum.

P 24
George Frederick Watts, OM, RA (1817–1904)
Lady Augusta Mary Holland (1812–89)
Exhibited at the Royal Academy in 1848
Oil. $31\frac{3}{4} \times 25$
Lent by Her Majesty the Queen

One result of Dickens's literary success was that Lady Holland, the famous Whig hostess, having assured herself that 'Boz' was presentable, invited him to dine. She found him 'modest and well-behaved' and Lord Holland considered him 'very unobtrusive, yet not shy, intelligent in countenance and altogether prepossessing'. After surviving the initial ordeal of the introduction, performed by Talfourd on 12 August 1838, Dickens grew to like and understand the dictatorial Lady Holland, and to enjoy the dinner parties at Holland House.

P 25
Benjamin William Crombie (1803–47)
Lord Francis Jeffrey (1773–1850)
Signed *BW Crombie*. Dated *1837*
Lithograph. $10 \times 5\frac{1}{2}$
Lent by the National Portrait Gallery

Lord Jeffrey, a founder of the *Edinburgh Review*, but long retired from its editorship, was already an admirer of Dickens's work when he met him in 1839; for his praise of *The Old Curiosity Shop*, see F 5. Dickens visited him at his home at Craigcrook on the Scottish tour of 1841, and they met regularly during Jeffrey's annual visits to London. Jeffrey frequently sent comments to Dickens about his novels as they appeared in monthly numbers; one such comment on *Dombey and Son* may have influenced the subsequent course of the story. He was godfather to Dickens's fifth child.

P 26
William Powell Frith, RA (1819–1909)
Portrait of the Artist at Work in His Studio
Painted in 1867
Oil. $24 \times 18\frac{1}{4}$
Lent by the National Portrait Gallery

Dickens met Frith for the first time in 1842 when he called to see the two paintings (see F 18) he had commissioned from the artist, who was at that time little known. In his *Autobiography* Frith recalled his first impression of the novelist: 'a pale young man with long hair, a white hat, a formidable stick in his left hand, and his right extended to me with a frank cordiality, and a friendly clasp, that never relaxed until the day of his untimely death'. Sixteen years later Frith, his reputation now firmly established, painted Dickens's portrait (see O 10).

P 27
After William Powell Frith, RA (1819–1909)
Derby Day
Signed in pencil *W.P. Frith* and by the engraver, *Aug. Blanchard*
Engraving. $19\frac{5}{8} \times 43\frac{1}{2}$
E.560–1969

Many of the features of Derby Day depicted in the painting – for example, the pickpockets, fortune-tellers, thimble-riggers and tumblers, and the hampers from Fortnum and Mason – are also described in an article on 'Epsom' written by W. H. Wills with assistance from Dickens, and published in *Household Words* on 7 June 1851.

The scene in the right hand corner is remarkably similar to an incident when Little Nell and her Grandfather were at the races with Tom Codlin and Short, in chapter 19 of *The Old Curiosity Shop*: 'The child bore upon her arm the little basket with her flowers, and sometimes stopped, with timid and modest looks, to offer them at some gay carriage, but alas! there were many bolder beggars there, gipsies who promised husbands, and other adepts in their trade.... There was but one lady who seemed to understand the child, and she was one who sat alone in a handsome carriage.... She motioned away a gipsy-woman urgent to tell her fortune, saying that it was told already and had been for some years, but called the child towards her, and taking her flowers put money into her trembling hand, and bade her go home and keep at home for God's sake'.

P 28
William Powell Frith, RA (1819–1909)
Sketch for the central section of 'Derby Day'
Signed and dated 1858
Oil. $11\frac{1}{2} \times 17\frac{1}{2}$
Bethnal Green Museum (Dixon Bequest)

P 29
Group photograph including portraits of the following: Marcus Stone, Mark Lemon, Augustus Egg, Charles Dickens Jun., Kate Dickens, Georgina Hogarth, Mary Dickens, Wilkie Collins and Charles Dickens. 1857
Lent by The Dickens House

P 30
Hans Christian Andersen
A Christmas Greeting to my English Friends
London, Richard Bentley, 1847
F.PB.159

P 31
Hans Christian Andersen
Danish Fairy Legends and Tales
2nd ed. London, Abbey & Co., 1852
With a lithographed portrait of the author as frontispiece
F.PB.160

'How much I should like to shake the hand of Boz, when I read his books I often think I have seen such things and I feel I could write like that,' wrote Andersen, before he visited England in 1847. Dickens was equally eager to meet the Danish fairy-tale teller, and, after their first meeting at Gore House, presented him with a set of his books. In 1857, after angling for an invitation, the Dane came to stay at the Dickens's new home, Gad's Hill, invited for two weeks but staying for five. The almost childish Andersen loved everything about the Dickenses. Charles was the greatest author in the world, Catherine, who took him to hear Handel's *Messiah* at the Crystal Palace, and to see the great Italian actress Ristori in the part of Lady Macbeth, was charming with her 'china blue eyes' and 'womanly repose'; the children were delightful.

During these summer weeks Andersen was quite unaware that he was overstaying his welcome, and was considered a 'bony bore' by Dickens's daughters, or that there was any strain in the relationship between Mr and Mrs Dickens.

P 32 [42]
Charles Allston Collins (1828–73)
William Wilkie Collins (1824–89)
Signed with monogram and dated 1853
Oil on panel. Arched top, $11\frac{5}{8} \times 9\frac{1}{8}$
Lent by the Fitzwilliam Museum, Cambridge

Wilkie Collins played the valet in Dickens's production of *Not So Bad As We Seem* in 1851, and with Dickens's help wrote two plays for the company: *The Lighthouse* and *The Frozen Deep*. A genial association developed between them. They spent several holidays together, once abroad (see note to P 34), and in Cumberland collaborating on *The Lazy Tour of Two Idle Apprentices*, a record of their adventures published in *Household Words*. In 1860 they collected material in Devon for 'A Message from the Sea' published in the Christmas number of *All the Year Round*. They also collaborated in 1867 on *No Thoroughfare*, which Collins afterwards dramatized for Fechter. In 1862, when Collins was ill, Dickens offered to help him complete *No Name*, then running as a serial.

The painter of this portrait, Wilkie Collins's brother, married Kate, Dickens's third child, in 1860.

P 33
Augustus Leopold Egg, RA (1816–63)
Photograph
Lent by the National Portrait Gallery

Egg designed the costumes for Dickens's second production of *Every Man in His Humour* in 1847 and took part in *The Lighthouse*. He made a sketch of Georgina Hogarth, Dickens's sister-in-law, who refused his proposal of marriage. (See P 42.)

P 34
Augustus Leopold Egg, RA (1816–63)
The Travelling Companions
Signed *Augustus Egg, R.A.*
Oil. $25\frac{3}{8} \times 30\frac{1}{8}$
Lent by the City Art Gallery, Birmingham

Egg, Wilkie Collins and Dickens spent two months in Autumn 1853 travelling together in Switzerland and Italy. Dickens was greatly amused by the way his companions conversed on art. 'To hear Collins learnedly holding forth to Egg (who has as little of that gammon as an artist *can* have) about reds, and greens, and things "coming well" with other things, and lines being wrong, and lines being right, is far beyond the bounds of all caricature.'

This picture was almost certainly painted in 1862, when the artist was travelling in Southern Europe and North Africa for reasons of health. The view is the coast near Mentone.

Note: the letter quoted is exhibited at [P 35].

P 35
Letter from Charles Dickens to Catherine Dickens, 21 November 1853
Lent by the Trustees of the British Museum

In this letter, written from Florence, Dickens describes the progress of his holiday with Collins and Egg. Besides lamenting foreign food and foreign hotels, he describes his companions in a highly amusing style. A passage on Collins as an art critic is quoted in the note to P 34. Dickens also remarks that 'Collins's moustache is gradually developing. You remember how the corners of his mouth go down, and how he looks through his spectacles and manages his legs. I don't know how it is, but the moustache is a horrible aggravation of all this ... He occasionally expounds a code of morals, taken from modern French novels, which I instantly and with becoming gravity smash'.

P 36
George Augustus Henry Sala (1828–96)
Photograph. c.1865
Lent by the National Portrait Gallery

Sala made his name as a journalist with his weekly contributions to *Household Words*, from 1851 to 1856. At the close of the Crimean War, Dickens sent him to Russia to write descriptive articles, which, because of Dickens's refusal to permit them to be published in volume form, were the cause of a temporary rift between them. In 1858 they were reconciled; Sala renewed his connection with *Household Words* and his articles on Russia were issued separately as *A Journey Due North*. He also contributed frequently to *All The Year Round*. Sala wrote one of the best obituary notices of Dickens for the *Daily Telegraph*, and afterwards expanded it in book form.

P 37
John Forster
The Life of Charles Dickens
Vol. I. London, Chapman and Hall, 1872
L.491–1970

This was G.A. Sala's copy of the book. On the title-page he has recorded his unfavourable and hostile judgement of it, and of its author. He was not the only friend of Dickens's later life who decried Forster's biography: Wilkie Collins, following G.H. Lewes, referred to it as 'the life of Forster with notices of Dickens'. In 1836 Sala was eight years old, and if, as he claims in a note on the title-page, he knew Dickens then, it was perhaps because his mother, an actress and singer, was working at the time at the St James's Theatre, where Dickens's early burlettas were performed.

P 38
Percy Hetherington Fitzgerald (1834–1925)
Photograph
Lent by the National Portrait Gallery

Dickens hoped that his eldest daughter Mary might marry Percy Fitzgerald, one of his 'bright young men' writing for *Household Words*. Mary, however, did not share his high opinion of Fitzgerald. In 1865 Fitzgerald gave Dickens an Irish bloodhound named Sultan.

After the author's death Fitzgerald wrote a number of works on Dickens including several on *Pickwick Papers*.

AMERICAN FRIENDS

P 39
Samuel Laurence (1812–84)
Henry Wadsworth Longfellow (1807–82)
Lettered *Published May 16, 1855, by George Routledge and Co. Farringdon Street, London*
Stipple engraving. $5 \times 3\frac{1}{2}$
F.P.113

A warm friendship sprang up immediately between Longfellow and Dickens; only four days after their first meeting at Harvard, Longfellow and Charles

Sumner took him for a long Sunday walk around Boston. Later in 1842 Longfellow stayed with him in London, meeting his friends and visiting theatres, and also being shown round the resorts of thieves and tramps. On Dickens's second visit to America they dined together on Thanksgiving Day. Longfellow, full of enthusiasm for his readings, found him as 'elastic and quick' as ever. On his death, the American wrote movingly to Forster: 'Dickens was so full of life that it does not seem possible he could die . . . I never knew an author's death to cause such general mourning. It is no exaggeration to say that this whole country is stricken with grief'.

P 40
After Gilbert Stuart Newton (1794–1835)
Washington Irving (1783–1859)
Engraved by George Parker for the *New York Mirror*, 1837. $10\frac{1}{2} \times 7\frac{1}{4}$
Lent by the National Portrait Gallery

Dickens admired Irving's work and, before they met on Dickens's first visit to America, Irving wrote to him with enthusiasm about his novels and encouraged him to visit the United States. During the three weeks Dickens spent in New York, he saw Irving, who presided at the Dickens Dinner held at the City Hotel, almost daily and visited his home Sunnyside in Tarrytown. The American 'wept heartily' when they parted after a meeting in Washington, not realizing they would meet again in Baltimore to sit long into the night drinking mint julep together. 'Washington Irving is a *great* fellow, we have laughed together most heartily.'

P 41
Cornelius C. Felton
Greece, Ancient and Modern. Lectures delivered before the Lowell Institute
Boston, Ticknor and Fields, 1867
Showing an engraved portrait of Cornelius Felton after H. Wright Smith
F.PB.2993

Cornelius Felton (1807–62), classical scholar and Professor of Greek at Harvard University, claimed to have been convinced of Dickens's genius since the publication of the first number of *Pickwick*. On Dickens's first visit to the U.S.A. he became his closest American friend. 'They have walked, laughed, talked, eaten oysters and drunk champagne together until they have almost grown together . . .'

wrote Sam Ward to Longfellow. Felton considered *American Notes* 'a capital book; lively, spirited, true and good humoured'. In May 1853 he visited Dickens in England. On Felton's death Dickens wrote to Forster, 'Poor dear Felton! It is 20 years since I told you of the delight my first knowledge of him gave me . . . and it is as strongly upon me to this hour . . .'

P 42
Letter from Dickens to Miss Burdett Coutts, 25 October 1853
Lent by the Pierpont Morgan Library, New York

After describing his journey to Italy with Wilkie Collins and Augustus Egg, Dickens writes of Egg's proposal of marriage to Georgina Hogarth. 'It would have been a good thing for her . . . But she said No, though they are very good friends. I took no other part in the matter than urging her to be quite sure that she knew her own mind. He is very far her inferior intellectually; but five men would be out of six, for she has one of the most remarkable capacities I have ever known. Not to mention her being one of the most amiable and affectionate of girls. Whether it is, or is not a pity that she is all she is to me and mine instead of brightening up a good little man's house where she would still have the artist kind of life she is used to, about her, is a knotty point I never can settle to my satisfaction.'

NOTES

NOTES

The Plates

1 (*left*) 16 Bayham Street, Camden Town (A 8)

2 (*below*) G. Harley and D. Dighton: Hungerford Stairs (A 13)

3 S. Laurence: Charles Dickens 1837 (02)

4 S. Laurence: Catherine Dickens 1838 (B 14)

5 G. Richmond: Charles Dickens junior (B25)

6 D. Maclise: Dickens's four elder children (E9)

7 (*left*) After J. E. Millais: The Black Brunswicker (with Kate Dickens) (B 28)

8 (*below*) D. Maclise: Girl at the Waterfall (Georgina Hogarth) (P 4)

9 (*right*) Mrs J. Barrow: Charles Dickens 1830 (B 6)

10 (*right*) Mrs J. Barrow: Frederick Dickens (B 7)

11 (*left*) D. Maclise: Dickens, his wife and Georgina Hogarth (o 7)

12 (*below*) D. Maclise: Dickens reading *The Chimes* to his friends (H 10)

13 (*above*) Phiz: 'Traddles makes a figure in Parliament and I report him', illustration for *David Copperfield* (B 3)

14 (*below*) Shorthand notes written by Dickens, *c.* 1850–60 (B 4: reduced)

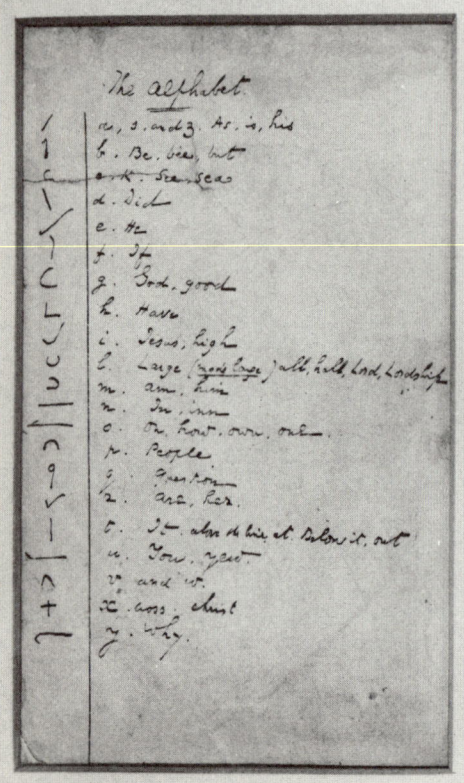

15 Advertising leaflet for *Bentley's Miscellany* (J 2)

Extraordinary Gazette.

SPEECH OF HIS MIGHTINESS

ON OPENING THE SECOND NUMBER

OF

BENTLEY'S MISCELLANY,

EDITED BY "BOZ."

On Wednesday, the first of February, "the House" (of Bentley) met for the despatch of business, in pursuance of the Proclamation inserted by authority in all the Morning, Evening, and Weekly Papers, appointing that day for the publication of the Second Number of the Miscellany, edited by "Boz."

16 (*left*) Anonymous: George Cruikshank (C9)

17 (*below*) G. Cruikshank: Drawing for 'Fagin in the Condemned Cell' in *Oliver Twist* (C67)

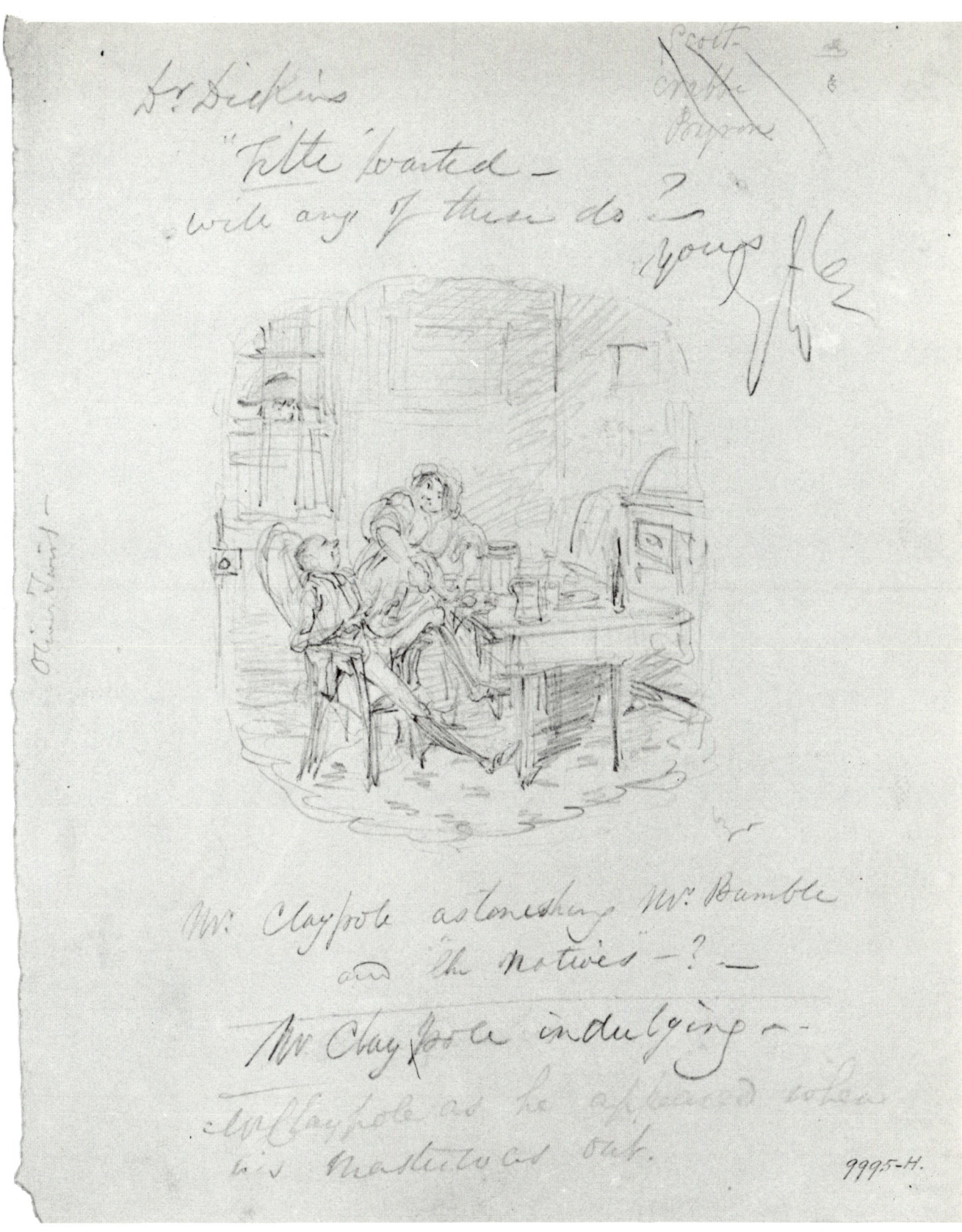

18 G. Cruikshank: Drawing for 'Mr. Claypole as he appeared when his master was out' in *Oliver Twist* (C63)

19 (*above left*) G. Cruikshank: Drawing for 'Mr. Bumble degraded in the eyes of the paupers' in *Oliver Twist* (C64: reduced)

20 (*above right*) G. Cruikshank: Drawing for 'The Burglary' in *Oliver Twist* (C62)

21 (*below right*) G. Cruikshank: Drawing for 'The Bloomsbury Christening' in *Sketches by Boz* (C13: reduced)

22 G. Cruikshank: Drawing for 'The Parish Engine' in *Sketches by Boz* (C20)

23 (*right*) R. Seymour: 'Enjoying Christmas' (C 42)

24 (*below*) Phiz: Drawing for 'Meekness of Mr. Pecksniff and his charming daughters' in *Martin Chuzzlewit* (F 31)

25 (*left*) Phiz: 'First appearance of Mr. Samuel Weller', illustration for *Pickwick Papers* (C 53)

26 (*below*) Phiz: Drawing for 'Major Bagstock is delighted to have that opportunity' in *Dombey and Son* (I 15)

27 (*below & right*) D. Maclise: Two sketches of John Forster (D 7)

28 (*below*) Facetious account by Dickens of Forster ballooning (D 6)

29 E. M. Ward and E. N. Downard: John Forster (D 15)

"thy precaution against fire, she had stationed in a basin on the floor, where it was glimmering away, like a gigantic lighthouse in a particularly small piece of water."

Mrs. Bardell faints in Mr. Pickwick's arms.

"'Oh, you kind, good, playful dear,' said Mrs. Bardell, and without more ado she rose from her chair and flung her arms round Mr. Pickwick's neck, with a cataract of tears and a chorus of sobs. 'Bless my soul!' cried the astonished Mr. Pickwick. 'Mrs. Bardell, my good woman—dear me—what a situation—pray consider—Mrs. Bardell, don't—if any body should come!—' —'Oh! let them come,' exclaimed Mrs. Bardell, frantically; 'I'll never leave you—dear, kind, good soul.' And with these words, Mrs. Bardell clung the tighter. 'Mercy upon me,' said Mr. Pickwick, struggling violently; 'I hear somebody coming up the stairs. Don't—don't, there's a good creature, don't.' But entreaty and remonstrance were alike unavailing; for Mrs. Bardell had fainted in Mr. Pickwick's arms; and before he could gain time to deposit her in a chair, Master Bardell entered the room, urshering in Mr. Tupman, Mr. Winkle and Mr. Snodgrass."

Mrs. Bardell Encounters Mr. Pickwick in the Prison.

"'His extravagance, Mr. Nickleby,' said Madame Mantilini in addressing herself to Ralph, who leant against his easy chair, with his hands behind him, and regarded the amiable couple with a smile of the supremest and most unmitigated contempt,—'His extravagance is beyond all bounds.' 'I have made up my mind to allowance him, and I say that if he has a hundred and twenty pounds a year for his clothes and pocket money, he may consider himself a very fortunate man.'
'Mr. Mantilini waited with much decorum to hear the amount of the proposed stipend, but when it reached his ears he cast his hat and cane upon the floor, and drawing out his pocket handkerchief, gave vent to his feelings in a dismal moan.'

Oliver Twist at Mr. Maylie's Door.

Mr. Giles held fast by the tinker's arm, (to prevent his running away, as he pleasantly said,) and gave the word of command to open the door. Brittles obeyed, and the group peeping timorously over each other's shoulders, beheld no more formidable object than poor little Oliver Twist, speechless and exhausted, who raised his heavy eyes and mutely solicited their compassion.

Little Nell and her Grandfather, the Military Gentleman and Mrs. Slum's Unexpected Appearance.

30 *Extra Boz Herald*, showing tableaux from Dickens's works (E 7)

31 J. W. Barber and O'Brien: the Tontine Hotel (E 15)

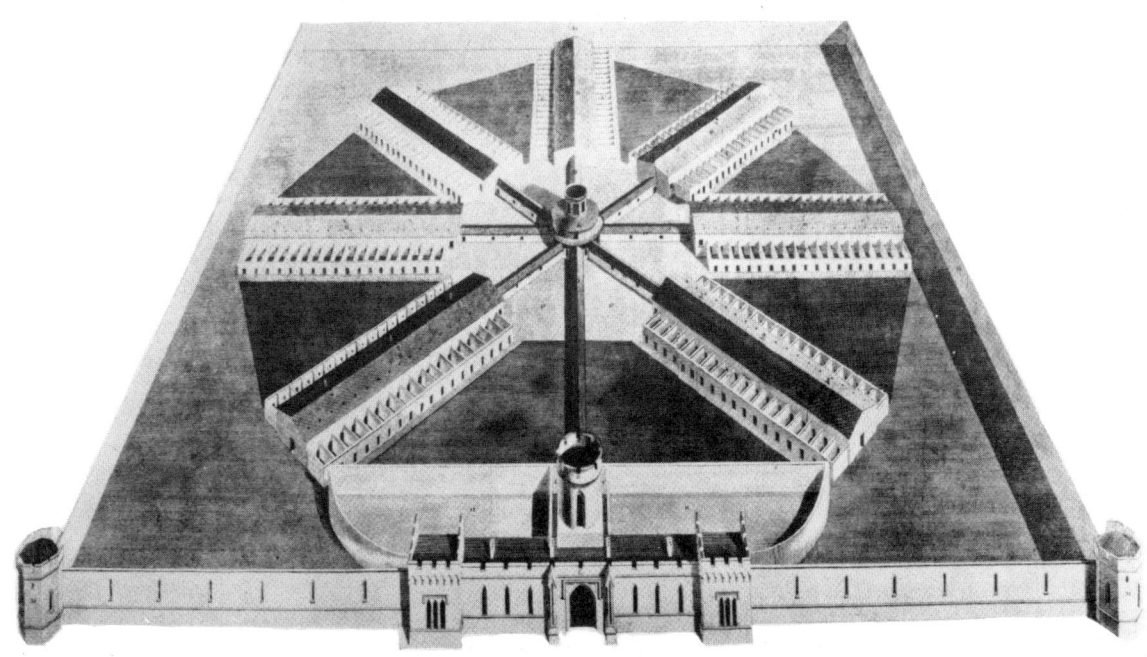

32 After John Haviland: Eastern Penitentiary, Philadelphia (E 12)

33 C. Stanfield: S.S. Britannia (E 10)

34 T. Creswick: Mount Tom and the Connecticut River (E 11)

35 After W. H. Bartlett: Niagara Falls (E 14)

36 A. Egg: Dickens in *Used Up* (G 43)

37 After C. R. Leslie: Dickens in *Every Man in his Humour* (G 13)

38 (*left*) D. Maclise: Macready as Werner (G 69)

39 (*below*) D. Maclise: Forster in *Every Man in his Humour* (G 15)

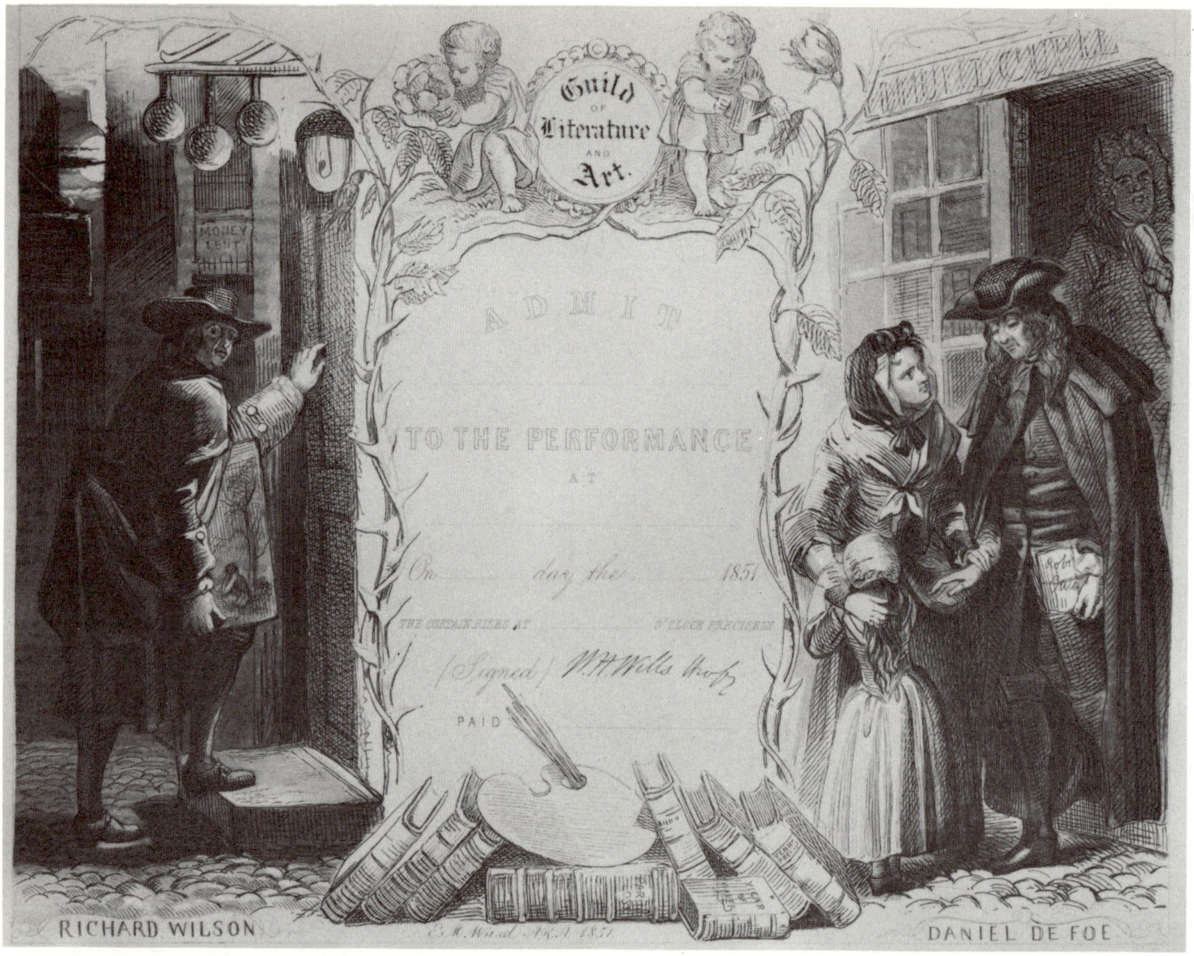
Guild of Literature and Art.
MONEY LENT
ADMIT
TO THE PERFORMANCE
AT
On day the 1851
(Signed) W.H. Wells
PAID
RICHARD WILSON
E. M. Ward A.R.A. 1851
DANIEL DE FOE

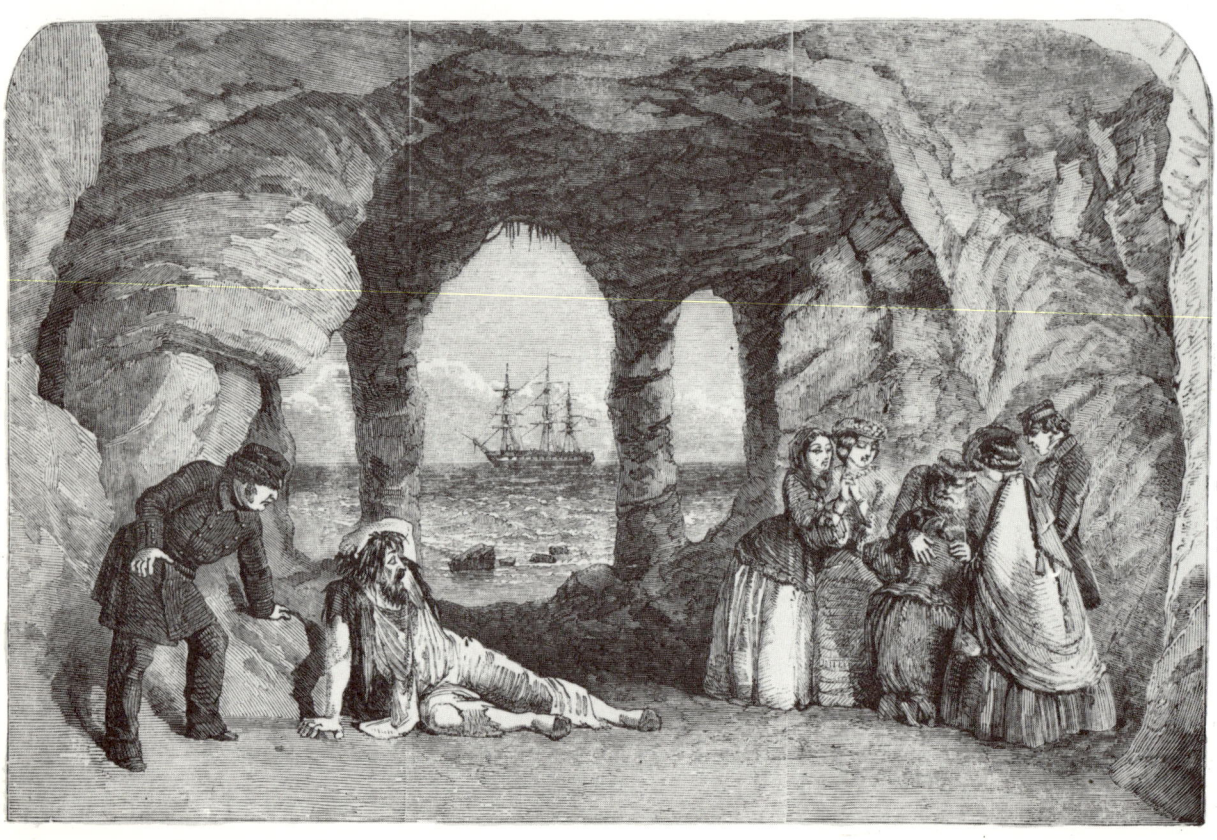

40 (*above left*) Admission ticket to the amateur performances 1851 (G 48)

41 (*below left*) Scene in *The Frozen Deep*, from the *Illustrated London News* (M 1)

42 (*below*) C. A. Collins: Wilkie Collins (P 32)

43 (*below*) W. P. Frith: Dolly Varden (F 18)

44 (*above right*) R. B. Martineau: Kit's Writing Lesson (F 9)

45 (*below right*) G. Cattermole: The Grave of Little Nell (F 8)

46 (*left*) W. M. Egley: Florence Dombey (I 12)

47 (*above right*) Letter from Maclise to Forster on the death of Dickens's raven (F 23)

48 (*below right*) D. Maclise: Drawing for 'The Tower of the Chimes' (H 8)

49 C. Stanfield: The Logan Rock (D 10)

50 W. P. Frith: Life at the Seaside (F 44)

51 Cartoon from *Diogenes* (I 25)

52 Phiz: 'The appointed time', illustration for *Bleak House* (I 19)

53 Illustration from G. Godwin, *London Shadows* (I 23)

54 Phiz: 'Mr. Guppy's entertainment', illustration for *Bleak House* (I 28)

55 Phiz: 'Tom-all-Alone's', illustration for *Bleak House* (I 28)

56 Playbill for Powell's Circus Royal (I 39)

57 H. Cole: Records in the Old Record Office (I 21)

58 A. F. Tait: Stockport Viaduct (I 34)

59 Overcrowding, illustration from *Sanatory Progress* (I 62)

60 Enon-Chapel Cemetery and Dancing Saloon, illustration from *Sanatory Progress* (I 66)

61 G. Doré: Drawing for an illustration to Hood's *Bridge of Sighs* (I 55)

was slowly opened, and the Dodger and Charley Bates entered and closed it behind them. "Where's Oliver you young hounds?" said the famous Jew, rising with a menacing look; "where's the boy?"

The young thieves eyed him, as if they were alarmed at his violence, and looked uneasily at each other, but made no reply. "What's become of the boy?" said the Jew seizing the Dodger tightly by the arm, and threatening him with horrid imprecations. "Speak out damn you, or I'll throttle you."

Mr Fagin looked so very much in earnest that Charley Bates who deemed it prudent in all cases to be on the safe side, and thought it might considered it by no means improbable that it might be his turn to be throttled second, dropped upon his knees and raised a loud, well-sustained, and continuous roar, something caused him to desist. He then pointed to the body, with an enquiring look.

"There's blood upon him". said Barnaby with a shudder. "It makes me sick."

"How came it there?" demanded Vardon.

"Steel, steel, steel!" replied the idiot fiercely, imitating with his hand the thrust of a sword.

"Is he robbed?" said the locksmith.

Barnaby caught him by the arm, and nodded "Yes"; then pointed towards the city.

"Oh!" said the old man, bending over the body and looking round as he spoke into Barnaby's pale face, strangely lighted up by something which was not intellect. "The robber made off that way, did he? Well well, never mind that just now. Hold your torch this way — a little further off — so. Now stand quiet while I try to see what harm is done."

With these words, he applied himself to a closer examination of the prostrate form, while Barnaby, holding the torch as he had been directed, looked on in silence; fascinated by interest or curiosity, but repelled nevertheless by some strong and secret horror which convulsed him in every nerve. As he stood at that moment, half shrinking back and half bending forward, both his face and figure were full in the strong glare of the link, and as distinctly revealed as though it had been broad day. He was about

63 Manuscript of *Barnaby Rudge* (K 2)

64 Manuscript of *The Chimes* (K3)

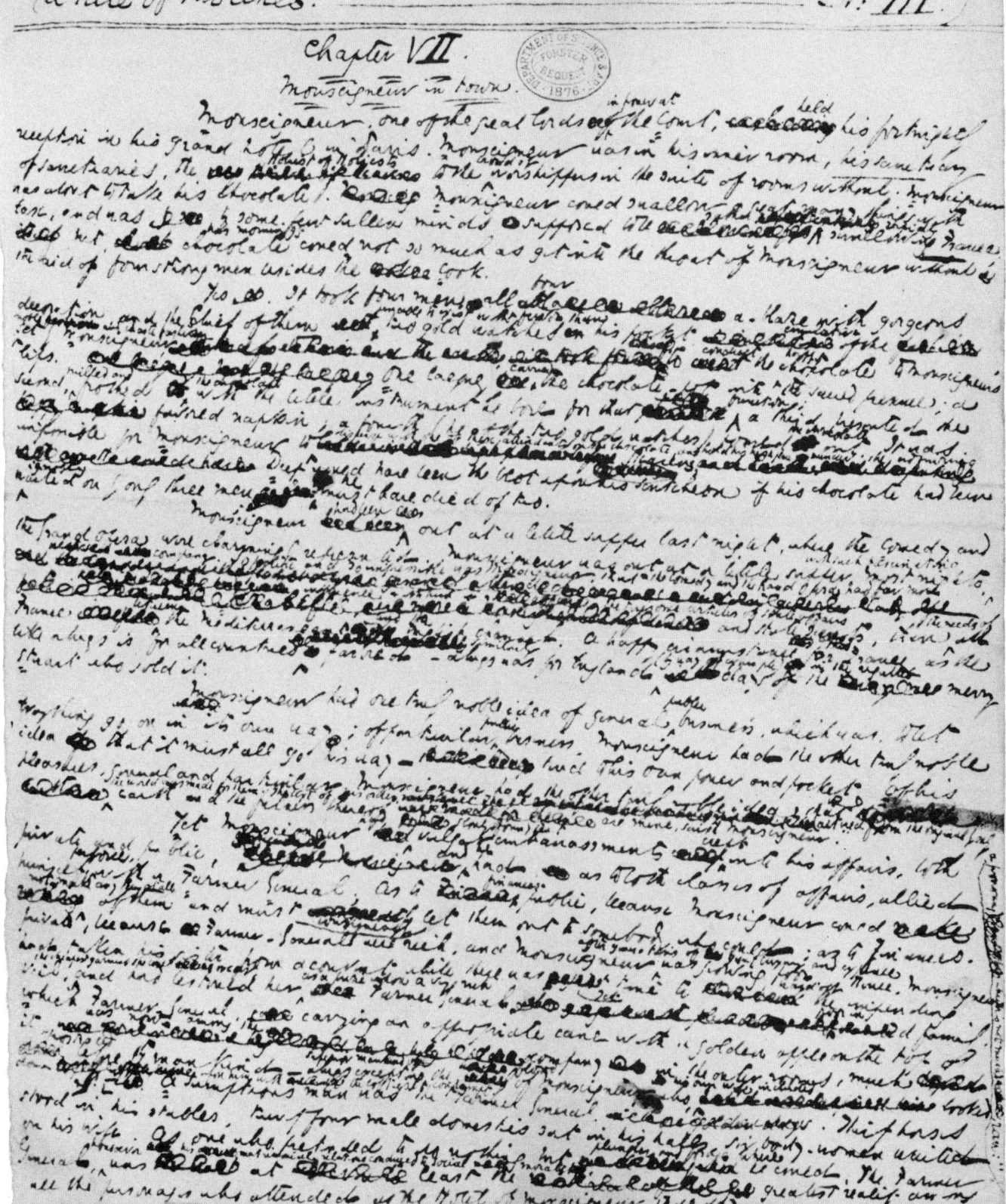

66 Plan for Number XVII of *David Copperfield* (K 21: reduced)

67 (*right*) Page from the corrected proofs of *Bleak House* (K 28)

404   BLEAK HOUSE.

(she was very firm)

for the firmest of us to be always guarded. There was domestic trouble and amazement, you may suppose; I leave you to imagine, Sir Leicester, the husband's grief. But that is not my present point. When Mr. Rouncewell's townsman heard of the disclosure, he no more allowed the girl to be patronised and honored, than he would have suffered her to be trodden underfoot before his eyes. Such was his pride, that he indignantly took her away, as if from reproach and disgrace. He had no sense of the honor done him and his daughter by the lady's condescension; not the least. He resented the girl's position, as if the lady had been the commonest of commoners. That the story. I hope Lady Dedlock will excuse its painful nature."

There are various opinions on the merits, more or less conflicting with Volumnia's. That fair young creature can't believe there ever was any such lady, and rejects the whole history on the thresh-hold. The majority incline to the Debilitated cousin's sentiment, which is in few words— "no business—Rouncewell's fernal townsman." Sir Leicester generally refers back in his mind to Wat Tyler, and arranges a sequence of events on a plan of his own.

There is not much conversation in all, for late hours have been kept at Chesney Wold since the necessary expenses elsewhere began, and this is the first night in many on which the family have been alone. It is past ten when Sir Leicester begs Mr. Tulkinghorn to ring for candles. Then the stream of moonlight has swelled into a lake, and then Lady Dedlock for the first time moves, and rises, and comes forward to a table for a glass of water. Winking cousins, bat-like in the candle glare, crowd round to give it; Volumnia (always ready for something better if procurable) takes another, a meek sip of which contents her; Lady Dedlock, graceful, self-possessed, looked after by admiring eyes, passes away slowly by the side of that Nymph down the long perspective, not at all improving her as a question of contrast.

(Bradbury — manage to bring this down, as I would rather not write more in. It can be easily done by bringing the previous chapter over, a little. CD)

68 J. Leech: Cartoon in *Punch* (L 16)

69 Phiz: 'The Sea Rises', illustration for *A Tale of Two Cities* (L 5)

VIEW OF A DUST YARD.
(From a Sketch taken on the spot.)

70 Illustration from H. Mayhew, *London Labour and the London Poor* (L15)

"A State Party."

71 R. Doyle: 'A State Party' from his *Bird's Eye Views of Society* (L12)

72 (*above*) L. Fildes: Study for an illustration for *Edwin Drood* (L 29)

73 (*below*) L. Fildes: Applicants for Admission to a Casual Ward (I 67)

74 G. Doré: The Lascar's Room in *Edwin Drood* (L24)

75 (*above left*) After D. Maclise: No. 1, Devonshire Terrace (C 83)

76 (*below left*) Tavistock House (G 55)

77 (*above right*) The Dining Room at Gad's Hill Place (M 13)

78 (*below right*) Anonymous: Cricket at Gad's Hill (M 15)

79 (*right*) Ellen Ternan (M 4)

80 (*below*) The Staplehurst Railway Accident (M 10)

81 (*above right*) Charles Dickens 1859 (O 15)

82 (*below left*) Dickens reading, illustration from the *Illustrated London News* (M 37)

83 (*below right*) Letter from Longfellow to Forster (M 28)

84 D. Maclise: Charles Dickens 1839 (04)

85 W. P. Frith: Charles Dickens 1859 (010)

86 Charles Dickens 1867 (o 20)

87 L. Fildes: Grave of Charles Dickens in Poet's Corner (M 43)

88 J. E. Millais: Dickens on his deathbed (M 39)

89 After L. Fildes: The Empty Chair (M 42)

Plan of the Exhibition

The rooms shown on the plan correspond to the sections into which the catalogue is divided.

- A Dickens's childhood
- B Early life
- C Early works
- D John Forster
- E Dickens's visit to America in 1842
- F Novels of the 1840s
- G Dickens and the theatre
- H Dickens and Christmas
- I Social novels
- J Dickens as editor
- K Dickens at work
- L Last novels
- M Final years
- N Personalia

The Library contains a selection of books by and about Dickens, which visitors are free to read and examine.

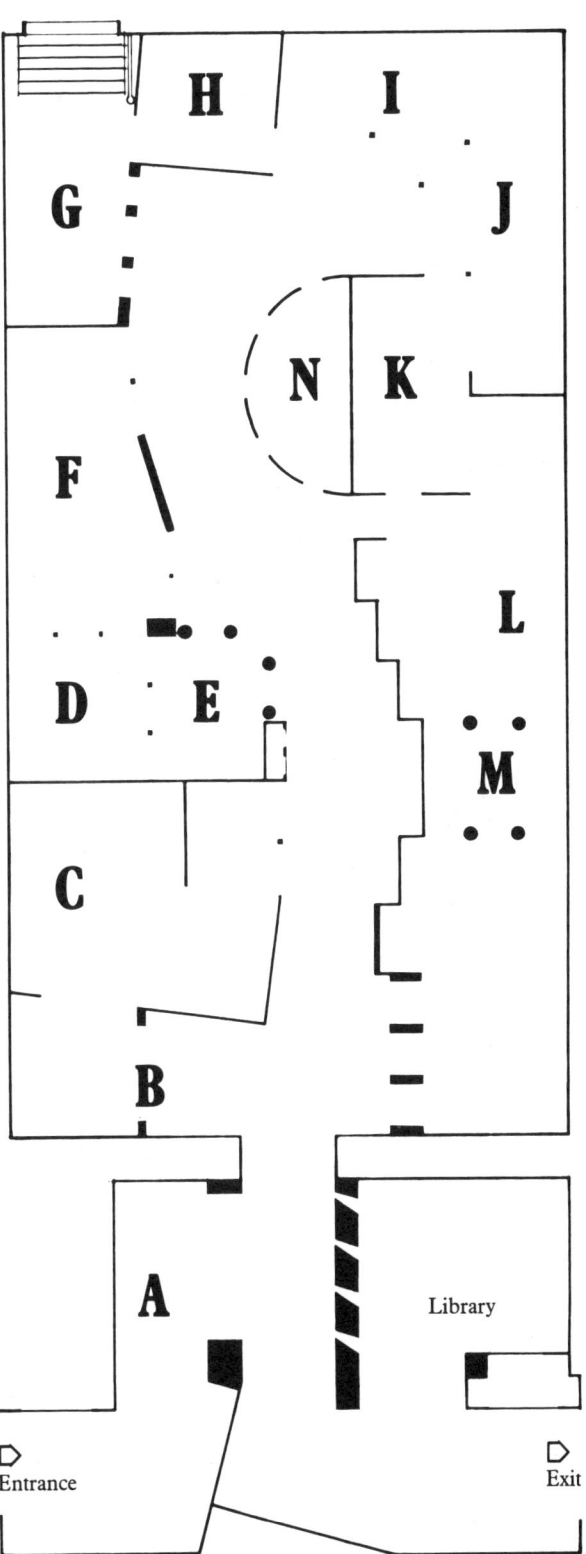

Exhibition designed by
CHRISTOPHER FIRMSTONE